Aiming High – Overland to

AIMING

HIGH

AIMING HIGH

Overland to the Himalayas
1971

Dr John Winter

Aiming High – Overland to the Himalayas 1971

First published as a paperback in 2014 by Appin Press.

Copyright: 2014 Dr John Winter

Copyright for this edition: 2021 Dr John Winter

The right of Dr John Winter to be identified as the author of this work has been asserted by him in accordance with the Copyright, Designs and Patents Act 1988.

A catalogue record for the 2014 paperback edition of this book is available from the British Library.

This Edition KDP ISBN: 9798772583586

All rights reserved. Apart from any fair dealing for the purposes of research or private study, or criticism or review, as permitted under the Copyright, Designs and Patents Act 1988, this publication may only be reproduced, stored or transmitted, in any form or by any means, with the prior permission in writing of the author, or in the case of reprographic reproduction in accordance with the terms of licences issued by the copyright Licencing Agency.   Enquiries concerning reproduction outside those terms should be sent to the author.

Dr John Winter: johnwinter049@gmail.com

Aiming High – Overland to the Himalayas 1971

Acknowledgement and thanks

All the photographic illustrations which are used in this book were taken by the author and other members of the Indrasan West Ridge Expedition 1971.

There is no information available to identify for certain which member of the team took each individual image. We were all using Olympus cameras to make a photographic record of the climb using Kodachrome film.

On our return to the UK the Kodachrome films were sent to a laboratory for development. Copies of the photographs, in the form of 35mm slides, were given to all the team members for their personal use in lectures and other activities.

The author has used a number of photographs which he took himself. In other cases the content of the image has made it possible to identify the team member who took a particular photograph. In such cases the team member's initials have been added to the caption. All images without such initials have been accredited to the team.

Should any team member consider that a particular photograph should be accredited to him in future editions of this book I would be very pleased, if he would like to contact me (E-mail: Page 3), to look into adding the appropriate accreditation.

My grateful thanks are due to all the members of the team who took these photographs. Back in 1971, in the days before digital photography, producing such memorable images was not easy.

Aiming High – Overland to the Himalayas 1971

FOREWORD

In 1971, forty three years ago, I was fortunate enough to get the opportunity to travel by road along the 'Hippie Trail' from England, through Europe, Turkey, Iran, Afghanistan and Pakistan, to India.

My companions and I were driving a lorry loaded, not with hallucinogenic drugs, but instead with a ton and a half of mountaineering equipment. We were heading for the Kulu Valley in the western part of the Himalayas and a mountain called Indrasan, known locally as The Throne of the Thunder God.

I kept a diary and, in 1972, after returning to England and resuming my career as a doctor, I wrote an account of my experiences.

The manuscript lay, unread and unpublished, upon a bookshelf in a spare bedroom until some American friends, encouraged by my wife, Susan, picked it up and read it. Their enthusiastic comments led me to read through it again for the first time since 1972. I have now reviewed and edited the manuscript, adding some of today's perspectives.

A great deal has changed since 1971. The overland journey through Iran and Afghanistan would now be very difficult, if not impossible. Mobile phones and satellite television have transformed communications and made our planet a much smaller place. In 1971 we spent many weeks out of touch with the outside world. Today it is possible to make a telephone call from

Aiming High – Overland to the Himalayas 1971

the summit of Everest, and television pictures can be transmitted to and from almost anywhere on the globe.

Forty three years on, this is a historical, rather than a contemporary, document.   I hope you enjoy reading it as much as I have enjoyed preparing it for publication.

John Winter

Ormskirk, Liverpool

August 2014

Aiming High – Overland to the Himalayas 1971

To Susan, who kept telling me that I should write.

And to Jim and Karen, who persuaded me that she might be correct.

"To the south-east we had a majestic view of the almost unclimbable peak, Indrasan (6221 metres/20,410 ft). Alongside Indrasan, the flatter, snow-capped summit of Deo Tibba (6001 metres/ 19,687 ft) could also be seen.

And yes, we did not even think about going to that avalanche, rock-fall and landslide prone area. There would be a number of hidden crevasses. Climbing Indrasan is tougher than Everest."

Quotation by the leader of an Indian Himalayan Association expedition to the region in 1994.

Aiming High – Overland to the Himalayas 1971

Glossary of Mountaineering Terms

Abseil – to descend a steep or vertical slope using a rope to control the descent

Arete – a sharp, steep ridge on a mountain

Ascender – a friction device which is used to ascend a fixed rope and reduce the risk of falling; also known as a Jumar which was one of the first designs

Belay – an attachment point, using a peg, a chock or a screw, on a rock or snow/ice face to reduce the danger of a fall

Bergschrund – a large crevasse between the upper part of a glacier and an ice cliff

Bouldering – climbing practice on large boulders at ground level

Buttress – a bulky, usually flat-surfaced outcrop forming a major part of a rock face

Carabiner (or 'crab') – a device for attaching a rope to a belay

Chock – a small metal block which can be jammed into a crack or crevice in a rock face to provide a belay point

Cornice – an overhanging ledge of snow, usually on a mountain ridge

Couloir – a steep gulley, usually filled with snow and/or ice

Crampon – a spiked device which can be strapped onto the sole of a climbing boot to provide additional grip on hard-packed snow or ice slopes

Elvis legs – an uncontrollable shaking of the knees caused by fatigue, often worsened by panic

Etrier – a webbing loop which can be attached to a fixed rope and used by a climber as a 'step' in which he can place his boot and take his weight

Fixed rope – a rope which is attached to a section of a climb and left in position

Ice axe – a metal axe with a flattened end for cutting steps in snow slopes and a sharp point for digging into ice

Snow screw – a long metal screw, usually tubular, which can be used to provide a belay point in firm, packed snow

Mantel-shelf – a climbing manoeuvre which can be used to get up onto a flat ledge or shelf by reaching up and then pushing down with the arms on the flat surface of the ledge

Neve – crumbly, granular ice formed by repeated freeze-thaw cycles

Peg – a metal device which can be hammered into a crack in a rock face, or into an ice surface, to provide a secure belay point

Pitch – approximately one rope's length, or the distance between two belay points on a climb – i.e. about 150 feet.

Scree – a slope surfaced with small, loose rocks, often found at the base of a rock face or cliff

Snow anchor – a triangular, metal device which digs into a firm, snow surface to provide an anchoring point for a rope at the top of a climb

Step cutting – using an ice axe to cut deep steps for safety on a steep, snow slope

Step kicking - using climbing boots, usually with crampons attached, to kick shallow steps into a steep, snow slope

Technical climbing – climbing steep rock faces using ropes and belays – as opposed to scrambling up less steep slopes without using ropes or belays for safety and protection

Top rope – a rope which is attached to the highest point of a climb to provide additional safety

Traverse – a horizontal pitch across a rock or snow/ice face

One

DOCTOR ON A MOUNTAIN

Saturday 8th May 1971. We all looked on as the grim-faced customs officer at the road border between Pakistan and India counted rupee notes and added them to the growing number which already sat on the metal desk in front of him.

"Two thousand one hundred rupees," he announced, as the last note was added to the pile. "You are aware that smuggling rupees into India is a serious offence? The penalties are severe."

The two couples who had been ahead of us in the queue of vehicles, and whose camper van had just been very efficiently searched, looked frightened and pale despite the tans they had acquired during their long overland journey from Europe. They were from London, and we had spoken to them earlier while we were waiting in the long line of vehicles for the customs check. We had all watched as some of the large, commercial vehicles were nodded through without a search; but other, smaller wagons and vans were carefully searched.

It was obvious to anyone that the four Londoners were very nervous. They had told us that they had visited a money-changer in Kabul, where rupees could be purchased at a rate that was several times better than the official exchange rate. The notes were hidden in an envelope which was taped underneath the spare wheel and, as we watched, it was found. Successfully smuggling such illicitly obtained rupees into India greatly reduced the cost of a stay in the country in sterling or dollar terms, but the authorities were well aware of the temptations which the currency dealers in Afghanistan offered to impecunious, overland travellers. At the Indian border, the searches and investigations of people who had passed through Kabul were usually very thorough.

"You will come with me please. One of my officers will take your vehicle."

A metal door closed behind them as the four, rather unhappy and dishevelled travellers disappeared from our view into a small, brick-built building. I thought I heard a couple of bolts slide into place after the door had closed but my imagination, heightened by the slight apprehension that I was feeling, may have been playing tricks with me. An officer in military uniform climbed into the camper van and drove it away.

It was twenty-three days, and almost six thousand miles, since we had left England. We were driving to the Himalayas for an attempt upon the unclimbed west ridge of a peak known as Indrasan. This was the last border between us and our destination.

We all stood alongside the lorry and trailer which had safely transported us, and our vast collection of food and equipment, across Europe and part of Asia. In an effort to create a good impression we had changed into clean white shirts and smart trousers a few miles short of the border and all our paperwork was tidily collected in a small leather attaché case. As far as we were aware everything was in order. We had already passed through ten international borders without any serious problems, and we had stopped at Lahore, in Pakistan, to pick up the permits we would need to cross into India; but the taxes and regulations which covered the importation into India of foodstuffs, and other items deemed to be of commercial value, were so complex that we felt certain that we would be in breach of one or more of the many rules if our lorry was searched. Our worries were compounded by the fact that relations between India and Pakistan were at breaking point and war could break out at any time. Most of the land border crossings between the two countries had recently been closed, and we could sense that the heavily armed, army officers who were stationed at the one or two crossing points that were still open, such as this one at Ferozepore, were twitchy and tense.

Apart from a number of rifle-carrying troops, who were stationed alongside the barrier which marked the route into India, the area was now deserted. The heat was sweltering, and our smart attire was in danger of losing some of its positive impact as our shirts gradually became soaked with sweat. Along with some of the fine dust which swirled around the holding compound, they started to cling to our perspiring skin.

After about half an hour the metal door opened again and a large, luxuriantly moustached and red-turbaned Sikh appeared, beckoning us to move up to the desk as he walked towards us.

"Your papers please."

The attaché case was handed to him and he unzipped it slowly before removing all the contents.

"While I look through these papers, you will please each fill out two forms for entry into India. All questions must be answered."

He lifted his head and looked each of us in the eye.

"In full, please."

In the official papers, which were about to be carefully studied, we had identified the contents of the lorry and trailer as being food and trekking equipment, for personal use only; and the purpose of our visit to India was stated as being to undertake a long, recreational trek in the Kulu Valley and surrounding hills. This was true, although we had deliberately failed to make any mention of Indrasan. The west ridge ran very close to the Inner Line, a restricted military zone in the mountains between India and China, and we did not want to run the risk of arousing suspicion in what was a tense military situation.

The Sikh officer eased himself gently into a wooden chair, with arms, which was behind the desk. He shuffled our papers around for about ten minutes, belching loudly every few moments as he did so. Then suddenly, and quite unexpectedly, as he was reading through our completed entry forms his face broke into a smile.

"Your papers indicate that you have driven here from Liverpool. That is right?"

We nodded.

"My brother has been to Liverpool," he continued, between smiles and belches. He clearly wanted us to appreciate that he was a cultured man who had knowledge of the wider world outside Ferozepore. "He liked Liverpool very much. The river and the buildings. Very grand. Like Delhi."

We suddenly realised that, sent to us like manna from heaven, we might have found a friend. And even better, he was a friend who appeared to be in a position of some authority. We enthusiastically agreed that Liverpool was indeed a very fine city. And Delhi too, even though none of us had ever been there. All was now smiles.

Our new friend studied each of our passports before placing them upon his desk.

"You are the doctor?" he asked, addressing me. The information had obviously come from my passport. He belched again, and raised his hand. "I must apologise. My digestion is very bad."

He then gathered the papers and passports together and arranged them into a neat pile, before placing them carefully back inside the attaché case and zipping it up.

"Everything is in order." He nodded his head several times before handing the case back to us. "You may go through. We do not need to search your lorry."

He stood up and waved at the guards, who immediately lifted the barrier.

We all thanked him profusely.

"Give him something for his wind." Tony, the leader of our expedition, whispered urgently into my ear.

As the others took their places in the lorry I presented our friend with a couple of packets of Alka-Seltzers from the medical kit.

"To help with your indigestion," I explained. He placed his hands together, as if in prayer, and bowed his head slowly and gracefully. The small gift had been accepted.

I swiftly joined the others and we drove off, giving our friend a cheery wave as we passed through the barrier. As soon as we were clear it closed behind us, and we gave grateful thanks for our safe passage. We had arrived in India.

= = = = = = = = = = = = = =

The long journey to India had first started nine months earlier, in September 1970, when I had received, in the post, a small advertisement for inclusion in a local medical magazine on Merseyside which I edited. Sent in by a person called Tony Johnson, it asked for applications for the position of medical officer on a planned Himalayan climbing expedition.

Having qualified as a doctor in 1969, I had just finished work at one of Liverpool's teaching hospitals. I was between jobs, and uncertain about exactly what I wanted to do next. The medical magazine was a small, part-time project which interested me, but I could not see it leading anywhere. I was spending my time doing a few part-time GP locums, which paid quite well, while I considered the future.

As I looked at the advertisement my imagination was fired. The Himalayas. Towering peaks. Incredible beauty. The drama of man against the elements. I had to admit to myself that I was tempted by the prospect. The only problem was that I had never as much as attempted the easy walk to the top of Snowden, at 3,560 feet the highest peak in England and Wales, let alone done any real climbing.

I began to prepare the advertisement for the printers but, try as I might, I could not drive the tantalising images that it provoked out of my mind. The whole idea of going on a Himalayan expedition would have been laughable, had it not been so obviously suicidal; but it would not be dismissed. I sat at my desk trying to decide what to do.

In desperation I tossed a coin into the air. If it came down heads, I would apply. What difference would it make anyway? They would certainly turn me down, and that would be that.

Thus it was that the following weekend I was sitting reading a photocopied brochure that had arrived through the post from the 'Indrasan West Ridge Expedition 1971'. Accompanying it was a letter inviting me to get in touch if I was still interested after I had read the material they had sent.

On the front page was the proposed itinerary.

INDRASAN WEST RIDGE EXPEDITION - 1971

15th April   Depart England.   Travel overland with all equipment.

5th May   E.T.A. West Pakistan/India border.

9th May   E.T.A. Kulu Valley. Manali.

10th May   Valley Base Camp outside Manali.   Arrange hire of high altitude porters and coolie gang.

11th May   Members of the expedition have a week to recover from overland travel and make acclimatisation and training climbs up to 12,000 feet.

19th May   Start walk-in to Base Camp.

23rd May   E.T.A. Base Camp in the region of Seri at 12,500 feet.

I became increasingly fascinated as I read on.

OVERLAND TO INDIA

We will travel overland to India as it will be cheaper and more interesting than going by sea. As we are carrying most of our food and equipment with us we are hoping to avoid usual shipping difficulties.

We shall leave England in April 1971 in a two ton lorry which will be needed to carry the seven expedition members plus the vast amount of equipment.   The route will be through Europe to central Turkey, via Istanbul and Ankara. From there we will pass through spectacular mountain scenery and over 9,000 foot passes to the plains of Armenia and south of Mount Ararat, legendary resting place of The Ark.   The next stage is desert, through Iran and into Afghanistan with its ancient capital of Kabul.   On to the Khyber Pass and the old North-West Frontier.   The names now ring of Kipling; Peshawar, Rawalpindi, Lahore, Amritsar and Mandi. From Mandi, negotiation of a road cut out of the very rock face of a precipitous gorge will lead us into the Kulu Valley, where we will drive along the banks of the Beas River, passing Nagar, an ancient settlement from which the whole valley was once ruled.   The distance from there to Manali is about twelve miles.

INDRASAN 20,410 FEET – THRONE OF THE THUNDER GOD

The mountain has so far received one brief skirmish and two serious assaults, but attempts on Deo Tibba, the Peak of the Gods at 19,687 feet, which forms the other side of the glacier col from Indrasan, have been numerous.

The first attempt to climb Deo Tibba was made in 1912 by Lt. Col. Bruce, followed in 1939 by a Lt. Roberts. In 1945 three Italian prisoners-of-war ascended as far as 18,000 feet but were foiled by the long approach. Further attempts were made in 1950 and 1952, the latter attempt, led by J. V. De Graaff, at last achieving the first successful ascent of the mountain.

The first tentative probe towards Indrasan was in 1958 when two members of an expedition, Bob Pettigrew and Basil Poff, reached the upper snow fields of the Malana Glacier, from which rises the summit cone of Indrasan. But this was a mere skirmish, too small scale to have any real hope of success.

The first serious assault was in 1961 and was made by the Derbyshire Himalayan Expedition, again with Bob Pettigrew as leader. This was a highly organised party which had other objectives, including the reconnaissance of peaks such as Ali Ratni Tibba and mapping the Kulu and Malana area. The expedition was based at the head of the Malana Nullah and began to seek a way onto the glacier. The plan was to put a camp on each of the three shelves of hard-packed snow which formed the approach route to Indrasan. Hopefully they would then be within striking distance of the summit.

On July 1st, two members of the team set off towards the west ridge of Indrasan, en route to the summit, but were forced to return, having reached no further than the crest of the ridge where the climbing was severe. They had found themselves switch-backing over numerous steep rock pinnacles, and they were exhausted.

The next day they repeated the attempt but once again, despite a swifter pace than on the previous day, they had to retreat, having halted at a point on the north face less than two thirds of the way along the ridge. Dennis Gray, in his book 'Rope Boy', explains that they had grossly underestimated the length and difficulty of the ridge in hoping that it would fall to a single Alpine-style assault. At the same time the two climbers felt that 'the climbing was of such difficulty that we could not envisage our Ladhaki porters, or even ourselves, carrying loads along it for additional camps or bivouacs.'

The second serious assault, and the one that reached the summit, was in the post-monsoon season in October 1962. A Japanese team from Kyoto University approached the mountain to the east of the route used by the British team. They regarded the west ridge as being too difficult to climb but, having established a camp at 18,045 feet, two members of the expedition, Y. Miyaki and K. Tomita, reached the summit by way of a snow field on the south-west face. The price they paid for their success was high. Oblivious to the time they had climbed on into the very late afternoon and nightfall forced them to bivouac near the summit with no tents or sleeping bags to protect them from the icy cold. In the sub-zero temperatures both sustained severe frostbite, losing fingers and toes, but somehow they managed to reach their camp again next day.

The impressive West Ridge of Indrasan is still unclimbed. This expedition hopes to make the first ascent by this route. Extreme difficulty is anticipated.

The members of the expedition will be:

Tony Johnson – Leader

Main Climbers - Geoff Arkless, John Brazinton, Roger Brook, Bryan Pooley and Geoff Tabbner

The brochure went on to outline the assault plan which had been worked out for the ridge, and gave further details about the area of the Himalayas in which Indrasan is situated, but I did not need to read any more. I had made up my mind. If I could persuade them to take me as their medical officer, I would go.

= = = = = = = = = = = = = =

My car came to a halt outside a magnificent, but now rather faded, Georgian mansion, just to the south of Liverpool city centre. It was one of a terrace of similar houses, built in the middle of the nineteenth century when the merchants of the city had grown wealthy on the profits of trade with America and the British Empire. Now too large for single families, they had all been divided into flats for students and other temporary residents.

I rang the top bell, one of six that nestled beside a great stone pillar that marked the left hand side of the entrance to the building. After a brief interval the door opened to reveal a dark-haired, tousled and slightly-built person with glasses.

"Tony Johnson?" I enquired. He was not anything like the intrepid mountaineer that I had imagined.

"Yes," he replied, smiling and shaking my hand. "It's very good to meet you. You must be Doctor John Winter. We're expecting you. Come on in. We're upstairs."

We climbed the stairs to a large room with a high ceiling. It had a comfortable and well lived in feel about it. In the middle of the room was a table, piled high with letters, brochures, files, folders and newspaper cuttings, plus an assortment of writing implements and rubber stamps. All the necessary paraphernalia of an expedition in the advanced stages of planning and organisation.

To the right of this disorganised mound of paper, on a couple of chairs and a settee, sat two men, and a young woman who was introduced to me as Laura, Tony's wife.

The two men stood up and shook me by the hand.

"Hello, I'm John Brazinton. Good to meet you. And this is Roger Brook."

John Brazinton was not tall, but he was obviously very strong in his arms and shoulders: a typical rock climber. He wore a tie-dyed tee shirt and a pair of purple Levis. Roger Brook was taller. He was quite slim, like myself, but he boasted a significantly more generous allowance of muscle than I could muster.

"Roger came up from Shrewsbury last night," said Tony. "We're just waiting for Geoff Tabbner. He's driving from Coventry this morning. He should be here soon I think. Fancy a coffee while we're waiting?"

Once the coffee was made we sat down to chat and get to know each other. I soon felt that I would have no problem getting on with the three who were present.

The sound of a bell in the hall downstairs announced Geoff Tabbner's arrival. Tony went down to open the outside door and, a few moments later, a figure who was much more like the mountaineer of folk-lore joined us in the room. Of medium build and bearded, with a ready smile and a tanned complexion, he wore a pair of faded denim jeans and a heavy tartan climbing shirt. Under his right arm was a bulky document case which he unzipped as he sat down. We were quickly introduced, and the meeting began. Apparently the other two members of the team were not expected.

Things had moved very fast in the three weeks since I had received the advertisement. After reading the brochure I had contacted Tony and explained my situation. He had seemed undismayed by my total lack of experience and confident that, if I wanted to join them, I could pick up some basic mountaineering skills in Scotland before we were due to leave for the Himalayas. I was rather less sure but, having convinced myself that he was the expert, I had agreed to come along to the meeting at which I now found myself.

Tony opened the proceedings by going through the finances. Everyone seemed satisfied, although there were some doubts expressed about the rather large sum which was anticipated under the heading of *'Newspaper Support'*. Even without this, however, the expedition seemed to be solvent. Just.

Geoff's turn next, and I learnt that the expedition lorry had not yet been purchased. He had, however, arranged to attend an auction of ex-military vehicles the following week and he was hoping to strike lucky there. It was agreed that he should be given a free hand to choose something suitable, as well as a blank cheque drawn on the expedition account.

'Food and Supplies' was John Brazinton's area of responsibility. His was a long and tortuous tale of discounts and percentages on carabiners, etriers, cagoules, ascendeurs, and a hundred and one other items of equipment which meant little or nothing to me. All

seemed to be on track and within budget, however, and it was now just up to the suppliers to meet their promises.

"Right," said Tony, "now for medical supplies. That'll be your department John. Perhaps, since we've got two Johns, you'd better be 'Doc' from now on."

They seemed to assume I was going. And I had decided. I was.

= = = = = = = = = = = = = =

For several weeks it was back to the everyday routine of medical work. I sought as many GP locums as I could find in an effort to build up some funds, and every evening was spent typing letters to pharmaceutical companies, requesting their support and assistance. Medical supplies are an expensive item on any budget. We would be a very long way from the services of hospitals or clinics and I had to try to beg or borrow sufficient drugs and equipment to cover the numerous medical problems and accidents that could arise in such an isolated situation. In return for any help which was given, I was more than happy to offer my services as a lecturer, on my return to England, at one or more of the medical meetings which pharmaceutical representatives arrange in order to liaise with the profession. Their feeling was that an illustrated lecture on mountain climbing, especially if given by a medically-qualified novice who had never previously been near a mountain, would certainly create plenty of interest. Several manufacturers therefore felt able to be very generous with donations and loans of the drug supplies and medical equipment which I would need to take with me to Indrasan.

Everything was going well when, quite suddenly, our plans were completely thrown off course by a postal strike. There were no e-mails in those days and, while we did what we could on the telephone and by making personal visits to prospective sponsors, mostly we just had to wait. And wait.

It was six weeks before the strike ended, by which time there were just four weeks left before our planned departure date. If we worked hard, we would have just about enough time to complete our plans. Had the strike lasted even a few days longer it would almost certainly have spelt the end of the expedition.

Two

SOME ROCK AND SNOW TRAINING

During the meeting in Tony's flat, John Brazinton had offered to take me to some sandstone cliffs, near Frodsham in Cheshire, to get some experience of rock climbing. So, on the following Saturday morning, clad as advised in a pair of worn-out cords and a couple of old pullovers which I did not mind ruining, I met John and one of his climbing pals outside his flat.

"I'm Pete." John's friend introduced himself as we walked towards his old Ford van. He was wearing a dark navy, roll top sweater which was well spattered with paint, and a pair of dirt-encrusted jeans that even a tramp might have discarded. The oldest of clothes were clearly the approved kit for rock climbing.

Pete slipped the van noisily into gear and we headed towards a dual carriageway which ran south out of Liverpool and which would take us over the Runcorn Bridge to Frodsham. With the accelerator pressed hard to the floor the van, which was at least as old and decrepit as Pete's trousers, trundled along at a steady sixty miles per hour, while our chauffeur seemed unconcerned by the periodic bangs and creaks that emanated from the chassis. He reassured us that he had wound an extra piece of chicken wire around the silencer before leaving the flat, so that item of equipment at least would not part company from our remarkable vehicle.

As we passed through Runcorn our driver suggested a brief detour to an old quarry.

"There are some great routes there. A hundred feet some of them are; and very exposed. It'd be fun."

I had done a little reading since agreeing to join the climbing fraternity and I had learnt that 'exposed', in climbing parlance, referred to the ability to see, from a perch on a rock face or mountain, the terrain far below onto which a climber might, in the event of a false move, be unceremoniously and painfully precipitated.

"I don't think so," said John after a moment's thought. "The holds there tend to be a bit flaky and loose, particularly towards the top. I think Frodsham'll be better for the Doc's first outing."

I nodded in full agreement and muttered a short prayer of thanks for his wisdom.

We reached Frodsham just as it started to rain. Not to be deterred, we parked the van and headed along a dirt track which led us uphill towards our objective for the day. The rain eased slightly as we were walking and I was able to see some red, sandstone cliffs through the trees and bushes which lined the track we were following. Although they were still a hundred feet or so above us, the cliffs looked encouragingly small.

We had been walking for about fifteen minutes when we came to a halt at the bottom of an overhanging sandstone bluff. A small group of girls, whose tee shirts announced that they were from a local youth club, were already swarming over a rock face to our right, and making it look very easy.

"If they can do it...." I thought to myself.

My two companions lowered their rucksacks and began to take out ropes and webbed safety harnesses. It all looked reassuringly competent and professional. Then, without any preamble, John reached up for a tiny hold above his head and pulled himself up the overhang using just his arms. As I watched, he lifted his legs and found a grip for his feet which were by then almost level with his shoulders. A couple more gymnastic contortions, during which the engorged veins on his arms betrayed the strength he was employing, and he was standing at the top, some thirty feet above me. His slightly taller friend then proceeded, perhaps a little less proficiently, to clamber up the same route.

"Throw us the rope, Doc, and we'll fix it at the top and guide you up."

I did as requested, and the two figures disappeared from view. A couple of minutes later they reappeared and the two ends of the rope snaked their way down the rock face, followed by the climbers. A couple of firm tugs reassured them that the rope was securely fixed.

"Okay Doc," said John. "The idea is that we keep that top rope tight and it stops you falling too far if you come off."

That sounded to me like a very sensible plan.

'With a top rope,' I had read somewhere, *'rock climbing is a very safe sport.'*

"Can you tie a bowline?"

The question from John was addressed to me.

My knowledge of knots was a little rusty but, with some assistance, I managed to tie the rope securely to the webbing belt and around my waist, using the recommended bowline. We then moved a few feet to the left of the overhang.

"You can do this chimney," announced John, consulting his Guide to the Buttresses of Frodsham and Helsby. "It's graded a 5A, but you should be fine. We'll make sure you don't fall off."

The first few moves were obvious. Good solid hand-holds, and ledges which supported even my size eleven feet as I ascended. The rope to which I was attached was kept reassuringly taut by John, and I felt I was doing quite well. Then I reached the chimney proper and came to an abrupt halt. It was, quite literally, a square chimney with one side missing. There was not a hand-hold or crack to be seen.

"You'll have to bridge it," called John. "Put your feet on the rock to your left and then lean out to get your back against the right hand wall of the chimney. Then you should be able to work your way upwards. Don't worry. If you slip you'll just be dangling on the rope. There's no danger of falling."

Very slowly I bridged the chimney as recommended.

"That's good."

The shout came from below me. It did not feel good but as I inched my way slowly upwards I began to understand exactly what I was supposed to be doing. Gradually it became easier, and I reached the top with a definite sense of satisfaction as well as relief. I had completed my first route. Not spectacular, and certainly not graceful. But definitely a first.

My companions followed me up the chimney without the benefit of a top rope. John made it look ridiculously easy, but Pete seemed to struggle a little on the middle section. Perhaps things were not completely hopeless.

The three of us stood at the top. The rain had cleared and we had a magnificent view, over the rooftops of Frodsham to the Mersey Estuary, and beyond to the Wirral and Deeside. I was gazing out, identifying familiar landmarks, when John interrupted my reverie.

"Right. Now we'll abseil down. We'll go first to show you how it's done, Doc. You wait here until we come back up again. I need to make sure you don't damage yourself."

With that he passed a doubled rope between his legs and over his right shoulder, before stepping backwards over the edge of the cliff. Pete followed as I watched, half-expecting disaster at any minute. If I expected disaster, it never materialised. Within a couple of minutes both John and Pete were back at the top.

"Your turn, Doc."

John showed me how to wind the rope around myself and, having checked carefully that it would not emasculate me, I stepped gingerly backwards towards the precipice.

"Get your feet firmly on the edge and then lean back slowly on the rope until you're almost horizontal. Then all you have to do is just walk down the cliff face, paying the rope out as you go. We'll be doing plenty of abseiling in the Himalayas, so it'll be useful if you can get the hang of it before we leave."

Two small steps and I was almost horizontal. It felt fine until, without thinking, I looked down. The Frodsham cliffs are no more than forty feet high but below them the hillside drops away quite sharply. The sensation at the top of the cliff was of being suspended hundreds of feet above the surrounding flat countryside. Out of the corner of my eye I could see a new motorway, winding like a pale grey ribbon across the patchwork of green and brown fields.

Then, even as I felt myself starting to panic, I took another step backwards and I was on my way down. To my surprise, once I was over the lip and committed to the descent, the frightening sense of exposure completely disappeared and I found I was really enjoying it. I walked my way down to the bottom of the cliff, feeling as secure as a fly on a wall, and immediately wanted to repeat the experience. The climbing drug was taking a hold upon me.

= = = = = = = = = = = = = =

The third week in March saw the end of the postal strike and requests from some of our sponsors for pictures of the whole team. The logical place to get together was North Wales, in Snowdonia, where I would be able to meet the other two members of the expedition. Bryan Pooley was a New Zealander, who had been in England and Wales for the past few months, and Geoff Arkless, the oldest member of the team, was a professional mountain guide.

We gathered at Geoff's house in Deiniolen, a small Welsh village which nestles at the foot of a peak known as Elidir Fawr, a few miles to the north-west of Snowdon. Geoff's wife, Breda, had been a member of the women's expedition to the Kashmir Himalayas during the previous climbing season, and our meeting dragged on into the early hours of the morning as every aspect of the plans we had made was discussed in the light of her valuable experience. The only member of our team with any previous Himalayan experience was Bryan Pooley, and he had been no higher than 19,000 feet.

Geoff Tabbner reported that we now had our transport, a sturdy Austin K9 lorry, an ex-military vehicle with a mere three thousand miles on the clock. Combined with a heavy duty military trailer, which he had also acquired, it should serve our purpose well and hopefully carry us all the way to India.

Everything was gradually falling into place. Everything, that is, except the food supplies. A number of sponsors in the food industry had been very generous in donating provisions, but there were some worrying gaps in both quantity and quality. Some of our dwindling financial resources would have to be allocated to filling the gaps. John Brazinton would work out what was needed and organise the necessary purchases.

This final item settled we retired wearily to our sleeping bags, each one of us hoping that nothing had been forgotten. There would be no time to make good any omissions after this weekend.

The next morning we had a brief photography session, with an appropriately mountainous and snowy background for the benefit of our sponsors, after which Geoff Arkless and I left to drive up to Scotland. The second part of my crash course in climbing was about to begin, this time as a member of the Advanced Snow Climbing Course which Geoff and a colleague ran in Glencoe each winter. I would have seven days to learn as much as I possibly could about survival in the high mountains.

It was a long drive and, after the late night we had experienced at Geoff's house, we were both very tired as we humped our kit into the Glencoe Bunkhouse at ten o'clock that evening. The other course members had already retired to bed and, after a quick drink of hot chocolate, we followed suit.

I slept well and felt surprisingly fresh as I set off with the other five members of the course for what Richard Stanley, Geoff's colleague, described as a brisk walk to loosen up our limbs. It was a beautiful morning and we drove to the eastern end of the Pass of Glencoe in the climbing school's Bedford van. The River Coe bubbled and sparkled alongside us as we headed towards Rannoch Moor with three mighty peaks, the sisters of Glencoe, towering high above us on our right. We were making for Meall a Bhuiridh where, according to Richard, some useful snow slopes were to be found, near the Glencoe Ski Area.

The appearance of a chair lift, with its steel pylons glinting in the sun as they climbed towards a distant ridge, revealed that we were nearing our destination. Sure enough, a few minutes later, we turned off the smooth tarmac road onto a cinder track which took us to the foot of the chair lift. A brightly-clad skier was making a rapid and effortless ascent of the peak in one of the chairs.

Richard must have read my thoughts for, as we got out of the van, he pointed towards a grass and heather-covered slope to the right of the pylons. "Ignore that ski-lift. We're walking up."

Before we set off up the slope Richard supplied me with an ice axe, all the others already having their own. As it was not immediately needed, I clipped it safely to my belt.

There was no snow on the lower slopes and we were able to make quite quick time up the damp, peaty hillside. Despite the fact that I regarded myself as being quite fit I was struggling to keep up with the pace which Richard was setting. The sun was hot and my shirt was soon wet with perspiration. My rests were just starting to become embarrassingly frequent when the slope began to flatten out and a small plateau appeared ahead of us. Steep, snow-covered slopes rose from the plateau on three sides.

Richard gathered us around him.

"Okay. Today I want you all to get some practice at using your ice-axe to stop yourselves from sliding out of control down a snow slope."

The snow was firm and, Richard having demonstrated how it was done, we spent much of the day climbing up the various steep slopes, kicking steps with our boots as we went, before throwing ourselves off the top and trying to arrest our fall by digging our ice axes into the snow. Achieving a rapid and effective stop was not as easy as it looked but I worked hard to master the technique, being well aware that, if it ever came to the real thing on a high mountain, it would be a very useful trick to have up my sleeve. By mid-afternoon I was satisfied that I was fully proficient on even the steepest of slopes and it was time to be heading back down.

The sun was setting behind the mountains in the west as we reached the van. We had not seen a cloud all day. The sky was a glorious blue and I was greatly looking forward to my next excursion into the mountains, being blissfully unaware of how relatively uncommon such perfect days are in Glencoe.

= = = = = = = = = = = = = =

The rain came at us in sheets, driven by a blustery wind from the bleak flatness of Rannoch Moor, as we made our way across the sodden, squelching surface of the valley below our objective for the day, Stob Dearg.   Rising to 3345 feet, this was the north-eastern summit of the Buachaille Etive Mor.

The choice for the day had lain between climbing the Buachaille and doing a bit of technical rock climbing on a group of cliffs known as The Etive Slabs. On Geoff's advice I had joined the party to the Buachaille. The Slabs involved rock work of a type I was very unlikely to come across in the Himalayas.

The path we were following wound around the contours of a slope which led to the beginning of a route up the Buchaille known as Curved Ridge.   The rain continued to lash down upon us as we reached some vertical cliffs which rose, almost sheer, for what seemed to be a couple of thousand feet. This was our route. The top three or four hundred feet were completely lost in thick grey clouds which clung to the cliffs and reached out over the whole of the valley. I could not see how anyone could contemplate climbing them in the prevailing conditions. The rocky walls, glistening wet in the all-pervading dampness and cold, seemed to breathe out a mysterious and frightening air which created an atmosphere that rejected our presence.

Richard had stopped.

"We'd better get together in the shelter of this boulder and chat about the climb for a few minutes, I think."

The four of us huddled in the lee of the rock to shelter from the torrential rain, which by this time had penetrated right through my waterproof hood and cagoule. The conditions meant that maintaining some speed was important, to avoid getting cold. It was therefore decided that we would climb Alpine-style, roped together in pairs. I would be with Richard, who would lead. I still had my reservations about the whole idea but, precise and methodical in everything he did, I was confident that Richard would get me up the Buachaille safely if anyone could.

He explained the basics of Alpine-style climbing.

"As we climb, each of us must keep a close eye on the person they are roped to. If it looks as though your partner is getting into trouble, and in danger of coming off, you must get your rope around a spike of rock or a ledge; anything that will do as a belay. If you're on a ridge, the best thing is to throw yourself off the other side to act as a counter-weight and stop your partner's fall. You must be prepared all the time for an emergency. Both your lives could depend on it because if you don't react quickly enough you'll both come off together."

I listened very carefully as he spoke, trying to commit every instruction to memory.

"Right. Let's get roped up and make a start on it. I think the weather might improve later."

The comfort that can be squeezed out of a 150 foot length of climbing rope is quite remarkable. I found myself climbing with almost total confidence, secure in the knowledge that, whatever I did, Richard would be very unlikely to make a mistake. Up and up we went, the climbing becoming progressively more difficult as we gained height. I avoided downward glances as much as possible but, on the occasions when it was unavoidable, the reassuring presence of the rope helped to preserve my peace of mind.

As we got higher, the moor beneath us slowly merged into the mist and rain, and finally disappeared from view altogether. The clouds swirled about us and, while I was quite glad that the giddy drop was hidden from sight, I was slightly sorry that the magnificent prospect across Rannoch Moor to the east was also lost with it. It seemed a pity to expend so much effort and see nothing.

We were now in a light-grey world of our own, completely surrounded by the thick clouds and mist. Time lost its meaning, and I had no idea how high up we were, or remotely how long we had been climbing. I just continued to pull myself automatically upwards, following where Richard led and all the time watching him closely in case of any slip. On his advice I stopped to belay myself around a convenient rock as he tackled what looked like a particularly tough section, feeding the rope out to him slowly as he ascended.

"Okay, John. You can come up now."

I knew that Richard would have found a secure belay on to the ledge which he had reached, and a couple of slips on the trickier bits did not concern me too much. A few moves, and I was able to heave myself up alongside him.

The ledge was wider than I had expected. Above it was a white slope, indistinct in the mist. The rain had turned to snow which was falling quite heavily and I realised that we must be near the top. Richard confirmed our position.

"Only a couple of hundred more feet to go now. We'll stop here for a rest and some lunch."

There was just the snow slope to negotiate and we would be on our way down. My exertions had completely banished all feelings of coldness and damp and I felt a little disappointed that the climb would so soon be over. I was enjoying myself.

The other pair of climbers, who had been following close behind, soon joined us on the ledge, which easily accommodated the four of us, and we feasted upon a traditional climbers' lunch of Mars Bars and apples; the former for their concentrated energy and the latter because they are easily eaten and light. We ate quickly for, within ten minutes, the warmth which our climb had generated was beginning to dissipate, and I was starting to shiver. It was time to move on.

The snow slope cannot have been steeper than fifty degrees at any point, but the prospect of losing our footing and sliding back over the precipice which we had just ascended made us extremely careful. The visibility was deteriorating by the minute, and white-out conditions soon prevailed. Visibility was down to just a few feet and, when the slope flattened out and Richard announced that we were on the summit, we had to take his word for it.

We did not stop, but carried on, still roped together, along the ridge which runs the length of the Buchaille Etive Mor, from the peak of Stob Dearg at 3345 feet, which we had just climbed, to the other main peak, Stob na Broige, at 3120 feet. A short walk along the crest of the ridge then brought us to an easy-angled gully which would take us back down to the moor.

At the top of the gully we removed our ropes. I watched as the others tried to glissade down the slope, and then followed their example. A glissade is like skiing, but sliding on the soles of one's boots rather than on skis. When it works it is a breath-taking experience which is all too quickly over. More often than not, however, it ends up as an uncontrollable slide and roll in which the soles of the boots play little or no part. On my first attempt I managed to stay upright for about fifty feet before hitting some softer snow and ploughing to an undignified halt. Subsequent attempts were little better.

As we reached the bottom of the gully, and began our walk back across the moor to the van, the clouds broke up to reveal a watery, late afternoon sun.

"I said it would turn out fine," said Richard.

None of us could honestly disagree. It had been a challenging day, climbing in the foulest of weather, but now that it was over there was a feeling of no little achievement, and very great satisfaction.

= = = = = = = = = = = = = =

The rest of the course passed quickly and without incident. The weather, true to form, continued to be wet and stormy and, on two of the remaining days, conditions were so bad that any thought of venturing into the mountains was out of the question. I had to be content with sitting inside and talking to Geoff about various aspects of mountain safety and climbing while, outside the bunkhouse, the low clouds hid the surrounding crags from sight and rain pelted down upon the valley.

It was still wet when I finally left the bunkhouse to travel back to Liverpool. As the peaks of Glencoe disappeared behind me I still felt far from confident about my ability to cope with what lay ahead, but I consoled myself with two thoughts. I now felt completely at home with the equipment which I would be using. And, even more importantly, I felt I had developed a much better understanding of how to look after myself in the mountains.

The statistics at that time indicated that one climber in eight failed to return from the Himalayas. I just hoped that I had learnt enough to make my personal odds a little more favourable.

Three

OVERLAND TO INDIA

We left Liverpool in our fully loaded lorry and trailer on a damp and foggy Friday morning in mid-April. Despite a tendency for the brakes to over-heat slightly we reached Dover without incident and caught the midnight ferry to Ostend. The ferry docked at four in the morning and, having snatched some sleep during the channel crossing, we headed straight off towards Brussels and the border between Belgium and Germany. After a very long day we finally reached Cologne, where we stopped for the night.

Early the next morning, while making steady progress along a fast autobahn, we were pulled in by the German traffic police, lights flashing, and told that it was illegal for a heavy goods vehicle to tow a trailer on a Sunday. Politely, but very firmly, we were instructed to pull in at the next service station and wait until after midnight before resuming our journey.

Those of us who had been doing the driving were, by this time, not at all certain about the safety and effectiveness of the lorry's braking system so we decided to make use of the unscheduled stop to replace the master brake cylinder with a spare which we were carrying with us. The task kept us busy for much of the day, after which we drove the lorry round the service station a few times to test the new system. It seemed to be slightly better, but the brake pedal was still soft with a tendency to lift slightly from time to time. Things were clearly not completely right but we were reluctant to waste more time by doing further work on the system, so we decided to see how things went.

Immediately after midnight we were on our way again. We crossed the border into Austria without any further problems and, having made up some time by means of another day of non-stop driving, we felt able to stop overnight just south of Salzburg.

Our route next day took us through spectacular, alpine scenery towards Villach, along winding mountain roads. The heavily-laden lorry struggled on the steep, uphill gradients, which reached one in five on some sections, and all of us except the driver were forced to get out and walk alongside the lorry to lighten the load. This did not slow us down much, for the lorry could not manage much more than walking pace on such hills, and the opportunity to stretch our legs amidst such beautiful scenery was no hardship. During our stop to work on the brake system Roger Brook had cobbled together some large, wooden wheel chocks for use in emergency and, as we walked along, four of us kept close to the labouring vehicle at all times, chocks in hand, ready to jam them behind the wheels should the engine stall and the lorry start to roll backwards down the hill.

Just short of Villach we reached the top of the final pass and commenced our descent, along equally windy and precipitous roads. On one particularly steep section, the lorry continued to creep slowly forwards despite the brakes being full on. The wooden chocks brought it to a halt but, fearful that the brakes might fail altogether, we stopped in the next lay-by to replace the rest of the braking system. Fitting new cylinders to all the wheels took the best part of twelve hours but under the circumstances we all felt that it was time well spent.

With a completely refurbished system, the brakes at last felt fine but even so, when we discovered that our planned route out of the Alps along a series of minor roads into Yugoslavia involved descending a one in three hill, we took a detour along a more forgiving major road which brought us down into Italy instead. This added several hours to our journey, but it ensured that we were able to leave the mountains behind us without further mishap.

Once we had crossed the border from Italy into Northern Yugoslavia a very modern motorway led us uneventfully across the flat plains, past Zagreb and onwards to Belgrade. As we motored further east the roads deteriorated, the smooth tarmac being replaced by old cobbles with numerous potholes. There were few private cars. The other vehicles on the road were mainly old agricultural wagons which trundled along very slowly from farm to farm, and huge trans-continental lorries which thundered past us at high speed en route to Tehran and the booming, oil-based economy of Iran.

So far, the various border checks had gone smoothly, but we were now approaching Bulgaria. We had been warned that the border guards there could be difficult, especially with vehicles that did not fit into their standard categories. Sure enough, after passing through the Yugoslavian exit checks, we were waved into a large compound behind the Bulgarian customs post.

"You will take all your luggage out and place it alongside your vehicle."

The fact that it would take us at least an hour to comply with this terse instruction was clearly immaterial to the uniformed guard. He had a machine gun in his hand, and he looked as though he would not need to think for very long before using it. In the early nineteen seventies the cold war was still a very real fact of life, and Bulgaria was a totalitarian, Leninist dictatorship. We had reached Winston Churchill's 'Iron Curtain'.

Without any argument we unlocked the lorry and trailer and began the long task of unloading our gear as the guard looked on, fingering his weapon. Just over an hour later, all our equipment and possessions were laid out on the ground, exactly as requested. The armed guard, and two others who had joined him, then climbed up into the empty lorry and began to kick and bang against the metal sides of the vehicle, before repeating the process with the trailer.

"They're checking for hidden compartments," whispered Bryan, who had crossed this border before. "They'll make us open the cases next."

Just as he had predicted, as soon as they had satisfied themselves that there was nothing hidden on the lorry and trailer the guards selected half a dozen of the wooden crates and indicated that they should be emptied of their contents. Four of the selected cases contained food, and two contained climbing equipment. After the contents had been tipped out, the guards tore open a couple of bags of our precious, dehydrated stew before pouring the contents out onto the dusty ground. Dry, shrivelled pieces of meat, potato and vegetable lay in a small mound until, using the toe of his boot, the man with the machine gun spread it out.

"Expedition, ya?"

We nodded.

"Okay. Now this. Open."

He kicked his foot against one of the large drums which contained our medical supplies.

I stepped forward, holding my passport open at the page which indicated that I was a doctor.

"Doctor," I said, pointing at myself, and then at the drum. "Medicines. For sickness."

Before opening the drum, I wanted to try and indicate that the numerous packs of pills, which he would see as soon as the lid was removed, were not illicit drugs being smuggled into his country.

His foot kicked the drum again.

"Open."

I prised the lid off the drum and the officer put his hand inside. He pulled out several packs of penicillin tablets and studied them for a few moments before looking at me and shrugging his shoulders quizzically.

"Antibiotics." I answered his implied question. "Antibiotics for infections. I am a medical doctor."

I again pointed at myself and held up my passport, hoping that words such as doctor and antibiotic were fairly universal and widely understood.

Without any hint of a smile, or any indication at all that he had understood me, the packets were returned to the drum unopened.

"Okay. Close."

The three men then indicated that we could begin the task of reloading all our equipment into the lorry and trailer. One of them held out his right hand.

"All passports, please."

We handed our passports to the men who turned on their heels and walked off into a nearby building without another word. Two hours later, with our equipment repacked and with our passports stamped with the necessary entry permits, we were ready to move on, somewhat apprehensively, into Bulgaria.

A newly-constructed highway, flanked by huge banners every couple of miles which announced that the road was a generous gift from the people of Russia to their communist comrades, took us across a dry and barren landscape, past Sofia, and on to Plovdiv. Most of the buildings we passed were functional and drab, but the citizens of every small town were making elaborate preparations for the parades and celebrations which were due to take place on the first of May to commemorate the revolution. Despite their obvious poverty, the people were expected to put on a good show. Grey concrete blocks of flats were festooned with bright red banners, many carrying pictures of Lenin, with the obligatory hammer and sickle. Huge posters, alongside the road and on every traffic island, depicted happy and smiling workers; the men with shirt-sleeves rolled up to show sun-tanned, rippling muscles, and the women with peasant clothing and fresh, healthy faces. The totalitarian images of state-enforced happiness were utterly depressing. It was a chilling, real-life version of George Orwell's Nineteen Eighty Four.

By the time we reached the outskirts of Plovdiv we were running low on fuel. Geoff Arkless, who had just taken over the driving from Bryan Pooley, made the mistake of entering a petrol station the wrong way. Within minutes the local police arrived, having been alerted to Geoff's misdemeanour by the garage proprietor who had appeared from his office as soon as the police car drew up. After a brief conversation between the policemen and the garage owner, accompanied by a lot of gesticulating and pointing in our direction, Geoff was led off, to the accompaniment of perhaps slightly unwise shouts from Bryan Pooley, who was relieved not to be the one in trouble.

"Send us a post-card and let us know what the weather's like in Siberia, Geoff."

As we watched, Geoff was pushed into the back seat of the police car. We were half-expecting him to be driven off, leaving our expedition one climber short, but after a few minutes he emerged again, looking a little shaken.

"They said they'll arrest me unless we pay a fine," he announced as he approached. "And no more wisecracks about Siberia, or we'll all end up in jail. One of them speaks quite good English."

Tony hastily paid the requested fine, which turned out to be the equivalent of about fifteen shillings, and we left the petrol station without filling up. The policemen had simply pocketed the cash, and it seemed highly unlikely that it would reach any official destination. We assumed that the garage proprietor would probably be getting a cut of the cash once we had driven on, and we were certainly not going to give him our business as well. We were carrying some spare fuel in jerry cans, and we would use them if we were in danger of running out.

As it turned out the next garage was only about five miles on, and we spent all the rest of our Bulgarian currency on fuel. The cashier, who was friendly and spoke almost perfect English, told us that if we had purchased some state petrol coupons at the border we could have saved ourselves twenty percent on the cost. It was not a huge sum of money but it was annoying that the border officials had chosen not to let us know about this arrangement. On our tight budget every penny counted, and this latest news convinced us that Bulgaria was not a place where we should hang about. We would get out of the country, and across the border into Turkey, as quickly as possible.

We reached the Turkish border late at night. It was almost deserted and, apart from the need to enter the details of the vehicle and trailer into our passports to prevent us selling it while we were in Turkey, there were hardly any formalities. We were through, and on our way to Istanbul, in less than fifteen minutes, the border officials obviously having decided that getting back to sleep was preferable to taking apart our lorry.

We drove on and reached the outskirts of Istanbul just as the sun started to rise. We were sorely in need of some sleep and a good shower, and Bryan knew of a camp site called Mocamp BP, about eight miles outside the city, with washing facilities and a self-service laundry. He had stayed there the previous year, and he was confident that it would be a good place to stop for forty eight hours of rest and recreation.

The first leg of our long overland journey was nearly over. Soon we would be leaving Europe and crossing the Bosporus into Asia. It felt as though the real adventure was just about to begin.

Aiming High – Overland to the Himalayas 1971

Communist Bulgaria in 1971 – behind the Iron Curtain *(JW)*

Four

ACROSS THE BOSPORUS

Istanbul, ancient Constantinople and city of the Blue Mosque, had a very Asian feel to it. Situated at one of the historic meeting points of the east and the west, it had always been a cosmopolitan melting pot. Modern buildings were springing up here and there, but they seemed to be part of an ongoing and natural evolution which would be unlikely to change the city's character.

In the old covered market the 'percentage boys', who made a living from the tips which they would get from the vendors in the event of a successful sale, took us to stalls where shelves and baskets held myriad different spices and exotic foods, many of which we could not identify. As we wandered along the bustling alleyways eager hands tried to pull us into shops. Salesmen chattered away as they attempted to interest us in leather goods, brass pots, filigree silverware, carpets, cloths and a thousand and one other exotic items. Several offered to buy the smart 'explorer' wristwatches, which had been given to us by the manufacturer in the hope that they would survive the extreme weather and temperature conditions in the high mountains. If they did, photographs of the watches in active use would be likely to feature in their future advertising campaigns. So, tempting as it was to turn the expensive timepieces into much needed cash, they were unfortunately not for sale.

As we were not really in the market for purchases, we soon discovered just how far below the original price the sellers were prepared to drop. The price of many items quickly fell to less than a third of the opening offer. Tony, in particular, tried to perfect his bargaining technique, for he knew that he would need to haggle hard if we were to avoid being overcharged for the many porters we would need to hire once we reached the mountains.

Early in the morning, after two days in Istanbul, it was time to head for Asia. As we drove along the waterfront we passed groups of labourers who were working on the foundations of Istanbul's first suspension bridge. Completion of this project was still a year or two away, so we were making our way to one of the ferries which, prior to the bridge being finished, was the only way to get a vehicle across the Bosporus, the narrow stretch of water which joined the Mediterranean to the Black Sea, and which separated Europe from Asia.

The Bosporus was half-hidden by a low, early morning mist as our lorry and trailer joined a ramshackle bunch of other vehicles in the queue for the short crossing. Once the ferry had been fully loaded it turned into the mist, sounding its foghorn as it cut through the water towards the far shore. In less than fifteen minutes Asia loomed into view and, as we looked back, the fortified walls of Istanbul gradually disappeared into the mist.

Our journey to India would take us along one of the ancient trade routes through old Asia Minor, Iran, Afghanistan and Pakistan. Iran, still ruled by the Shah of Persia, was a friend of the west, as was Pakistan, once part of British India. Afghanistan, by contrast, was then a mysterious and little known place, an Islamic country nominally ruled by a king, Muhammad Zahir Shah, but in practice controlled by a number of rival war-lords, each with their own territory which they ruled as they saw fit. The situation was not unlike England in the middle ages, when it was the feudal barons who really held sway over people's everyday lives, rather than the king who was based far away in London.

Afghanistan is a harsh and mountainous land with cold winters and long, hot summers. Situated in a land-locked, but strategic, position between Russia and China to the north, India and Pakistan to the south and east, and Iran and the other Middle Eastern countries to the west, it has been fought over by many nations and empires over the years, none of whom have been able to subjugate it for very long. For twenty or thirty years prior to 1971 it had largely been left in peace, but from the nineteen eighties onwards the lessons of history would be ignored and it would be invaded once again, first by the U.S.S.R., and then by the U.S.A. and Britain. As their armies tried in vain to assert effective control over the country, previously unheard of places such as Kabul and Kandahar would become household names throughout the western world.

After disembarking from the ferry we pushed on through Eastern Turkey, passing the capital, Ankara, and heading towards the southern coast of the Black Sea. The journey was uneventful. To obtain fresh fruit we bartered with local farmers, exchanging cigarettes for oranges and apples. It was still spring and the weather was pleasantly warm as we followed the coast, passing empty beaches of black sand and driving along the top of steep cliffs. After an overnight stop near a town called Trabzon, during which we slept under the stars around the lorry, knives in hand in case of thieves, we turned inland into the mountainous eastern region of Turkey which would lead us to the border with Iran.

As we climbed up to a pass at 7,500 feet we saw army camps and many NATO troops, both American and Turkish. Notices warned us that stopping and taking photographs was strictly prohibited. The border with the U.S.S.R. was a mere fifty miles away to the north-west and the whole area was on permanent military alert. As we left the restricted area Bryan pointed out Mount Ararat, one of a number of mountain peaks which could be seen in the distance to the north. Numerous photographs were taken, only for another, much larger, volcanic cone to come into view, some thirty miles further on, with a smaller cone alongside it.

"Sorry lads. The last mountain wasn't Ararat. That's definitely it. And the one alongside it is Little Ararat."

Bryan's change of opinion was not gracefully received, for our previous photographs could not simply be erased from our cameras. Digital photography, and the luxury of being able to shoot off numerous pictures and see the results instantly, before deleting the unwanted ones, was far in the future and between us we had wasted almost a whole roll of our valuable supply of 35mm Kodachrome film.

These 'mountains of Urartu' in eastern Turkey were, according to The Bible, the legendary resting place of Noah's Ark. Mount Ararat itself is the highest peak in the region at just under 16,000 feet. A dormant volcano, it is permanently capped with snow, and a large glacier winds down the north- eastern side of the mountain from the summit snowfield, covering the black larva on the upper slopes. Expeditions have been mounted over the years to try and find the remains of the Ark but, despite some claims of success, no convincing trace of the ancient vessel has ever been discovered.

Several ancient texts, in addition to The Bible, contain references to a great flood, so it is very likely that some sort of major disaster once occurred in the region. Recent underwater explorations have found evidence that the Black Sea was almost certainly once a fresh water lake which was suddenly inundated in around 5000 BC. The waters of the Mediterranean Sea, which had risen as the glacial sheets covering Northern Europe slowly melted, are thought to have broken through a land barrier, catastrophically flooding the lake and the surrounding valleys. The lake's water level rose by several hundred feet as a torrent of water, two hundred times as powerful as Niagara Falls, continued to flow through the breach for some three hundred days, transforming the previous fresh water lake into what is now the Black Sea. By the time the deluge finally came to an end, the Mediterranean Sea and the Black Sea were joined together by the Bosporus, and any human settlements which may once have been on the shores of the lake had been totally destroyed. They now lie three or four hundred feet under the sea. The story of the flood may be based upon a historic event, but if a wooden ark ever came to rest on Mount Ararat, it would, by now, have been eroded away by the weather, or ground into dust by the constantly moving glacier. It is not likely that any remains will ever be found.

We had been warned that these mountains were bandit country, and that it would be unwise to stop for any reason. There were stories of lorries being fired upon and hijacked, and we were told that some of the drivers of the big intercontinental lorries had rifles stowed away in their cabs to protect their valuable loads. The roads were appalling but, being mindful of this danger, we kept up a steady pace, stopping for nothing despite the numerous large potholes. As we passed through small villages local youths threw stones at the windscreen of our lorry to try and make us stop, but without success. And any bandits who took pot-shots at us from the surrounding hills must have missed, for we emerged from the mountains unscathed. By six o'clock in the evening we had reached the Iranian border.

The Turkish border police were surly and awkward. Even though the registration numbers on our vehicles clearly matched the entries in our passports, they pretended to be unconvinced that the lorry and trailer were the same ones that we had brought into the country.

It was possible that our transit through customs would have been much easier if we had slipped a few dollars into one of the passports before they were handed over for checking, but we had no spare money. One of the customs men flicked through all the passports, as if looking for something, but we pretended not to understand. It was with ill-grace that they eventually cancelled the relevant pages with official rubber stamps and waved us on our way.

The contrast, when we reached the smiling Iranians, could not have been more marked. They politely advised us that we would need to purchase a government-approved insurance for our vehicle, at a nominal cost, which would be valid for a single transit of their country lasting up to one month. There were no searches, and no requests for *baksheesh*, or bribes. We emerged from the customs area onto a silky-smooth, tarmac road, the edges of which were crisp and clearly marked.

Unlike Eastern Turkey, Iran was unmistakably affluent with well-maintained shops and houses. Golden statues of the Shah of Iran, Mohammed Reza Pahlavi, seemed to be everywhere. It was obvious that we were now in a country which had grown wealthy on the proceeds of its enormous oil reserves. Supported, as he was, by America and the other western nations, it seemed that the Shah was in an impregnable position. The Pahlavi dynasty had ruled Persia for many years, and the vital strategic interests of the west, with its need for a reliable supply of oil, would, it seemed, ensure that he would never be allowed to fall. As long as the oil dollars continued to flow into the country, and enough of them found their way to the ordinary people to improve their standard of living, all would surely be well.

Next day, after an overnight stop just beyond a town called Maku, we reached Tabriz, a university town. The main street was thronged with people, who were going in and out of shops which looked very western. Many of the older women still wore traditional dark blue and black veils which covered their faces, leaving only their eyes showing, but the young students were all in jeans, tee-shirts and mini-skirts. Were it not for their uniformly dark, straight hair and middle-eastern complexion, they could easily have been mistaken for the undergraduates of any European or American university. The contrast between the youngsters and their elders was stark and, although we did not think much of it at the time, it was a pointer to the rapid changes which were taking place in a country whose official religion was still the very traditional, Shi'a Islam. This rapid westernisation, and what was seen as the malign influence of Britain and the United States upon the politics and the economy of the country, was anathema to the religious community and, less than ten years later, everything would change. The Shah would fall, and Iran would become an Islamic Republic led by the Ayatollah Khomeini.

The road from Tabriz to Tehran, the Shah's capital city, took us through irrigated valleys where numerous crops were being cultivated. What looked like cherry blossom trees were heavy with pink and white flowers, and tall, thin cypresses made some areas feel almost like Tuscany. Unlike Italy, though, the valleys we were following were narrow, green ribbons, threading their way through an otherwise arid landscape of dust-brown hills and rocky mountains, which rose ever higher as we neared the capital.

As the number of houses and other buildings increased, the road which we were following ran alongside a section of the Trans-Asian Railway. This was a project which had been started in the 1960s with the hope that Singapore and the Far East could be connected by rail to Europe. The dream was that such a line would transform transport and trade across the whole region. It was seen as a modern version of the old Silk Road, but whether it will ever be completed is uncertain. Forty years on, the practical and political problems which would need to be overcome seem insuperable.

The distance from Maku to Tehran was about four hundred and fifty miles and, after spending several nights by the roadside, we were keen to reach Gol-e-Sahra, an official campsite on the western edge of Tehran which had been recommended to us. It was a long journey, even on the good Iranian roads. Despite having made an early start, it was four o'clock the next morning before we finally came to a halt outside the entrance to the campsite. We had been on the road for almost nineteen hours, and we were desperate for sleep, but the steel gates were locked and chained. Roger and Geoff Tabbner wanted to move on and find somewhere else but, from what we could see through the railings, the facilities looked excellent and, by a five to two majority vote, it was decided that we would wait outside until morning. It proved to be a wise decision. When we got inside, four hours later, we were welcomed by a good restaurant, a hot breakfast, plentiful showers and a large, modern swimming pool. As the total cost was the equivalent of just one pound per day, we could afford to stop there for at least a couple of nights.

At the campsite, as well as relaxing and catching up on some much needed sleep, we were able to exchange stories and information with other travellers. Some of them were Australians, who were doing the overland journey the other way, from Sydney via Singapore and India, to London. As they had very recently passed through India, Pakistan and Afghanistan, the advice they were able to offer us was both up-to-date and invaluable.

One couple, who were travelling to Britain in a flower-painted VW camper van, described how, when changing money at the border between Afghanistan and Pakistan, they had been advised by the Afghan border official that if they waited half an hour, until the border office closed, the exchange rate would move from the official government rate of about ten Afghanis to the dollar to the black market rate of thirty to the dollar. When they expressed some doubt about waiting, the official immediately stood up and moved the hands on the wall clock, which had no cover, forwards by half an hour. He then declared that the office was closed and the black market exchange rate was applicable.

They also warned us that the penalty for being caught smuggling drugs into Iran from Afghanistan was death by firing squad, the sentence being carried out at an army barracks near the border, possibly without trial and often within twenty four hours. They had checked their camper van very carefully before crossing the border, as packs of drugs might have been taped to the underside by Afghanistan-based smugglers whose accomplices would then retrieve the packets when they had safely reached Iran. They had heard that a couple of Americans had recently been caught with some drugs attached to their vehicle and, despite their protestations of innocence, they had been summarily shot. We took note that on our way back to Europe we would need to make a very thorough check.

Together with this couple and another group of Australians we travelled by taxi into the centre of the city on our second evening. Tehran in 1971 was a bustling metropolis. In the centre of the city there were wide boulevards which were busy with modern cars, and as we looked down the side streets we could see modern-looking shopping and commercial areas. Unlike the more provincial towns, where there was still a sense of the old Iran, the capital city seemed to be almost completely westernised. Men and women of all ages wore standard western clothes, and most of the cars were American and European in style. The shops and hotels in the city centre were smart and well looked after. The streets were clean and almost completely free of litter. There was a relaxed and friendly atmosphere, and the city felt safe.

We ate in the restaurant of the Hotel Marmar on Avenue Zahedi, the hotel having been named after the Marmar Palace, which was then the home and imperial palace of the Shah. The restaurant was not as palatial as its name but it looked clean and the chelow kebabs were excellent. Chelow kebab is the national dish of Iran, consisting of steamed, saffroned basmati, or Persian, rice, topped with butter and served with grilled tomatoes and kebabs. After placing a dish of rice in front of me the waiter went back to the kitchen and reappeared, holding two skewers of kebabs in his left hand and a large piece of nan bread in his right hand. The kebabs, one lamb and one minced chicken with parsley, were placed on top of the rice, followed by the nan and, with the nan bread pressed firmly down to hold the skewered meats in place, the skewers were deftly withdrawn. With a flourish and a bow, the waiter then left us to enjoy our meal. The traditional beverage to go with this dish is *doogh*, a sour, fermented yoghurt, but we all opted for bottled Coke.

Next morning it was time to take leave of our relatively luxurious stopover in the Gol-e-Sahra campsite. Despite not getting back from the Hotel Marmar until about 3 a.m. the previous night, we had planned an early start, but the campsite manager had gone into Tehran, taking our passports with him. He did not return until mid-morning and by the time we were on the move the traffic in the centre of Tehran was chaotic. Vans and cars weaved and meandered along the wide streets, taking no notice at all of policemen, traffic lights, or other road users. Fortunately our heavy, ex-military lorry was sturdy enough to intimidate other drivers, and we emerged from the chaos without incident.

Our route now took us along the southern edge of the Elburz Mountains, a range of jagged snow-capped peaks averaging 9000 feet in height. To our north, hidden from us by the mountains, lay the Caspian Sea, the largest lake on the planet, but we would be driving south-east, away from the sea and towards the Dasht-e Kavir. The Dasht-e Kavir, also known as the Kavir-e Namak or Great Salt Desert, is a large and arid region which lies in the middle of the Iranian plateau. Its climate is almost completely rainless, and daytime temperatures can reach 50 degrees centigrade in the summer while, even in mid-winter, the temperature rarely drops below 22 degrees. As in all desert regions the nights are cold, and the temperature in the early hours can drop below freezing.

To save time we had decided to follow a dirt road which ran along the northern edge of the desert, rejoining the main road just before the ancient city of Mashed. This route would take us on a two hundred and fifty mile journey along a road which would at best be a dirt track and which might, at worst, disappear altogether beneath wind-blown sand and dust. It turned out to be rougher than we had expected. Hard ridges of baked mud and salt, covered with numerous rocks and pebbles, made the going extremely uneven and we had to experiment to find the least uncomfortable method of covering the ground. By a process of trial and error we managed to establish that, at a constant speed of between 40 and 45 mph, the lorry rode most of the bumps without too much trouble, the only problem being the clouds of dust that were thrown up and blown into our vehicle, making progress both hot and uncomfortable.

The late start from Tehran meant that we were still deep in the desert as night began to fall. In the fading light it became increasingly difficult to differentiate the road from the surrounding desert sands and it was clear that we had no choice but to stop for the night. We had not seen another vehicle or person since venturing into the desert, so we reasoned that there should at least be no need to worry about bandits or thieves.

After a cool night we woke at dawn to continue our journey. In the early morning light the desert stretched out as far as the eye could see in all directions. Despite the harshness of the landscape, there was a curiously hypnotic beauty about the place. It would be easy to underestimate its dangers. Huge hills of sand stretched out along the southern horizon, piled up by the strong winds which can appear without warning in such flat, desert regions. In places the fine sand, which covered most of the surface of the desert, had been blown away to reveal a thick crust of salt beneath which, it was said, lay treacherous, quicksand-like areas of salt marsh. In the long distant past this region lay beneath a salt sea which had become land-locked as a result of movements of the earth's crust. As the water slowly evaporated a dry, salty marshland was left behind. Our route, skirting the northern margin of the desert, kept us well away from the most dangerous parts of the salt marshes but there was still an acute awareness, as we thundered noisily along the ill-defined, ridged track, that whoever was driving needed to remain very alert and avoid wandering off the edge of the road, for it would not have been wise to get stuck in such a hostile place. It was something of a relief when, after a full morning of non-stop driving, we found ourselves back on the main road.

By lunchtime we had reached Mashad, which used to be a major oasis on the ancient Silk Road. Numerous major poets and religious figures in Iranian history had made it their home in centuries past, and it was in Mashad that the great Iranian poet, Ferdowsi, had composed the national epic Shahnameh, The Book of Kings, between 977 and 1010 A.D. This classic poem, consisting of some 50,000 couplet verses, tells the story of the Persian Empire from the creation of the world until the Islamic conquest of Persia in the 7th century, and it is still an important part of the cultural identity of both Iran and Afghanistan.

The city boasts major landmarks such as the Shrine of Imran Meza, the largest mosque in the world. Dominating the city like a huge medieval cathedral, the shrine has a shining, white facade which is covered with coloured, abstract designs, figurative art not being permitted by Islam. The tall, square entrance to the private, inner courtyards was richly painted, and through it we could see a huge, golden dome, sitting between tall, lavishly decorated, minarets. It would have been well worth stopping there for a while, but we had a mountain to climb and there was time only to take a few photographs before we had to move on towards the next border.

It was not possible to cross into Afghanistan at night, so we made camp about forty miles short of the border and slept under the stars. When we reached the well-kept buildings which marked the crossing point, at about eleven the next morning, the Iranians were, once again, straightforward and efficient. Our vehicle insurance was checked, our passports were stamped, and we were through.

The border between Turkey and Iran *(JW)*

Aiming High – Overland to the Himalayas 1971

Dust devils - Great Salt Desert – Iran *(JW)*

Five

AFGHANISTAN

The entry into Afghanistan, though, was markedly different. The border officials appeared to be having a siesta when we arrived and we had to sit in the lorry, hot and dusty, while a fierce wind whipped the sand on each side of the road up into the air, forming great clouds that obscured the sun and infiltrated every nook and cranny of the vehicle and our clothes. The customs post itself consisted of a pair of brick buildings, one on each side of the road which stretched ahead for unbending miles across the desert. The buildings were old and poorly maintained. Scrawny livestock wandered around and, when we were eventually permitted to enter and sit at a desk inside one of the customs offices, a couple of hens pecked away at the mud floor around our feet. The border police were polite and relaxed, but there was a huge mound of administrative paperwork to be completed, largely, it seemed, for the purpose of keeping people occupied. None of the officials appeared to care what we actually wrote in response to the questions on the numerous pieces of paper. The forms just had to be filled in.

Most of the questions concerned our lorry and trailer. According to the rules any vehicles entering Afghanistan had to be exported, rather than being left behind or sold. The lorry and trailer were to be entered on Bryan's passport, which he was not entirely happy about as he would be unable to leave the country without them, but the passport officer, who spoke quite reasonable English, suggested that if our lorry were to break down in the mountains and be abandoned, that would be a perfectly acceptable reason for not exporting it. Having received this reassurance Bryan agreed to his passport being stamped with the vehicle details and the necessary box was ticked. All was well. The papers had been completed according to the rules and officialdom was satisfied.

Formalities over, we needed to change some money. Tony pulled some dollars out of his case and, having satisfied himself that we were getting the 'best' exchange rate, he bought enough local currency to pay for the fuel we would need while passing through Afghanistan.

Having politely thanked the customs officials for their assistance, we were climbing back into the lorry ready to drive off when one of the men suddenly appeared alongside the passenger door.

"You have hashish?"

The question was asked in a friendly rather than an aggressive manner. In any case, as we had just left the Shah's Iran where the penalty for carrying drugs was death, the answer was obviously no, as we explained.

"Okay. So you want hashish?"

The customs officer thrust his hand into his coat and pulled out a lump of hash the size of a small loaf, wrapped in paper.

"Five dollars. Grade A, Afghan hashish. Best quality. You take."

We indicated to him that none of us were smokers and that there was therefore no point in us accepting his undoubtedly very generous offer.

"Three dollars."

He thrust the brown lump of hashish through the open window.

"Three dollars. Very good price. No smoke, so you eat. Cook in cake and eat. Three dollars."

We looked at each other.

"Two dollars then. Last price. Two dollars. Here, you take, now."

For two dollars we could almost afford to throw the hashish away once we were out of sight of the customs post so, to avoid upsetting him and maybe creating unnecessary problems, a couple of dollar notes changed hands and we were on our way. To use President Bill Clinton's famous phrase, we might have tried it, but we did not inhale. Although the effect may have been largely psychological, the Grade A hashish certainly made our journey through Afghanistan more interesting.

There is just one main highway in Afghanistan which runs from the border through Herat, south-east to Kandahar, and then northwards towards Kabul. The western and northern sections of the highway were built by the Russians. These two sections were then linked together by an American-built road, which passed through Kandahar in the south of the country. The Americans had constructed a conventional, single carriageway, tarmac road, but many of the Russian-built sections were long and straight, much wider than even the largest of lorries would ever need, and surfaced with thick, reinforced concrete slabs. These parts of the road, we were told by an American aid worker in Kandahar, were capable of taking the weight of tanks, and even aircraft. They had been designed by the Russians for a future invasion.

We drove into Herat, in the middle of the afternoon, along a tree-lined avenue. The trees looked like sturdy, drought resistant conifers, planted there to try and prevent the heat and dust of the surrounding desert from blowing into the town. Picturesque as the conifers were, the shops behind them were just simple, mud-built structures, with open fronts in which myriad items for sale were displayed. All the shops seemed to be selling the much same thing; basic cooking pots, carpets and wooden furniture.

As we neared the centre of the town we could see, ahead of us, the castle of Pai Hessar. It, too, seemed to be built from mud bricks, and it looked as though a good rainstorm would wash it away but, as it had survived for several hundred years at least, it was presumably sturdier than it looked. It was difficult to believe it had been built by Alexander the Great, as the locals claimed, but maybe it was not impossible.

In the heat of the afternoon, there were not many people out on the streets. The few wheeled vehicles which we saw were simple wooden carts, piled high with battered goods and pulled along either by hand or, in a couple of cases, by a scrawny donkey. There were a number of mosques in the town, some of which were clearly very old. They were all surrounded by minarets, the older ones of which were leaning over at seemingly impossible angles. These ancient minarets had lost all their tiles and they were presumably no longer in active use as it looked as though they could collapse at any minute.

The people we saw were all dressed in traditional Afghan costume. There was no sign of any western dress. Some of the women wore cotton trousers, known as tombaan, together with an overdress, and a head-covering which looked like a scarf or pashmina. Other women wore full length black or deep blue veils, keeping most of their faces covered. These veils, or burquas, were similar to those we had seen in the more provincial parts of Iran. The men, most of whom were strikingly handsome in appearance with rugged, sun-weathered faces, wore white turbans, roomy over-shirts and jackets, and traditional loose trousers, wide over the upper leg and narrower towards the ankle.

We stopped for an hour in the town, keeping a close eye on the lorry and taking turns to wander around the shops to exercise our legs, but there was nothing of sufficient interest to detain us for very long. By early evening we had left Herat behind us and pulled off the road for an overnight stop. We set up camp on a sandy plain which was covered with what seemed to be wild lavender bushes, the scent of which was carried gently towards us on the warm, evening wind as we sat and ate a meal of rice and stew before settling down for the night.

The highway which we were following traced a broad arc, passing to the west, and then to the south, of the mountain ranges which occupy almost all the central part of the country. This mountainous terrain, harsh and difficult to penetrate, was clearly visible from our camp. Because of these mountains, overland travel in the interior of Afghanistan is very difficult. They form almost impenetrable barriers that divide the country into numerous regions, each inhabited by different tribal groups. The mountains also provide the ideal terrain for guerrilla warfare, as many mighty armies have discovered to their cost over the centuries. Small, mobile groups of fighters are able to emerge from their rocky lairs and inflict significant damage upon their numerically superior and better equipped opponents before melting away again into the countless caves and valleys which are hidden away in the rocky hills.

During the whole of next day's journey to Kandahar we saw no more than three or four other motor vehicles on the road. A couple of ancient and gaudily-painted buses passed us heading for Herat, heavily loaded with local passengers. Several men, who had been unable to squeeze themselves inside, were perched up on the roof-rack along with their luggage which was wrapped in black cloth and secured to the rack with string. With so much weight on the roof the buses looked dangerously top-heavy and unstable. They rolled alarmingly from side to side as they approached us down the middle of the road, before swerving to the right hand side with just seconds to spare and careering past us. The only other traffic on the road consisted of heavily laden donkeys and camels, carrying goods to and from market. They walked obediently, just ahead of their owner, making their slow and steady way along the side of the highway.

Opportunities to refuel were infrequent, even on this main west-to-east highway, and whenever we came across a petrol station, which usually consisted of little more than a couple of pumps sitting alongside a few spartan huts in the middle of nowhere, we filled up our tank and all the spare jerry cans.

As we drew up alongside a pump, someone would appear out of one of the huts. The pump indicators used Arabic numerals, which we had taken care to learn. Zero was a single dot, and it was essential to make sure that the smiling, and seemingly helpful, pump operator had actually set the indicator to zero before he started pumping the fuel into our tank. To the side of each pump was a long lever which had to be pulled backwards and forwards by hand to deliver the fuel, there being no electricity available to operate it.

As well as being hand-operated, the pumps usually had no cover over the mechanical dial which indicated the quantity of fuel which was being dispensed. If not watched very carefully the attendant would sometimes try and use a spare finger to change the numbers in his favour by spinning the dial surreptitiously as he pumped away. We rapidly learnt that the best way to prevent such tricks was for one of us to lean casually against the pump, facing the man, and lift a cautionary finger if there was any movement of his spare hand towards the dials. An innocent smile and a shrug of his shoulders, usually accompanied by a side to side movement of his head, would indicate that he knew we were on to him. The transaction would then proceed amiably and without any problems.

As we neared Kandahar, which is situated in the south of Afghanistan and therefore has a warmer climate, we were averaging just over forty miles an hour along the well-made road. Things were going well when, at about two in the afternoon and without any warning, there was the sound of a muffled explosion from beneath the bonnet. The lorry ground to a halt. As soon as the bonnet had been opened it was clear to Geoff and Bryan what had happened. The sustained speed, combined with the afternoon heat, was causing our fuel to vaporise. Once the engine had cooled down a little they rigged up an improvised, cooler for the fuel delivery system, using crepe bandages, elastoplast, and the windscreen-washer tube. This, we hoped, would keep the problem under control until we reached the cooler air of the mountains.

Once we were on our way again we began to see occasional large tents pitched on the flat terrain between the highway and the hills. These tents were the homes of the *Kuchi* nomads. The Afghan/Persian word *'Kuchi'* means 'those who go on migrations', although the city-dwellers of Kabul tended to use the term *'Kuchi'* as a derogatory as well as descriptive term, much like the English word 'gypsy'. These nomads traditionally had a wandering lifestyle, moving from place to place with their families to seek fresh grazing for their livestock, but by the 1960s and 1970s many of the nomads tended to spend at least part of the year in one place, making a living by selling items such as meat and goat milk. A few individual herd-owners still clung to a totally nomadic lifestyle and they referred to themselves as *'Maldar'*, or *'Maldar Kuchi'* meaning migrating herd owners.

About two miles outside Kandahar lay an area known as Manzel Bag, an extensive government-owned, walled complex of modern houses, gardens and recreation areas. Known locally as 'Little America', the area was built as a residential zone for the foreign workers of the American Morrison-Knudson (Afghanistan) Construction Company who had been constructing an irrigation canal system in Helmand Province with the aim of improving the crop yields of the local farmers and encouraging them to move to a western style of farming. Sadly the project was not as successful as had been hoped. The newly irrigated land proved to be too saline for traditional crops, and many of the local farmers were forced to return to growing the opium poppy which thrives in almost any type of soil and is relatively drought resistant. In the absence of any viable alternative, the cultivation of the opium poppy seems destined to remain one of Afghanistan's main economic activities, and the best hope for the future may lie in diverting as much as possible of the crop to the production of legitimate, pharmaceutical products such as morphine, and away from illicit, black market heroin.

Manzel Bag was still being used as a U.S. Aid Base, and we were due to stop there for a meal at the invitation of Graham Craig, a New Zealander who was working with the Americans at the Base, and who Bryan, as a fellow New Zealander, had got to know during his previous visit to Afghanistan.

The city of Kandahar had been in slow decline from the late 18th century, having previously been a major cultural and government administrative centre, but by the mid-20th century it was starting to expand again, having become a major producer of wool, figs, pomegranates and apricots.

Graham and his wife Norma were expecting us, and we enjoyed a very welcome, home-cooked meal. We also made the most of the opportunity to have a hot shower and wash away the desert salt and dust which had accumulated over the past few days. We were not permitted to stay overnight in the compound so, at eleven in the evening, it was back on the road again, to put a few more miles on the clock before spending another night under the stars.

We reached Kabul at three o'clock the next afternoon after a spectacular drive through increasingly mountainous scenery, following the sturdily constructed Kandahar-Kabul highway. Kabul lies in a narrow valley at 5,900 feet above sea level, making it one of the highest capital cities in the world. It was founded over 3,500 years ago and, until the middle of the 18th century it had always been proudly independent. In 1747 it came under the control of the Durrani Empire, the rulers of which were based in Kandahar, followed, ninety years later, by the British. In the course of the First Anglo-Afghan War, the British Army invaded the city, only to sustain thousands of casualties in a subsequent ambush at nearby Jalalabad. In retaliation the British burnt Kabul to the ground before retreating back into India through the Khyber Pass.

The British forces continued intermittently to harass the city from India until the 1920s when, British resolve having been weakened by the First World War, Amanullah Khan drove them from the city and began a process of modernisation.

By the 1960s Kabul had become known as the Paris of Central Asia as it started to transform itself into a modern, European-style city with cinemas, cafes, formal gardens in the French style, schools, libraries, a university, and fine boutiques.

As we drove into the city the weather was clear and cloudless, as is the case for at least three hundred days each year. The surrounding peaks of the Hindu Kush Range, still largely snow-covered, were outlined against a deep, blue sky. Our plan had been to call in at the Pakistani Embassy, where we hoped to be able to collect the permits we would need in order to cross the border into India. Unfortunately the embassy was not easy to find and, despite apparently helpful directions from various local citizens, many of whom seemed to speak some English, we had no success.

"The Embassy for Pakistan? Let me think. Ah yes, I have it. You know the river? Yes? Well, the embassy is in that direction. Close to the river, I am sure."

After we had been given four or five completely different sets of directions, each time with no sign of the embassy turning up, we realised that we were the unwitting victims of a culture of helpfulness. The locals seemed to feel they had to offer some sort of information for the sake of politeness, even if they had no idea at all where the embassy was situated. By the time we eventually stumbled across it, the embassy was closed for the day. We would have to get our permits in Lahore, one of Pakistan's eastern border cities, instead.

Taking turns to guard the lorry, we took a wander around the city centre, during which we called in at the local market and surreptitiously watched the black market money-changers as they negotiated deals involving all the many currencies whose official rates were artificially maintained and bore little relationship to open market values. Many of the deals seemed to be with Indian businessmen, who at the time were prevented, by their government's currency exchange controls, from converting their rupees into hard currencies such as the US dollar. They would sit down with briefcases full of rupee notes, which had been smuggled out of their country, and happily accept deals at half, or even a third, of the official exchange rate in order to obtain precious, internationally accepted dollars. The rupee notes would then be sold to overland travellers, who were on their way to India, at a much better rate than was obtainable at banks within India. On each deal, the money-changers took a very generous commission. Although the trade was illegal, the money-changers were running little risk, while the businessmen had almost certainly paid out plenty of *baksheesh* to ensure that their passage out of India, with the rupees, was as risk-free as possible. The greatest risk was being taken by the travellers, who had to smuggle the black-market rupee notes back into India through customs. The penalty, if caught, could be a long stay in an Indian jail.

Most of the goods in the bazaar, in the older part of the city, were cheap, and poorly made. Afghan coats, which were very fashionable in London at the time, were on sale for as little as two or three dollars, the drawback being that the hides from which they were made had almost certainly been cured in camels' urine. When such coats were first purchased they seemed to be fine, but after a few weeks they would gradually start to smell. The stallholders, of course, were always happy to offer cast-iron guarantees that their coats were properly cured, reasoning that the most of the unlucky purchasers would be many miles away by the time the problems began to develop, and not in any position to complain. Undeterred, Roger bought one, his reasoning being that if he struck lucky it was a bargain and, if not, he could always take it back on our return journey.

The modern shopping area was much more up-market, but the transformation into an eastern version of Paris was still very much a work in progress. Although the shops had a surprisingly varied selection of western goods and the pavement cafes looked inviting, the overall feel of even the most modern parts of the city was still unmistakably Asian. As was the case in Tehran, many of the residents of Kabul seemed to have a keen awareness of the world outside their country, even though this was long before satellite television, mobile phones and the internet made the world a much smaller, and more inter-connected place.

Many of the men and women wore western clothing, and mini-skirts were by no means an uncommon sight. In 1971 Kabul was well on the way to becoming a peaceful, well-educated and progressive city. Fifty years of progress would be brutally halted just a few years later by the Soviet invasion in December 1979, and the subsequent series of events has resulted in some areas of Kabul being laid to waste, setting the clock back many years. To those of us who were privileged to glimpse what might have been, the destruction of the city is immeasurably tragic.

Having stopped overnight at a camp site in Kabul, alongside the main water reservoir above the city, we left in the middle of the morning, following the Kabul River eastwards towards Jalalabad, and then on into Pakistan, by way of the Khyber Pass.

The border area between Afghanistan and Pakistan has long been regarded as one of the most dangerous and lawless places in the world. Afghanistan has never recognised the internationally agreed border, known as The Durand Line, claiming that large parts of north-west Pakistan, the so-called Pashtun tribal areas, should be Afghan territory. The ongoing border friction, which in more recent years allowed Al Quaeda and other similar organisations to establish safe havens in the disputed zones, is attributable to tribal links which date back centuries. The ancient lands of the Pashtun people, who not unreasonably regard themselves as a distinct nation, were cut in two by The Durand Line, and Pashtun nationalists have long been demanding that the whole disputed area should be declared an independent state, to be known as Pashtunistan. Afghanistan and Pakistan are unlikely to accede to such demands, contenting themselves with blaming each other for failing to deal properly with the militants who move back and forth across the porous borderline.

This was the region we would have to pass through in order to reach Peshawar in Pakistan.

The route from Jalalabad to Peshawar, which crosses the border at Torkham before climbing over the Khyber Pass and dropping down onto the plains of Pakistan, has been used for centuries by both traders and armies. Countless camel caravans, loaded with oriental goods, have passed along it, wending their slow way to the markets of Afghanistan, Persia, Asia Minor and beyond. The troops of powerful empires, including those of Alexander the Great and Genghis Khan, have marched along it on their way to new conquests. As we passed through it, having reached Torkham Gate in the early afternoon, it felt like a strangely familiar, and truly historic, place.

The formalities on both sides of the border were straightforward, and we were not long delayed. The two Pakistani Army Officers who had inspected our passports told us that the Khyber Pass, being in what they termed a 'tribal area', was very dangerous, even though it was nominally under their control. We were instructed not to stop under any circumstances, and never to stray away from the road. As long as we were through the pass and safely in Peshawar by sunset, the risks were not too great; but should our vehicle break down and strand us in the pass overnight they made it clear that they could not guarantee our safety, and nobody would come looking for us. No-one was allowed to enter the pass after nightfall.

The distance from Torkham to the summit of the pass at Landi Kotal was only just over three miles, but the road was narrow and steep. It curved back on itself time after time. As we wound our way along the road, climbing ever higher up the pass, we could see the twisted remains of the tracks of the British-built Khyber Pass Railway, constructed after World War One and now totally disused. Even in its broken state, the railway still looked very impressive.

Bridges had been constructed across steep ravines and tunnels had been blasted through obstructing ridges. We passed memorials which had been cut into the rocky hillsides and engraved with the names of men who had lost their lives far from home in the many battles which these hills had witnessed. Disused hillside forts still clung to the strategic viewpoints upon which they had been so laboriously constructed from brick and stone. More recent relics, concrete obstacles known as dragons' teeth, were evidence of the measures which had been taken during World War Two to forestall any attempt by German tanks to use the pass to break through into India. Our passage through the Khyber Pass was a three dimensional, illustrated lecture upon a pivotal part of world history.

Our trusty lorry did not let us down, and we drove into Peshawar at just after five in the evening. It turned out that we were the very last vehicle to complete the journey that day.

We had descended five thousand feet since leaving Kabul, and the heat on the plains of Pakistan, even in the evening, was intense. Peshawar used to be a heavily fortified, border citadel and, as we drove past the old city, the remains of the high walls which once surrounded and protected it, punctuated by sixteen gates, could still be seen. Unsurprisingly, in such a volatile border region, one of Peshawar's main cottage industries is gun manufacture. Numerous small workshops turn out perfectly serviceable, working copies of many of the world's most formidable small arms.

All kinds of weapons, from Kalashnikovs to high-velocity rifles, were on open sale in markets around the city, and we spotted several men walking along the side of the road with rifles in their hands and heavily-loaded ammunition belts slung across their chests. There was no obvious sign that they had any intention of using their lethal armoury, but we nevertheless decided to drive on, and get well clear of the border area, before we made our stop for the night.

Very shortly after making this resolution we were flagged down by some armed men, wearing police uniforms, who had set up a road block. We seriously considered not stopping, but happily they were genuine policemen who were simply making a routine check on the illegal importation of fresh fruit from Afghanistan. Once we had assured them that we were not carrying any fruit, we were waved on our way.

The next day was equally hot and it was not long before our fruit-free status was compromised by the urgent roadside purchase of a sack of watermelons and a crate of locally bottled Coke to quench our thirst. The Coca-Cola Company is said to have a strict, and very effective, policy of closely monitoring the quality of the water supply to its bottling plants throughout the world, but in order to take no chances I suggested that two or three Sterotabs should be dissolved in each bottle before it was gulped down. The deliciously moist flesh of the watermelons, safely protected from germs inside its thick, green skin, I passed as safe to consume untreated.

Because of the tension between Pakistan and India since the 1965 war, and the possibility that further hostilities could erupt at any time, we were unable to go beyond Lahore without a military permit. The consulate in the city was closed until the following morning so we treated ourselves to a stay in the Park Luxury Hotel. The main attractions of the hotel were a secure garage, in which we could park the lorry and trailer without charge, and a very reasonable rate of just one dollar for a room. For the princely sum of two dollars we reserved two executive rooms for the night, each sleeping up to four people and justifying its 'executive' status by the presence of a large ceiling fan. In the hotel bar, cold beers were unfortunately priced at an exorbitant fifteen shillings for a small bottle so we reluctantly had to stay sober.

Our military permits were issued to us at ten o'clock the next morning, and by noon we were waiting in the hot, dusty queue for our last border check. Just twenty three days had passed since our misty departure from Liverpool, and we would hopefully be entering India very shortly. Ahead of us in the queue were two couples in a camper van. As we were soon to observe, their long journey was about to be brought to an abrupt end.

Afghan Elder – Herat *(JW)*

Ancient Minarets - Herat *(JW)*

Donkeys loaded with sacks of grain near Kandahar *(JW)*

The Russian Road heads to Kabul from Kandahar *(JW)*

Aiming High – Overland to the Himalayas 1971

Sunset - Indian Palace near Amritsar *(JW)*

Six

THE HIMALAYAS

The road was narrow and bordered by thick hedges on each side. Were it not for the heat and the humidity we could have been in rural England, but in fact we were driving northwards on the Indian side of the disputed border with Pakistan.

After leaving Lahore, armed with the permits we needed to cross into India, we had been forced to make a long, southerly detour to Ferozepore as there was only one border crossing still open between the two countries. On both sides of the border there were clear signs of the tension which had existed since the Indo-Pakistan War, six years earlier, in 1965. Troop encampments and camouflaged airstrips every few miles made it obvious that more trouble was on the way, and the increasing tension between India and Pakistan eventually came to a head eight months later, in December 1971. The second war resulted in the creation of Bangladesh in the east but, despite some fierce fighting in the region through which we were driving, it failed to resolve the long-standing dispute over Kashmir and the border in the west.

Dusk was falling as we drove into Amritsar, the City of the Golden Temple. The distance from Lahore to Amritsar, as the crow flies, is a mere thirty miles but, because of our long detour south, the journey had taken us seven hours. Amritsar is named after the pool, fed by an underground spring, in which the original golden temple was built in the sixteenth century. The word literally means 'pool of ambrosial nectar', the drink of the gods. The outer walls of this most sacred temple of the Sikh religion are decorated with gold leaf and it sits upon a jewel-encrusted platform in the middle of the pool. Its proper title is Harmandir Sahib, The Abode of God, and it was intended to be a sanctuary of great beauty and sublime peacefulness, where people of all religions could gather and meditate. The temple and pool are almost completely surrounded by other religious buildings, and it was difficult to obtain anything more than a glimpse of the sumptuous gold façade as we drove past. The streets around the religious complex were thronged with people, for the Golden Temple is a major pilgrimage destination for Sikhs from all over the world.

There being nowhere to make camp in such a densely populated city, we stopped at a hotel in the northern outskirts with the name 'AMBASSADOR' emblazoned in large neon letters across the front. As had been the case in Lahore, its most attractive feature was an adjoining private car park in which we could leave the lorry and trailer, hopefully without attracting too much attention from local residents.

It turned out that we were the only guests, and we were received royally. Nothing was too much trouble for the Sikh owner, who personally supervised every aspect of our brief, overnight stay. We had a room each and when, at breakfast, we casually asked whether he had any orange juice, someone was immediately dispatched to the market to buy a sack of oranges, from which the freshest of juice was squeezed. Dinner, bed and breakfast cost just eighty rupees (about four pounds) for all seven of us. At just over ten shillings a head (fifty pence in decimal coinage), it was the best value we had ever come across.

May 9th 1971 was a Sunday and we spent a good part of the morning trying to obtain a detailed road map of the area, for we had only the vaguest idea which route to take in order to get to Kulu.

Everywhere we stopped the answer seemed to be the same.

"No maps, Sahib. Army take them all away. In case Pakistani spies buy them. Many road signs gone too."

Eventually, in a small general store, we found a diagrammatic map which, although it was not to scale and seemed to have been sketched out roughly by hand, was detailed enough to show us that we needed to head towards a place called Pathankot. From there a journey of a hundred miles or so, following what was shown as the only road in the region, should bring us to Mandi, a hill town which we knew lay just south of the Kulu Valley. Hopefully we could not go wrong.

The miles passed by quickly, taking us further and further north through countryside that stretched out in all directions, almost completely flat. Then, suddenly and dramatically, in the far distance we glimpsed the foothills of the Himalayas. It was an incredible sight. One minute everywhere was relatively flat, and then, within no more than an hour, the whole of the distant horizon had reared up to form rolling chains of green hills that rose progressively higher until they seemed to touch the sky. And far beyond the hills, as we drove closer, we could just make out the shape of huge mountains.

It was easy to imagine the earth's thin crust being crushed and pushed upwards as the continent of India, which had once lain far to the south, drifted inexorably northwards and collided with Asia. That great collision, like a slow-motion car crash, created the Himalayas and the high Tibetan plateau and, as India continues to push north-eastwards at a rate of about five centimetres each year, the mighty peaks are pushed imperceptibly higher.

We had to pay a toll of fifteen shillings to enter Himachal Pradesh, a notice alongside the toll gate informing us that we were 'entering into the mountainous and most beautiful state in the whole of India'. The relatively straight, albeit quite narrow, highways, which we had been drumming along at forty-five or fifty miles an hour since leaving Amritsar, were now behind us. The road ahead rose steeply as it made its way over ridges and then plunged down into deep valleys. We were forced to engage four-wheel drive and crawl up the steeper sections in first gear while, on the long, downhill runs it was often difficult to decide whether to use the gearbox to slow the heavily loaded vehicle, or risk overheating the brakes. Quite often the best solution was to use both.

By nightfall we had reached Mandi, the delightful former capital city of the Punjab Hill State, situated on the banks of the Beas River which ran southwards out of the Kulu Valley. It was not a big place, and it was known as a city because of its former status, not for its size. The houses nestled together, clinging to steep, wooded hillsides on both sides of the river. Dak bungalows were generally regarded as good, and relatively inexpensive, places to stay, and there was no difficulty in locating one. Perched on a small hill, overlooking a lazy bend in the river, the dak bungalow in Mandi occupied a prime spot.

The old dak bungalows, scattered all over the hills of India, were one of the mainstays of the Indian tourist industry. Dating from the days when travellers in the northern regions were mainly colonial administrators, fleeing from the stifling heat of the plains to spend their summers in the hills, the bungalows offered simple, overnight stopping places for the officials and their entourages.

The *chaudikar*, or caretaker, welcomed us. As on the previous night, we were the only guests but, being a government-controlled guest house, there was a non-negotiable room rate of one hundred rupees per night. We suggested eighty, the same price as we had paid in Amritsar.

"I am sorry, Sahib. I am not permitted to reduce the rate for the room. It is written on the chitty. Inside the door. It is official rate. It cannot be changed."

We asked to see his biggest room.

The chitty was there, as he had said, pinned to the back of the door but, looking at it closely, there appeared to be no specified limit on the number of people who could use the room.

"That's fine, thanks. We'll have this room."

"Very good, Sahib. Follow me, now. I will show you the other rooms."

"No, just this one thanks. We'll all sleep in it if that's okay. There's nothing on the chitty that says we can't, is there? We'll use our own sleeping bags, so you won't have to wash any sheets."

The chaudikar made a brief pretence of thinking about our offer, but it was clear that he liked the idea of his workload being reduced.

"Okay, Sahib. Sheets stay clean. Big help. Cooked breakfast extra. Two rupees. Each man."

We had a deal. Six of us slept in the room, while Bryan spent the night in the lorry to guard our equipment. The risk of it being stolen was almost non-existent in such a place, but we did not want to take any chances at all on what we hoped would be the last night of our long journey.

Since leaving Amritsar we had climbed to an altitude of three and a half thousand feet, and the evening air was refreshingly cool after the suffocating heat of the plains. The reason for the great affection which the British rulers had for these foothills during the days of the Raj was becoming clear. In the days before air-conditioning, no senior official from Britain could be expected to work in Delhi or Calcutta during the hottest months of the year, so most of the administration of British India moved north into the much cooler foothills. Shimla, one of the best known of the summer hill towns, was just forty miles away to the east.

It had been another long day. Almost four weeks of non-stop travelling had made us weary, and it was a great pleasure to drift off to sleep in the certain knowledge that the marathon journey would very soon be over.

The morning dawned fresh and still. The sky was cloudless and there was not a breath of wind in the air as we sat on the verandah of the bungalow and looked down upon a platoon of soldiers, clad in bright red and black uniforms, who were being drilled on a tree-lined, grassy square in the middle of the town. A couple of other men, wearing the same uniform, were exercising a pair of horses which trotted around the perimeter of the square. A little further away a game of hockey was in progress. This was the romantic India of Kipling, elegant and relatively affluent, and quite different from the crowded cities and the grinding poverty of the plains.

Breakfast over, it was time to hit the road again on the final leg of our journey. Our final destination lay no more than forty five miles away, so we should reach it well before nightfall.

Until 1926 the only road from Mandi into the Kulu Valley had climbed up into some intervening mountains and over the 6,760 foot Dulchi Pass before dropping down into the valley. This road was invariably closed by snow for several months in the winter, leaving Kulu isolated, so a new road was constructed along the Mandi-Largi gorge which the Beas River had carved out for itself over many thousands of years. It was a magnificent piece of engineering. In some places the road was, quite literally, cut into the side of the gorge and we were forced to walk in front of our lorry to keep watch and ensure that it did not become wedged against the overhanging rock. The narrowest section, between Pandoh and Aut, was controlled by a one-way system, traffic being allowed to pass in each direction on a two-hourly rota. This part of the gorge was a dark and forbidding place. The rock cliffs rose vertically for many hundreds of feet above us, while the Beas River, some fifty feet below, swirled and foamed its way along a narrow, rocky channel. Very high up, on the far side of the river, where the cliffs became less precipitous, it was possible to make out some small patches of green vegetation, but in the lowest part of the gorge the rocks were bare.

We reached Aut safely, our lorry having suffered nothing worse than a minor scrape as the roof touched a particularly low overhang. The road now crossed the river by means of a suspension bridge. As we approached it we all had very serious doubts about the strength of the structure, and whether it would support the weight of our heavily loaded lorry and trailer, but there was no alternative route.

Bryan Pooley, who was driving, decided we had to risk it.

"Everyone out. I'll take it across. There's no point in us all ending up in the river if the bridge gives way."

We all piled out and watched anxiously as Bryan inched his way onto the bridge. As it took more of the weight of the lorry, the wooden planks which made up the roadway started to sag alarmingly, bringing a pair of officials running out of a hut on the far side of the river.

"No. No. Please Sahib. Go back, You must go back."

They were soon standing at the end of the bridge, waving their arms and gesticulating up at Bryan. As the lorry reached the middle of the span the whole bridge seemed to shudder. One of the officials covered his face with his hands, as if he could not bear to watch.

"Stop, Sahib. Now. Stop."

But it was too late. The front wheels of the lorry touched the far bank and, with one further press on the accelerator, Bryan was safely over. We all ran across and jumped back in.

"No problem," announced Bryan. "It was fine. And the lorry'll be much lighter on the way back."

Next stop Bajaura, and the Kulu Valley.

By curious coincidence it is thought that the first Englishman ever to see the Kulu Valley was a Liverpool veterinary surgeon, William Moorcroft, who was born just north of Liverpool, in Ormskirk, a market town in which I now live. He and another man, George Trebeck, passed through the valley in August 1820, en route to Leh and Tibet, where they hoped to negotiate some trading arrangements on behalf of the East India Company. Their story is preserved in their diaries, published as 'Travels in the Himalayan Provinces of Hindustan and the Punjab.'

Bajaura, at the northern end of the gorge, was once a heavily fortified stronghold, guarding the region against invaders. As we drove out of the gorge and passed the town, the cliffs on each side became less steep and the legendary, fertile valley of Kulu came into view. The whole of the valley is a paradise. The rich soil which is washed down from the mountains supports numerous varieties of trees and flowers and since the mid-nineteenth century, when it was first inhabited by a colony of English settlers, it has supported a flourishing fruit-growing industry, which is centred upon the small town of Kulu. Apples, plums, cherries, apricots, and even pomegranates, can be grown with ease in the temperate climate.

By the start of the twentieth century there were about ten large estates in the valley, whose owners led an idyllic life, watching their fruit ripen in the semi-tropical sun as the trees were fed and watered naturally by the afternoon rain and the many small streams. In their spare time they were able to indulge in hunting and fishing to their hearts' content for the surrounding hills were rich with game. Deer, red and black bears, and ibex flourished in the foothills, and higher up, in the mountains proper, it was possible to spot the very rare, snow leopard. Pheasant and duck, and half a dozen other species of game bird, were abundant in the area, and in 1909, to add the final icing to the sportsmen's cake, trout were introduced into the Beas River, so successfully that within a few years the local fishermen claimed that it was possible to catch twenty trout in as many minutes.

It was a paradise that was enjoyed by no more than a few hundred people. It could not last, and with the new road and the coming of the motor car in the nineteen twenties everything began to change. Local tourists made the journey from the plains in increasing numbers and, by 1971, the Kulu Valley was starting to rival the Vale of Kashmir as a holiday venue for the more affluent city-dwellers of India. The changing character of the valley, together with the political changes which came with India's independence, caused some of the landowners to sell up and return to England, but several active estates still remained, and it was to one of them, Johnson's Orchards, that we were heading.

We passed through Kulu town at midday, by which time the moist air from lower down the valleys, warmed by the sun, was rising up into the surrounding hills and forming heavy, black thunder clouds, a daily weather pattern with which we were to become very familiar. Peals of thunder echoed faintly in the far, high distance. The Thunder God, from his throne on Indrasan, was acknowledging our arrival.

Johnson's Orchards were located about six miles beyond Kulu, and we brought the lorry to a thankful stop alongside a painted, wooden sign on the left hand side of the road which announced that we had reached our destination. The lorry had served us well, but every one of us was heartily sick of the drumming of the huge wheels, and the monotonous, deep rumble of the four litre engine. We were glad to be at the end of our journey.

We hoped to be able to camp in the orchard for a few days while we prepared for the mountains. The equipment had to be sorted into loads, and porters had to be hired to carry them on the three day walk to the planned site of Base Camp. The owner of the orchards, Jimmy Johnson, was a long-standing friend of Bob Pettigrew, one of the sponsors of our expedition, who had been the leader of the unsuccessful 1961 attempt upon Indrasan. He had kindly written to Jimmy Johnson, seeking permission for us to leave our lorry and trailer on his land while we were in the mountains.

Tony walked up the driveway towards a large villa which was visible from the gate, taking with him a copy of the letter which Bob Pettigrew had sent.

Ten minutes later he returned.

"Pettigrew's letter never arrived. But Jimmy Johnson was in and he said he's more than happy to let us camp in his orchards. And we can leave the lorry here as well."

An hour and a half later we lay inside two green tents which we had erected, and contemplated the torrential rain which had started to fall. The lorry had been emptied of all its contents, which were now covered with a huge tarpaulin, and the trailer stood on its own, in the open, as we waited for the downpour to stop.

"Hope it's not the bloody monsoon," muttered Bryan in the curious New Zealand Welsh accent which he had acquired during his time in Snowdonia.

"If it is we might as well start packing the lorry up again now. Sure looks like the monsoon to me. Are you sure you've got your dates right, Tony? I'm sure the Everest climbers had to be off the mountain by May, and I reckon . . . . . "

We never found out what he reckoned because a well-aimed clod of earth cut him off in mid-sentence. Fortunately he was just winding Tony up. The monsoon does not reach the western part of the Himalayas until early July. At least it had never done so before.

Approaching the Himalayan foothills *(JW)*

Mandi-Largi Gorge and Beas River *(JW)*

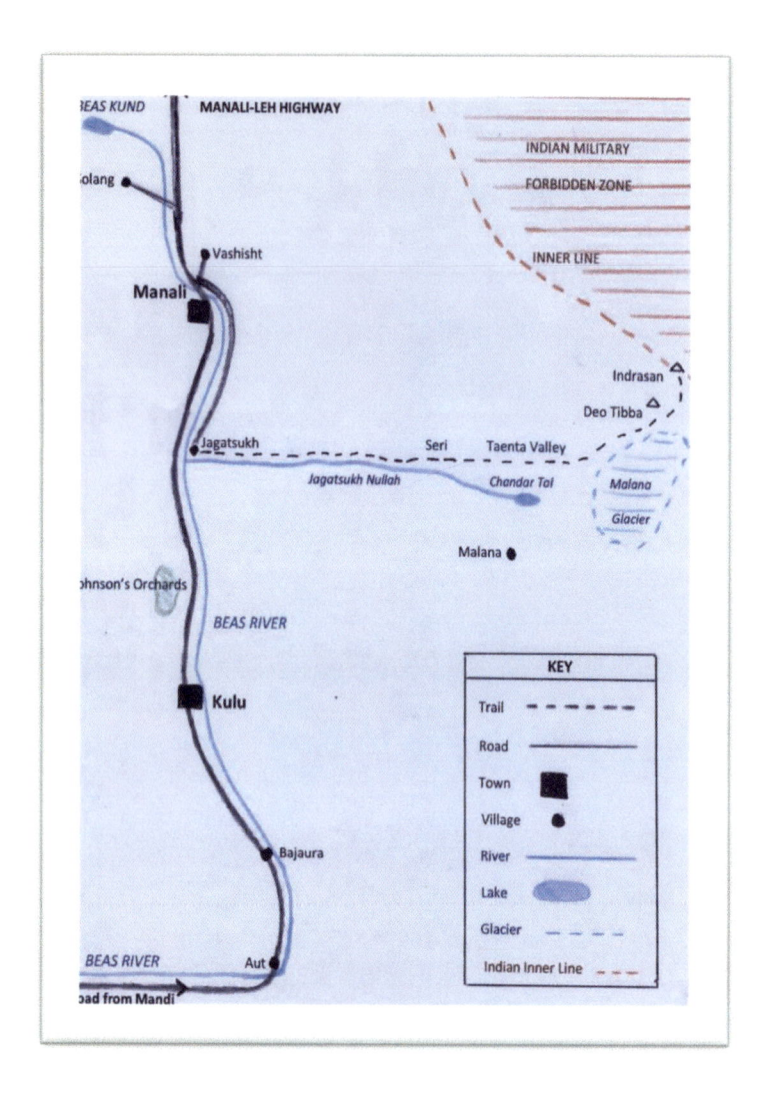

Sketch Map of the Kulu Valley and the Trekking Route to Indrasan

(not to scale)

Seven

PREPARING FOR THE MOUNTAINS

Jimmy Johnson was the most generous of hosts. Not only did he allow us to use his land, after our unexpected arrival, but he also put at our disposal his orchard manager, Tarra Chand, together with his jeep. And he instructed his staff to open up one of the large fruit-storage barns, so that our lorry and trailer could be securely locked away, along with any other items which we did not need, while we were up in the mountains.

As if all that was not enough, he and his charming Indian wife entertained us to dinner every evening at a large table which was laid out on the lawn outside their house. We started with drinks at seven thirty, followed by a feast of Indian cooking. At least seven different dishes, each one highly spiced and curried, would be presented to us, and the festivities would eventually draw to a close around midnight.

A worse way of preparing for a challenging mountain climb I could hardly imagine, but a more enjoyable way of spending those last few days would have been difficult to find.

Unfortunately there was also work to be done. Hangover or no hangover, one and a half tons of equipment and food had to be arranged into sixty pounds loads for the porters to carry. And the porters were yet to be recruited.

Without the help of Tarra Chand we would never have completed all the necessary arrangements in the five days which we had allowed. Precious time would have been lost finding out who to contact but, as it was, on the afternoon after our arrival, Tony and I jumped into the jeep with Tarra Chand and roared off up the valley to Manali, where Tarra said he knew someone who should be able to supply all the porters we would need.

We took the main road through Manali and crossed the Beas River on a new bridge which had been built just above the town. Signs of rapid change were everywhere. Yellow bulldozers and other sophisticated road-building machinery lined the road. Gigantic earth-movers looked as though they had been designed, quite literally, to move mountains. We passed an inscription, carved into a huge block of Himalayan rock, which proudly proclaimed 'LEH-MANALI HIGHWAY. HIGHEST MOUNTAIN ROAD IN THE WORLD'. An engineering triumph, no doubt, and a boost for tourism in the area, but it would sadly allow motor vehicles to reach a place which the ancient chroniclers regarded as 'the end of the habitable world'. The main driving force behind the decision to build the road was the Indian Government's constant fear of invasion from China. Once completed it would provide a way for Indian troops and heavy armour to be moved rapidly into the strategic border region should the need arise.

Just after Manali we turned off the main road and climbed up a steep track for about ten minutes. Tarra Chand then brought the jeep to a halt.

"We'll have to walk from here, I'm afraid. This is as far as the road goes."

He pointed to a narrow path which wound its way up an even steeper hillside.

"Do you see that village up there?" he asked. "That is Vashisht. I know a man called Wongdhi who lives there. He should be able to find the porters you will need."

As we made our way up the path we could see that the village lay on a flat area at the foot of a towering, granite cliff. Above us, on both sides, were hills, thick with pines and Himalayan deodars. Swathes of green in every possible shade were broken up only by long, vertical scars where landslides had exposed the underlying soil and red-brown rocks. Far below us the foaming torrent of the Beas River tumbled down the middle of the valley. And straight ahead, occupying almost the whole of the northern horizon, was the most majestic sight of all. The great, snow-covered ridge above the Solang Nullah dwarfed the green foothills. The top of the ridge had been visible from Manali, lower down, but up here at Vashisht it revealed itself in its full glory. The eternal snows of the Himalayas. The view was breathtaking.

The village of Vashisht was a ramshackle collection of small houses, constructed from wood and stone in the traditional, two-story, Himalayan style. A verandah encircled each house at first floor level on which were stored the cone-shaped baskets, or *kilta*, used throughout the region to transport goods along the winding mountain trails. The roofs were all tiled with what looked like slate. Each house had, alongside it, an area enclosed by a low, stone wall within which were gathered various simple farm implements, along with small piles of fodder, presumably for animals, even though there were none to be seen.

We walked between the houses into a central, communal courtyard, at the far side of which was a *chai,* or tea, stall. Tarra Chand pointed to a couple of benches alongside the stall.

"Please wait here for a moment. I will see if I can find Wongdhi."

He disappeared behind one of the houses. An elderly woman, who stood behind the *chai* stall fingering a battered, enamel pot which presumably held the tea, eyed us up, slightly curiously, before speaking.

"Chai, Sahib?"

Tony and I both indicated our thanks, but shook our heads. We had no idea where the water she was using had come from, or whether it had been properly boiled, and we did not want to risk an attack of dysentery just before the start of the expedition.

We sat in silence and awaited Tarra Chand's return. We did not need to wait long. He re-appeared within five minutes, accompanied by a sturdily built, older man whose face was a cross between Indian and Tibetan. There was a third, much younger man with them.

Tarra Chand introduced the older man to us as Wongdhi. Tony appeared to have heard of him, and very soon I was to learn that Wongdhi had achieved international mountaineering fame when he made the first ascent of Jannu with a French team in 1962. Jannu, a notoriously difficult mountain to climb because of the need for some very tough rock climbing at high altitude, is in the eastern Himalayas, near the border between Nepal and Sikkim.

The story of the French expedition, along with Wongdhi's exploits, is recounted in Lionel Terray's book 'At Grips with Jannu.' Published in 1967, it is a gripping account of the first ascent of one of the world's most challenging mountains.

The younger man who had arrived with Wongdhi turned out to be Tarra Chand's nephew, Dharm Chand.

"You will take *chai*?"

Without waiting for our reply Wongdhi ordered tea for the whole party. In India it was impossible to contemplate tackling a subject as complex as the hiring of porters without some tea to keep everyone going.

We moved to a small table, which seemed to appear from nowhere, and the strong, lukewarm brew was served in dirty, chipped cups. Tony and I made a pretence of drinking ours, while the other three consumed several cups with gusto.

It was our first experience of negotiation, Indian style. Tarra Chand and his nephew listened patiently as Wongdhi launched into a long preamble in broken English, little of which seemed to be relevant to the subject in hand. Tony and I were eager to get things sorted out but, each time we made as if to interrupt, Tarra Chand motioned us into silence with a wave of his hand.

Eventually, after an introduction which had embraced the weather, life in England, mountains, French cuisine, Delhi, and a synopsis of his exploits as a climber in Nepal, Wongdhi reached into a folder which he had placed upon the table and pulled out a sheet of paper headed 'SHERPA GUIDE SCHOOL'. On it were listed the current rates for porters.

There were clearly no flies on Wongdhi. His list of rates covered every possible aspect of mountain climbing, from the hire of porters to the provision of guides for inexperienced trekking parties. There was even a list of charges for the loan of boots, ice-axes and ropes, plus a host of other items which he had almost certainly acquired from the large expeditions he had been associated with in the past.

Ordinary porters, whose role was simply to carry equipment as far as Base Camp, would cost us ten rupees per day for each man. High altitude porters, who would remain with us throughout the climb and assist with the back-breaking task of ferrying food and equipment to the higher camps on the mountain, would be paid fifteen to twenty rupees per day, depending upon experience.

After much haggling over numbers and discounts, we settled upon fifty two ordinary porters, who would be hired for three days, plus two high altitude porters at fifteen rupees a day. We would also take a cook who would be in charge of all the food preparation and other routine chores at Base Camp. The cook's wage would be ten rupees daily.

The presence of Tarra Chand's nephew was explained when Wongdhi announced that he was an experienced climber who would be our head 'Sherpa', or *sirdar*, at a fee of thirty rupees daily.

In order to avoid extra charges for equipment, we agreed that we would supply our high altitude porters with any items of gear which they did not already have themselves.

We took our farewells after a meeting that had lasted almost two hours. In England the whole transaction would have taken perhaps fifteen minutes. Nevertheless, we now had the porters we needed, and we could concentrate on other vital things.

Back at Johnson's Orchards, we started to collect together some clothing and other equipment for the porters.

"You weren't going to take your single boots up with you were you, Bryan?" shouted Tony as he unearthed a pair of climbing boots.

"No. Sling 'em in the lorry."

"That's okay. They'll do for one of the porters."

The process was repeated with every other item of surplus gear until we had accumulated a substantial pile of sleeping bags, pullovers, waterproofs, thick socks, and other sundry, but serviceable, items.

"I hope they'll be good enough," mused Tony. "A lot of expeditions these days provide a full set of brand new gear for their high altitude porters and sirdar. Dharm Chand's coming over here tomorrow to meet everyone and pick up his gear."

Tony continued to be slightly concerned, but the general consensus was that, although the equipment was second hand, it was all quality stuff. And most importantly it was all in good working order. It should be fine.

= = = = = = = = = = = = = = =

Dharm Chand arrived at Johnson's at half past five the following morning, having travelled down the valley from Manali on the first bus. Obviously well used to rising early, he was surprised to find us still asleep in our tents. Our excuse was that it had been another heavy night at the Johnson's house. Dharm Chand's English was very good and, when we explained the situation, he apologised for waking us so early and happily disappeared to join his uncle, Tarra, for breakfast.

When we surfaced, a few hours later, and went through the equipment with him, Dharm Chand was very pleased with all the equipment, except for the sleeping bags. They were, admittedly, far from new, but they were very good quality and we eventually persuaded him that they would do the job.

He also brought news from Wongdhi. The porters had all been arranged, and they would meet us in three days' time at the village of Jagatsukh, ready to begin the trek to Base Camp. Jagatsukh lay on the eastern side of the Beas River, a couple of miles downstream from Manali, and it had been selected as the meeting place on Tarra Chand's advice.

The route to Indrasan Base Camp passed through the village before climbing up into the mountains by way of a valley known as the Jagatsukh Nullah. Tarra Chand reasoned that if we took our lorry across the river, using the new bridge at Manali, we could drive all the way to Jagatsukh, using a dirt road which ran along the far bank. This would cut out the long walk from Johnson's Orchard to the village, and save a day on the approach march.

Wongdhi and Dharm Chand would be picked up en route to Jagatsukh, at the bridge in Manali, while Tarra Chand himself would accompany us to Jagatsukh and then drive the lorry back to the orchard. These arrangements seemed perfect, and they were quickly agreed upon.

We now had just three days to complete the mammoth task of packing, weighing, and listing all the loads for the porters, before loading them onto the lorry for the short trip to Jagatsukh.

Our assault on Indrasan was about to begin.

Aiming High – Overland to the Himalayas 1971

The march-in from Jagatsukh to Base Camp and the route up the mountain

Black circles mark the camps   B.C. = Base Camp   A.B.C. = Advance Base Camp

Mountain Camps: I = Camp I   II = Camp II   III = Camp III   Camp IV on ridge not marked

The porters selecting their loads at Jagatsukh *(JW)*

Eight

THE MARCH-IN

Saturday, May 15th. We were woken at four by Tarra Chand and by quarter to five we were on our way. Dawn was breaking beyond the mountains to the east as we drove towards Manali for our arranged rendezvous with Wongdhi and Dharm Chand. After we had picked them up we would cross the river and double back along the far bank to Jagatsukh, where the porters would be waiting.

The atmosphere in the lorry was tense and expectant, and there was little conversation. We all seemed to be lost in personal thoughts, wondering perhaps what lay before us in the coming weeks. Looking down the valley we could see a violent electrical storm raging in the hills, the clouds grey and heavy and the forked lightening illuminating the southern sky. It all served to increase the sense of awe and slight bewilderment that I was feeling.

To the north, through a gap in the pine-covered hills, there were occasional glimpses of the dazzling white ridge above the Solang Nullah. The sun had not yet hit the valley but the ridge, reaching up to thirteen or fourteen thousand feet, was already basking in brilliant sunlight, outlined against the deep blue of the sky beyond.

Manali nestles towards the head of the Kulu Valley at a height of about six thousand feet. As we drove through the town, the shops and huts which we passed were bathed in an eerie half- light. There was an air of benign decay about the whole place. Here and there houses made out of wood were shored up with makeshift scaffolding, and many of the slate roofs were patched with corrugated iron sheets. It looked like a long abandoned township in a Western movie.

Despite the very early hour there was considerable bustle and activity around the large barn-like building which served as the bus station. The first bus was about to leave on its meandering journey down the valley to the town of Kulu and there was a great scramble for places. One thing the British certainly did not leave behind them was the habit of queuing.

We stopped by the bridge across the river where we had arranged to meet Wongdhi and Dharm Chand. It was a quarter to six, exactly the arranged time, but there was no sign of either of them. We waited ten minutes and, when they had still not put in an appearance, Tony announced that he was off to look for them.

It was beginning to look as if we might be faced with a long wait. We had skipped breakfast, apart from some tea and coffee, in our hurry to get away from the orchards on time and I was starting to feel empty. A further half hour passed without any sign of activity and I could tolerate the increasing pangs of hunger no longer. I just had to find something to eat.

I set off the way Tony had disappeared, telling the others I would be straight back. The main street was already busy and I stopped at a small cake stall on my left. There I purchased four sweet pastries and a packet of what appeared to be arrowroot biscuits.

The stall seemed to be clean and I calculated that the items I had chosen should be safe to eat. The pastries I ate on the spot, and I slipped the biscuits into my jacket pocket. They would be very welcome later.

When I got back to the others Tony had reappeared with the elusive Wongdhi and Dharm Chand. Standing with them and engaged in earnest discussion was John Banyon, the representative in the area of the Himalayan Institute. Known to all the locals as Burfy Sahib (Snow Man), Mr Banyon was an influential figure. His family had lived in the valley since the eighteen seventies, when his English grandfather was effectively the ruler of the Upper Beas Valley. We had met him one evening at Jimmy Johnson's and, when Tony had bumped into him as he was looking for Wongdhi, he had wisely enlisted his assistance.

Wongdhi's non-arrival was rapidly explained. From an unknown source he had heard a rumour that we were not climbers at all, but British spies who had been sent to infiltrate the forbidden area near the border with China. Indrasan sat right on India's defensive Inner Line, which ran parallel to the Chinese border and delineated a strip of territory, some one hundred and fifty miles wide, into which no unauthorised access was permitted. The Indian fear of a Chinese invasion across the passes from Tibet was very real, and Wongdhi had decided that he was taking no chances. Even with John Banyon's invaluable support it took more than an hour of pleading and reasoning to convince him that we were not up to mischief and intended to go no further than the summit of the West Ridge of Indrasan.

By the time we eventually reached Jagatsukh the valley was out of the shadow of the hills and the sub-tropical sun was already pushing the temperature up. It was going to be a hot start to the march-in to Base Camp.

Despite his worries, Wongdhi had not cancelled the porters and to our relief they were all still waiting for us, standing in the central area of the village with their carrying-ropes and sleeping blankets over their shoulders. There was a flurry of activity as we drove up to them and started to unload the equipment sacks. The experienced ones amongst them cast a professional eye over each load, picking out the easiest to carry, and once they had been given permission to select their loads they moved rapidly from one sack to another, lifting them up and expressing approval or disgust, as appropriate, at the weight.

We watched with great interest, for we had carefully weighed each load on a spring balance before leaving the orchards and we knew that they were all within a pound or so of the generally accepted sixty pound maximum weight.

Within half an hour we had all the porters lined up with their loads while Wongdhi was busy making a list of who was carrying what, so that we should be able to identify the culprit if anything went missing. They were a motley bunch, ranging in age from about fifty down to twelve or thirteen years old. Wearing the grey and brown woollen tunics that were standard dress in the Beas Valley, most of them were bare-foot and many looked incapable of carrying the hefty loads up into the mountains. I knew, however, that there was usually no other way of transporting goods from village to village in this region, so they must be well used to such hard labour. Here and there Wongdhi would exchange heated words with groups of men who thought they had ended up with extra-heavy loads and were apparently trying to extract extra payment by threatening to go on strike. We had been warned about such labour troubles on approach marches and a mental note was made of the potential trouble-makers so that we could keep a close eye on them.

By mid-morning all was ready. Dharm Chand led the way as the long procession of porters, with the seven of us spaced out amongst them to keep things moving, snaked its way out of the village and up the rocky pathway that was the start of our route. We had scarcely gone a hundred yards when two of the porters in my section stopped at one of the tiny houses on the very edge of the village and indicated by sign language that they were stopping for a meal before going on any further. They would catch us up.

I had no choice but to acquiesce and hope that, in the event that they failed to reappear, Wongdhi's list would prove to be accurate. I watched them disappear with their loads into the house, and then had to hurry to regain my place in the file.

The path initially wound its way around the edge of cultivated terraces that covered the slopes immediately above the village, but very soon we were heading up the unspoilt Jagatsukh Nullah, a deep valley cut into the hills by a fast flowing tributary of the Beas River which carried melt water from the glaciers high in the mountains. Our path followed the left hand side of the valley, with the river far below us. It was well worn, being the route used by the villagers to take their cattle up to the lush pastureland higher up the valley. Nevertheless there were many places where a carelessly placed foot risked a headlong fall into the rushing torrent below.

There were occasional short, flat stretches for relief, but the overall progress was relentlessly upwards. The unwieldy pack on my back lurched from side to side and the shoulder straps, well padded though they were, rubbed and cut their way into my shoulders. The sun climbed towards its highest point in the sky and as noon approached I felt very hot and extremely weary.

My mind went back to the week in Scotland, but happily it was not the same. In Scotland I had endured a series of wet, cold and sometimes miserable trudges. Here the weariness was but a small part of an unforgettable experience. I could lose and ignore my tired limbs by concentrating on the magnificence of the scenery that was all around me. The river we were following was breathtaking in its power and beauty, yet it was dwarfed into relative insignificance by the size and majesty of the hills and cliffs through which it had cut its way. It felt good to know that it is hard for man to develop and spoil such wild places. My hope was that before long I would reach a place that was truly too remote ever to be tamed and civilised.

Looking back down the valley all sign of human habitation had disappeared. The village of Jagatsukh was well out of sight, and the few wooden huts which we had passed since then had merged into the pines that covered the hills that surrounded us. I had started the day about halfway down the column of marchers, walking behind the three porters who were carrying the medical equipment, but by the time we had been on the move for an hour the original tidy arrangement had been abandoned. Instead of moving in an orderly single file, the porters had redistributed themselves into small groups. Some would set off at a very fast pace until they were quite exhausted, when they would collapse to the ground and chatter in twos and threes for five or ten minutes. They would then be ready for another burst of activity. Others preferred to proceed slowly and steadily without taking any rest stops. I found myself adopting a combination of the two methods.

I proceeded slowly and took rests. Nevertheless I seemed to be passing as many people as were passing me, so I was happy with my progress.

By half past twelve we had covered about five miles and we were passing through a heavily scented pine forest. I had got my second wind and I felt as though I was moving well. I seemed to have found my best pace and was just setting myself up for a steady afternoon's walk when the path flattened out and I found myself in a wide grassy clearing in the forest. The clearing was dominated by a mighty tree, the trunk of which must have been thirty feet in circumference. Beneath its canopy were gathered all the members of the expedition apart from Geoff Arkless and Dharm Chand who were bringing up the rear of the column, making sure that none of the porters ran into problems.

"You okay Doc? That's it for today," grinned Tony.

The half a dozen porters who had reached the spot were sitting down to rest, their loads already off their backs and propped up against the tree. I wandered over to a nearby rock and followed their example, balancing my pack against the rock to relieve myself of its weight before slipping the straps off my shoulders and letting the whole load drop to the ground. My pack, on Dharm Chand's advice, was slightly lighter than the loads being carried by the porters by even so it felt good to be rid of it. Suddenly forty pounds lighter, my body seemed to float. I pulled off my light cotton shirt, which was soaked with sweat, and lay down upon the grass. Now that I had stopped, a great weariness was overtaking me.

We all sat and soaked up the sun for about an hour as the rest of the porters arrived in dribs and drabs. Their loads were deposited in the centre of the clearing so we could count them, each one with an individually coloured cord or thread around it so that the carrier could identify it correctly the next day. The loads were counted, and all were present. The men who had stopped for a meal at the start of the march had caught up with us.

At around two o'clock the last two porters, who were carrying the big frame tent, arrived and those of us who had some energy left began to erect it. The camp site was soon a hive of activity. A number of campfires had been lit as little groups of porters gathered to prepare their evening meal of dahl and rice.

Our own cook was also hard at work and I watched him, squatting back on his heels Indian fashion, as he prepared our food. He seemed to be significantly older than the rest of our group and I wondered whether he would fit in. All the way up from Jagatsukh he had worn a heavy, woollen jacket. How he had managed to remain cool on such a warm day was beyond me. Now, in addition to the jacket, he had donned an enormous, ex-army greatcoat and a beret. The collar of the coat was turned up, and only his brown, heavily-lined face was visible. Dharm Chand had said he was seventy years of age, and he looked every one of those years. I honestly could not see him surviving the rigours and the cold of living at high altitude for a number of weeks. It was difficult to understand why Wongdhi had chosen him. Perhaps his cooking was too good to miss?

As his food preparations progressed it became increasingly clear that no such reason existed. When, at last, the food was ready it turned out to be nothing more than a just-about-edible meat and rice curry, but of much greater concern was the fact that his knowledge of basic hygiene seemed to be almost non-existent. My attempts, as he was preparing the meal, to explain the importance of issues such as keeping his hands clean were frustrated by his very limited grasp of the English language. For the sake of our health I, as the doctor, was going to have to keep a very close eye upon him.

During our meal the sun had disappeared behind some banks of grey cloud and the air had become noticeably cooler. In the distance we could hear rumbles of thunder which gradually became more frequent and louder. The usual afternoon thunderstorm was on its way. The porters began to gather together their meagre belongings and move towards some rocky cliffs at the edge of the valley, where some small caves would offer them shelter. Sure enough, within ten minutes, the sky over our heads was black, and large droplets of rain began to fall. It seemed that the storms we had heard every afternoon during our stay in Johnson's Orchards were going to match in scale the gigantic hills amongst which they arose.

The loads would have to be kept dry. A huge tarpaulin had been brought from England for just this purpose, but nobody knew which load it was in. A hasty perusal of the inventory revealed the answer. We had left it behind in the lorry. There was nothing for it but to manhandle all the loads into the frame tent but, with sixty loads and our own packs crammed inside, there was not much room to spare. As we squashed into the tent to take shelter, our cook squatted stoically by the fire outside, partly protected by an umbrella, and brewed up some very welcome cocoa.

Fortunately the storm was as brief as it was ferocious and by four o'clock the clouds had melted away to reveal a late afternoon sun. The rocks very quickly dried out and we all sat and watched as the sun dipped slowly down into the valley which we had ascended earlier. It had been a long first day, and it was time for an early night.

Aiming High – Overland to the Himalayas 1971

Heavily loaded porters on the march-in to Base Camp *(JW)*

Nine

ONWARDS TO BASE CAMP

"Chai, Sahib."

The speaker was Tashi, our second high altitude porter, who grinned broadly as he watched me struggle to full consciousness. In his right hand he held a steaming mug of hot tea which he handed to me once I had freed my arm from the sleeping bag. It felt like a scene from every Himalayan book I had read; six o'clock in the morning and early morning tea provided by a 'Sherpa'.

I lay there and sipped the hot brew. Lifting the tent flap I could see that outside all was activity. The porters were already milling about waiting for their loads. Today's march would be longer and they were keen to get started before the sun reached its full ferocity. The sky was a cloudless, deep blue once again and, although the sun had yet to make an appearance from behind the hills to the east and there was still a slight nip in the air, all the signs were that it would be another hot day.

I dressed, or rather added a pullover and breeches to the garments which I had left on overnight, and joined the others outside. They were already breakfasting on some thick porridge and jam, and a further cup of tea, which would have to keep us going until we pitched camp again. The gluey mixture was very filling, and it would sustain us for several hours, but I was glad I had a pack of Glucodin available to fill any energy gap which might arise during the march. As I packed my load I made sure it was easily accessible, near the top.

The load itself was thankfully some ten pounds lighter than the previous day. We had all felt that we were carrying too much, especially as some of the porters had been overheard congratulating themselves on having such easy loads to carry and, during the overnight stop, we had all sneaked some of our personal gear into the general equipment loads. We would have felt bad about the deception had it not been Dharm Chand who came up with the idea.

By seven o'clock the large frame-tent had been dismantled and packed away, and Tashi was carefully stamping out the remains of the camp-fire. There were still six or seven loads sitting in the clearing, which were yet to be collected by their carriers, but D.C. was confident they would soon appear. Geoff Arkless would wait for them and bring up the rear, while the rest of us would set off. The air had warmed perceptibly in the hour since I had woken and I was keen to get going. I swung my pack onto my shoulders. Despite the reduced load it still felt heavy, and the straps rubbed on the chaffed, bruised areas on my shoulders from the day before. A few minor adjustments made the discomfort more bearable, and then I was on the move again.

I muttered under my breath, one-two, one-two, one-two, as I tried to find the slow, steady rhythm which had served me well on the first day. The track meandered up a shallow slope which led from the flat camp site towards a steep hillside, populated by enormous pines. I looked ahead to where the trees traced a delicate pattern against the sky, lining up along the crest of a ridge which seemed to mark the limit of this particular valley.

The end of the valley had not looked that far away, but four hours passed before I was able to stand upon the crest of the ridge and look down upon a valley which was much wider and greener than the one out of which I had just climbed. The previous valley had been narrow, and slightly claustrophobic, with high cliffs on both sides. The sudden widening of the panorama made the sense of discovery seem very real.

It had been a long, tough climb to reach this vantage point and I sat down to rest. The pine forest through which we had passed had chosen a strange place to lay down its roots. The hill we had ascended was almost vertical in places and, as we wound our way up the zigzag path, it was possible to reach out and touch the upper branches of trees whose roots were perhaps a hundred feet lower down. In some places the path disappeared beneath a tangle of cast-off branches, covered in slippery moss. How the villagers managed to coax their cattle along such a hazardous route without losing them was difficult to understand.

Quite near to the place where I was resting, the river tumbled over the ridge on its headlong journey down the deep valley to Jagatsukh. Thousands of gallons of icy water swept through rock channels, forming miniature waterfalls and fountains from which a fine mist floated towards me. The granite rocks had been eroded over the centuries, by the gentle but relentless friction of the water, to form countless strange and beautiful shapes. In the middle of the fiercest stretch of water a solitary rock stood like a giant mushroom, its stem almost completely worn away. Beyond it another boulder had been hollowed out to form a quiet bay into which some of the water would meander for a brief rest before committing itself to the steep drop towards the valley.

I could have continued to sit and watch the ever-changing river waters, but I knew that if I took too long a rest I would struggle to carry on. Reluctantly I left the sweet smell of the pines behind me and followed the path as it dipped down towards the wide valley floor. Ahead of me I could see a line of dark shapes moving slowly across the pasture. It was our porter vanguard. They were making good progress, for I estimated that they were at least an hour and a half ahead of me.

Closer to me I was able to make out the figure of Geoff Tabbner, who seemed to have stopped for a breather. I caught up with him, and he was soon bemoaning the inadequacy of our breakfast.

"Pooley and Johnson may be able to walk all day on a plate of porridge, but I blooming well can't."

I felt the same, and opened up my pack in order to take out the Glucodin. Together we sat and poured liberal helpings of the sickly powder into our palms, washing it down with what was left of the fluid in our water bottles. We gave the Glucodin a few minutes to be digested and then set off with renewed energy and enthusiasm, maintaining a steady pace across the almost imperceptibly rising pastureland. Ahead of us the valley curved gently round towards the south. The trees were becoming noticeably sparser, and we guessed that we must be nearing the tree line. The overnight camp could not be too far off, for we had to stop where the porters would still be able to collect the wood they needed for their cooking fires. The following day, with an early start, they would be able to reach the site of Base Camp and then return to below the tree line, having successfully completed their job.

By one o'clock the sky was becoming overcast again and rain was beginning to fall. Geoff and I both had umbrellas with us and we hastily put them up. These umbrellas were rapidly proving themselves to be one of the most useful pieces of equipment we had brought with us. Just as had happened on the previous day, the temperature dropped quickly, making us feel distinctly cool.

We hurried on a little faster, still wearing the shorts and tee-shirts which had served us well in the heat of the day, but the increased effort was enough to make us both feel breathless in the thinner air and we soon dropped back to our original slower pace. We were now at about twelve thousand feet and, even at the slower pace, we noticed that we were breathing more deeply and quickly to compensate for the relative lack of oxygen in the air.

We left the wide valley behind us and began to cross a rocky moraine, making our way between large boulders. The hills on each side closed in as we moved on, and before very long we were once again hemmed in by granite cliffs on both sides. Thin, grey wisps of cloud clung to the cracks and ledges high above our heads.

Then, quite unexpectedly, in an area which had been partially cleared of the ubiquitous boulders, we came upon a rectangular enclosure surrounded by rough, dry stone walls, about two feet in height. In the centre of the enclosure was a paved floor, fashioned from numerous large, flat stones, and, standing in the middle of the paving, was a black rock, about eighteen inches in height and perfectly smooth. This centre-piece was garlanded with flowers, all freshly cut from the pastures and plaited into simple wreaths. We realised that this must be one of the shrines where porters could offer flowers and other gifts to the mountain gods to ensure their safe return from the dangerous mountain realm which they were about to enter. We stopped a few moments, to offer our own prayers, and then hurried on.

The misty rain continued to fall and it was much colder without the sun to warm us up. We kept on the move until, in a flat area just ahead of us, we caught sight of the others. Many of the porters were already gathered around camp fires which had been lit in the shelter of the large rocks and boulders which were scattered around. We were not so fortunate. The porter carrying the canvas sheeting for the large tent had not yet put in an appearance. The metal framework of the tent, which had arrived and been assembled, stood in the centre of the flat area like a giant spider, but until the canvas arrived there would be no shelter. I quickly donned further pullovers and wind-proofs to shield myself from a brisk wind which whistled along the valley with no trees to lessen its force. The heavy rainstorm which had threatened earlier had fortunately not materialised, for I was quite wet and chilly enough in the biting wind and the intermittent light showers of rain.

Some hot food was the number one priority. Tashi and our cook were already out searching for wood to start a fire but I guessed they might be some time, for the only woody vegetation in the immediate area seemed to be some gaunt bushes which had no foliage and very few branches. To occupy ourselves while we were waiting we constructed a rough and ready cooking shelter out of tent poles and a groundsheet.

The two woodsmen returned surprisingly quickly with sufficient fuel for our overnight stay and they very soon had a fire going. We gathered around it for some warmth while awaiting the arrival of the canvas for the large tent. By five o'clock it had still not arrived and, to avoid further exposure to the elements, we decided to break open another load and erect three of the mountain tents. Within twenty minutes we were sheltering inside the snug little tents and eating a very welcome, hot supper.

By six-thirty the following morning we were on the march once more. The terrain was now very bare, the only features being some spartan grass and countless boulders of every shape and size. We were passing through the desolate landscape which marks the boundary between the lower slopes, with their trees and luxuriant vegetation, and the high, snow-covered mountains. It was not a place to linger and I was glad when, after an hour or so, the valley opened out to reveal a long, wide basin.

For the past two days we had been following the river as it ran swiftly past us down a narrow, V-shaped valley, along the increasingly deep channel which it had cut out for itself over many thousands of years. As we entered the wider valley the river changed its character, slowing down to meander the length of the basin and overflowing its now poorly defined banks to form a swampy marshland in which spiky grasses flourished. We had reached the place known to the locals as Seri.

At the far end of this wide valley, a mile or more distant, was a rocky cliff, almost vertical, from the top of which the waters which formed our river tumbled in a single, glorious cascade. From where I stood I estimated its height as at least three hundred feet, but it was difficult to be sure with no objects of known size, such as trees, against which the height of the waterfall could be compared.

On the right side of the cliff I could make out some steep, snow-covered slopes which glared brightly, forcing me to put on my sun glasses. It was obvious, even to my inexperienced eye, that the snowy slopes offered the only practicable route out of the valley and, sure enough, the long line of porters which stretched out ahead of me started to turn towards them. Some delicate negotiations with the representatives of the porters were going to be required as Wongdhi had warned us that if we hit snow the men might refuse to go on without footwear and snow-goggles. To cover such an eventuality we had brought with us as many spare pairs of boots and shoes as we could find, as well as some extra snow-goggles, but we certainly did not have enough to kit out all of the men. As I made my way across the valley I could see everyone milling around at the foot of the snow slopes. Negotiations had already begun.

We raided the loads for every piece of footwear we could find and, miraculously, by lending out our own shoes, boots and sandals we managed to find all of the men something to put on their feet. Goggles, though, were more of a problem. We gave out every pair we had but, even after we had taped all our spare lenses onto the faces of the porters who were still without goggles, there were a few without any eye protection. After a lot of haggling it was decided that those without goggles would be paid an extra two rupees as compensation. It was a reasonable solution. We had to get the loads up to Base Camp somehow and, while there would be a certain amount of uncomfortable glare from the surface of the snow, much of the slope was facing away from the sun at this time of day so it would be in partial shadow. The real risk to the porters' eyes would be in the later afternoon when the sun would be shining directly onto the slope but, well before then, they should all have dumped their loads at Base Camp and returned safely to the site of the previous night's camp.

Bryan Pooley and Roger Brook led the way up the slope, cutting big steps in the snow with their ice axes to make the ascent easier for the heavily laden porters. We did not want to risk losing a man, or a load, at this stage. I stood at the bottom and watched as the procession wound its way upwards, numerous dark shapes zigzagging back and forth across the slope as they followed the easiest gradients.

The rest of the party waited until the last porter had arrived from the overnight stop before starting up. The steps, made slightly bigger by each of the sixty or so pairs of feet which had preceded ours, were now like buckets. Some were so deeply trodden that it was difficult to move up to the next one, and we soon decided that it would be sensible to cut a fresh trail alongside the one which had been so well used by the porters.

As we climbed the slope we moved above the thirteen thousand foot mark. The air was getting thinner all the time, causing those of us who were more used to sea level oxygen levels to gasp for each breath. The porters, living as they did at six thousand feet, were less affected by the altitude and were moving better than any of the main climbing party, despite their heavier loads.

Before long I was pausing to take deep breaths about every fifteen paces, and my throat and lungs seemed to be burning in the thin, dry air. It felt like an age before the long and winding ascent up the snow brought us level with the top of the rock barrier and we began to traverse across the slope towards it. Our ascent had opened up the view to the west and each time I stopped for breath I was able to gaze all the way down the Jagatsukh Nullah, up which we had marched for the past three days. Gazing further, into the far distance, it was possible to make out numerous snow-capped peaks on the far side of the Kulu Valley. The waterfall, now that I was closer to it, was a magnificent sight as it tumbled over the cliff and fell precipitously towards Seri, feeding the river below.

The sun was starting to melt the hard crust on the surface of the snow and, as we crossed the top of the slope, the steps began to collapse beneath our weight. There was no danger involved, just the laborious and energy-sapping process of hauling oneself up from a position knee or even thigh deep in soft snow. The last of the porters had now reached the cliff-top ahead of me and disappeared beyond. Floundering in the snow I had fallen about fifty yards behind my companions. It would have been no distance at all at sea level but, with the effort that each step now required, it felt as though the gap was unbridgeable.

I forced myself on and, at last, I too was at the top of the cliffs. As I followed the well-trodden trail around a rocky spur, I found myself looking down upon what I knew must be Taenta Valley, the site which had been chosen for Base Camp. The wide, flat floor was about three hundred yards in width and some two miles in length, while the side walls climbed slowly upwards to meet steep ridges that enclosed the valley and formed an almost circular basin. The whole area was covered by a thick blanket of snow, with just a few gigantic, dark boulders, poking through the otherwise uniformly white surface, their tops smooth and domed, like skulls. There was no sign of the river which fed the waterfall, and I supposed that it must be coursing somewhere beneath the thick snow.

Ahead of me, in the very centre of the valley, the porters were already milling around excitedly as their names were checked off against the list. They had worked hard, and their payment of fifty rupees was well earned. I joined them, breathless and exhausted, some thirty minutes later. The porters who had been accounted for were already setting off on their return journey, waving their goodbyes as they disappeared.

It was strange to see them go. With their constant chatter and movement they had made even this remote place seem like a busy railway station. Now, as the last of the stragglers gave us a final cheery wave, a complete silence descended upon the valley.

We had arrived.

Aiming High – Overland to the Himalayas 1971

Base Camp – May 1971 *(JW)*

Ten

THE FIRST FEW DAYS

"Come on lads. We'd better do something even if it's only have a brew and get something to eat."

The speaker was Bryan Pooley.

We were all lying on a couple of groundsheets, spread out in the middle of the ton and a half of equipment which was piled up, haphazardly, around us. Almost an hour had passed since the disappearance of the last porters, an hour that had been spent in complete inactivity. The rapid increase in altitude, almost nine thousand feet in three days, had taken its toll on every one of us. At 13,700 feet the lack of oxygen in the air seemed to be making it very difficult to recover from our long climb.

To add to our discomfort the sun was now blazing down from a clear, sub-tropical sky, sending the temperature in the enclosed valley into the eighties. We had opened a few umbrellas in an attempt to shield ourselves from the fierce ultra-violet rays, but there was no easy way of avoiding the considerable reflection from the bright surface of the snow. Nobody was specifically short of breath, but a physical and mental lethargy that would not be shaken off had overtaken us all. At the back of our minds was the certain knowledge that we ought to be getting on with pitching the tents before the inevitable afternoon clouds started to roll in from the lower valleys, but no-one could find the energy to make the first move. Even Bryan had slumped back down again, having lifted himself up on one elbow to speak.

After a few more minutes of silence one or two voices murmured agreement with Bryan, and our cook was asked to get some snow melted for a stew; the first positive action since our arrival. The snow seemed to take an age to melt but at last the dehydrated meat was cooked and eaten along with the usual rice and, as the sun sank lower in the sky causing the temperature to fall a little, we at last found the energy to stir ourselves into activity.

The big frame tent, the sort of standard model can still be seen in thousands on every camp site in Britain and Europe, was assembled first. It would serve as a general storage and cooking area, and also as a refuge where we could sit and eat in relative comfort. Our plan was to make Base Camp as pleasant and luxurious as possible, so that a couple of days there would be a restful and recuperative break from the rigours of life at higher altitudes.

We were not entirely confident about the ability of the tent to withstand the fierce weather conditions which might arise, even in such a relatively low and sheltered valley, so we packed the bottom edges of the canvas with snow to make it as windproof as possible. A couple of ropes were then passed over the top and tied to heavy boulders on either side to hold it down in the event of severe gales.

Satisfied with the result, we grouped four smaller, sleeping tents around the main tent. The equipment loads were unpacked and covered with canvas, and the sixty eight food boxes were left stacked in the open, ready to be carried up to the higher camps.

By the time we had finished the sun had almost set. As it finally disappeared the temperature fell precipitously. I could feel the rapid change on the exposed skin of my face and hands and, within a few minutes, it had dropped below freezing point.

I had not expected such dramatic extremes of temperature. I knew the high mountains were cold, but the daytime temperatures, which continued to climb into the seventies and eighties when there was no cloud cover, were a surprise. Many times in the coming weeks I would find myself carrying loads up the mountain wearing just a tee-shirt, my pack frame festooned with the items of woollen and weather-proof clothing which I had discarded.

Our elderly cook was now at work again, producing a light evening meal which we could consume before retreating from the freezing cold into our tents and sleeping bags. I watched him carefully. His clothes were far from clean and, despite the firm instructions I had previously given him, he continued to pick his nose and teeth and wipe his hands on his trousers as he prepared our food. He would have to be replaced.

I spoke to Tony.

"The cook's got to go, I'm afraid, or we'll all be going down with food poisoning. I've been keeping an eye on him and he's not got the first idea about hygiene. I've tried to get through to him, but either he doesn't understand me or he just doesn't get it."

My views on our cook did not come as any surprise. Tony had been watching him too.

"He's not our only problem," added Tony. "I had a word with Dharm Chand about Tashi on the way up this morning. Apparently he's never been higher than twelve thousand feet before, and he's got no high altitude portering experience at all. Wongdhi usually only hires him out to amateur trekking parties who come here on package holidays for a couple of weeks."

"Maybe Wongdhi thought we weren't really serious about climbing the west ridge?" I suggested.

"Possibly. Or maybe he thought we'd take one look at it and chicken out. He said to D.C. that he didn't think it'd ever be climbed. Even though he's climbed Jannu, he thinks the west ridge is impossible. And I'll tell you something else. Wongdhi told D.C. that his job was to guide us. I had to make it very clear that we appreciate his local knowledge, and that we'll certainly listen to him, but I'll be making the decisions. We're paying him to help us, not to tell us what we can and can't climb."

We both watched the cook as we carried on talking, trying to work out how best to tackle the problem. He was peeling the remaining fresh vegetables which we had brought up with us from Jagatsukh, while Tashi was busily cooking some rice in a pressure cooker. The solution to our difficulties suddenly seemed perfectly obvious to both of us. Why not make Tashi our cook, and send the old man back down to Wongdhi with a note saying that we needed another high altitude porter?

Our decision, which would take immediate effect, was relayed to the two men by Dharm Chand, who had become our official interpreter. Tashi seemed to be very pleased, despite the fact that his pay would drop from fifteen to ten rupees a day. He told D.C. that he was relieved that he would not have to do any serious climbing, and that he would work very hard to make sure we were well fed.

The old man also took the news well. As he pulled his heavy coat ever tighter around himself to ward off the cold, he said that he was not sorry to be leaving. He had never been so high in the mountains before and he was finding it much colder and more unpleasant than he had expected. He would be glad to return home first thing in the morning. He assured us that, as soon as he reached Manali, he would explain to Wongdhi that Tashi had been given his job and tell him that we needed another porter - a man with previous high altitude climbing experience.

= = = = = = = = = = = = = =

By the time I dragged myself out of my sleeping bag next morning our first cook had left. Tashi was preparing breakfast and, as I looked on, it was clear that his ideas of hygiene were very different from those of his predecessor. We would face many dangers in the coming weeks, and it was reassuring that at least one unnecessary hazard had been successfully eliminated.

Apart from Tashi, I was the first to wake. While waiting for the rest of the team to appear I sat in the entrance of the big tent and looked out at the magnificent scenery that surrounded our little camp. We had certainly chosen a spectacular setting.

The great ridges of granite and snow that encircled us soared two thousand feet towards the deepest blue sky that I had ever seen. As my eyes followed the tops of the ridges I could see huge tongues of ice poking out over the valley. These hanging glaciers, pushed remorselessly forwards by the accumulation of snow higher on the mountain, were able to ignore the law of gravity at this early hour of the morning but, as the day wore on, the melting action of the sun would release gigantic blocks of ice which would crash, suddenly and unpredictably, down to the valley floor in huge ice and snow avalanches. We would need to keep well clear of them. To the right of our tents, still hidden from sight beneath a white blanket, a stream known as Duhungan Nullah carried the water from the rapidly melting glaciers and snows down the valley, feeding the waterfall which we had passed the previous day.

Very soon the sun would appear from behind the ridge at the head of the valley. The snow on the valley floor and surrounding slopes would act as a very efficient reflector, magnifying the heat. Despite having spent much of the previous day under a shielding umbrella, my skin was slightly sunburnt. Even the usually highly effective glacier cream, which we had all been applying liberally to our exposed skin, afforded little protection against such an onslaught, and I resolved to spend as much time as possible, over the next forty eight hours, under canvas. This would hopefully give my skin a chance to build up some natural protection.

The day ahead was to be spent planning the first stage of the assault upon Indrasan, while we gave our bodies time to get used to the low atmospheric pressure and the reduced oxygen levels. At that time it was believed that for every one thousand foot increase in altitude above twelve thousand feet, a period of at least two days was needed to acclimatise. It was thought that the crucial factor was the altitude at which the climber sleeps. He can ascend as far as he is able to during the day, but he must always descend for the night and sleep at the altitude to which he is fully acclimatised. Failure to allow sufficient time for acclimatisation significantly increases the very real risk of developing altitude sickness. In mild cases the symptoms may be no more serious than a bad headache, shortness of breath and general malaise for a few days. In severe cases, however, the initial symptoms may progress to life-threatening cerebral and pulmonary oedema, when the lungs and brain start to fill with fluid, and death can be frighteningly rapid. The only effective treatment is to achieve an increase in both barometric pressure and oxygen levels as quickly as possible. In practical terms this means making an urgent and rapid descent to a lower altitude.

Like many other illnesses, altitude sickness affects one person more than another and it is impossible to predict who will suffer from it and who will not. Even the fittest of people may succumb, and it would be one of my tasks on Indrasan to make sure that the accepted rules for acclimatisation were understood and followed.

All the rest of the team, with the obvious exceptions of Dharm Chand and Tashi, were also feeling the effects of the sun, and we were content to spend most of our time sitting inside the big tent, out of the sun, discussing the problems which lay ahead.

From Base Camp the high ridges immediately around us obscured any view of what lay beyond them, but we knew the basic geography of the hidden terrain from information which Bob Pettigrew had passed on to us. The mountain rose in two great steps to the base of the west ridge. The first of these steps, and the initial problem that would have to be overcome, was the ridge which we could already see at the eastern end of the valley. A successful ascent of that ridge would allow access to the upper snowfields of the Malana Glacier. Those snowfields would have to be crossed to reach the bottom of the second great step, at approximately 16,000 feet. This second barrier took the form of a massive two thousand foot ridge which would take us up to a plateau, at 18,000 feet. From there the final part of the climb, the west ridge itself, should be visible and, hopefully, accessible.

The foot of the first ridge was at least a mile and a half away across the gently rising valley floor. It was obvious that the first priority was to establish an Advance Base Camp below it, from which supplies could be ferried up to the top relatively easily. There would then hopefully be a good site for what would be Camp 1, somewhere near the top of the ridge. Further planning would have to be left until Camp 1 had been established and a full assessment of the barriers beyond it had been carried out.

Since Advance Base Camp would only be four or five hundred feet above the altitude of Base Camp, we decided that anyone who felt up to it could carry a light load up to the proposed site next morning, as a first step towards establishing the camp. Geoff Arkless and Geoff Tabbner were the only ones who felt that they were not quite ready for such a carry. They were both suffering from headaches and loss of appetite, typical early symptoms of altitude sickness, and it was decided that they should rest at Base Camp, to allow time for further acclimatization, before attempting any further climbing.

It was traditionally thought that the best age for climbers to go to the Himalayas was in their early to middle thirties. This was possibly because few people, in the past, had gained sufficient mountaineering experience to be invited on an expedition much before that age. With the exception of Geoff Arkless, who was in his mid-thirties, we were all in our early twenties. Roger Brook and I were the oldest, at twenty four, and the average age of our group, including Geoff Arkless, was just twenty three years of age. We were by far the youngest team ever to have been assembled for a major Himalayan climb.

The team as a whole seemed to be acclimatising quite well, despite the minor symptoms which the two Geoffs were experiencing, but it was early days. The physiological challenges, to which a younger body should in theory respond better, were only just beginning. The tests of mental stamina - the cold, the exhaustion, and the isolation - were yet to come. It would be our ability to cope with mental stress, and not just physiology, which would decide the ultimate success or failure of the expedition.

= = = = = = = = = = = = = = =

Tashi woke us at four-thirty the following morning. This ungodly hour of reveille had been decided upon by Tony, who insisted that a later start would result in us floundering up to the ridge in soft, wet snow. The journey would be much easier while the snow crust was still frozen hard as a result of the sub-zero, overnight temperatures.

Like all the others, I had left most of my clothes on overnight. Dressing was merely a matter of adding an extra pullover and wriggling into my heavy climbing breeches. I had worn my soft, inner boots inside my sleeping bag, and I reached out, under the tent flap, to where I had left my hefty, outer boots. The thick leather was frozen solid. With great difficulty I forced my warm feet into the boots, but lacing them up was out of the question. The laces were like twigs, with tiny icicles hanging from them. I would have to wait, until the warmth of my inner boots had softened the outer boots a little, before the laces could be securely tied.

Outside it was barely light. My exhaled breath hung like clouds in the still, cold air. Even with several layers of clothing to protect me, it felt incredibly cold. I walked over to the big frame tent, my unlaced boots crunching and squeaking on the crisp, frozen surface. The ridged, Vibram soles left almost no impression upon the icy snow.

I found Tashi on his own inside the tent, hunched up over a primus stove cooking up some porridge. He looked absolutely frozen. He did not have the benefit of down clothing and double boots and, even though he had a plentiful supply of pullovers and heavy woollen socks, he was making full use of the heat which was coming from the primus to keep himself warm.

The others soon joined us and we ate a comforting breakfast. All the loads had been prepared the previous evening and they were arranged in a line outside the tent entrance. During breakfast I had decided that I would like to try skiing down from the site of Advance Base Camp after I had completed the carry, so I went outside to add a pair of short, mountaineering skis to my pack. It would mean carrying a little extra weight, but I hoped it would prove worthwhile. I tried to release the knots which held the pack together, but they were frozen hard and immovable. Skiing would have to wait for another day.

The route up to Advance base Camp was a long, slow plod. Had it not been for the altitude, and our semi-acclimatised state, it would have been a very gentle, and enjoyable, hill walk. The first half mile, along the floor of the valley, was almost flat, with just a slight incline as we neared the cliffs on the northern side of the basin. I had set off with Tony and Bryan, leaving Roger, John and D.C. to follow on. We covered this first section fairly quickly, but ahead of us lay a more testing slope.

We threaded our way between a group of boulders, each of which towered thirty or forty feet above our heads. Beyond the boulders the slope became considerably steeper, stretching upwards for about four hundred feet. At this early stage of the expedition I was far from fit, and the acute breathlessness which I was feeling forced me to stop. Before tackling the slope I would have to take a short rest.

I leant against the last of the boulders, too tired to be bothered with taking my pack off, and watched as Tony and Bryan plodded slowly on. For ten minutes I followed their progress as they meandered backwards and forwards, from side to side across the slope, gradually, painfully, inching their way upwards. Their ascent was snail-like, and before long they too were stopping for rests; for only a couple of minutes each time, but with increasing frequency as they climbed higher.

Feeling refreshed I set off in their wake. They had ascended perhaps a hundred feet as I watched. It did not seem much, but as soon as I started up the slope I knew I was not going to be able to keep up with them. Ten paces and my legs were pleading for another break. Try as I might to ignore their demands, I was forced to give in. I stood there, panting and bent forwards, with my hands on my knees to distribute the weight of my pack as evenly as possible.

I would have to devise a system; set myself targets and stick to them despite the pain. I decided upon thirty paces between each rest and, by forcing myself to complete the full number of paces before allowing myself to stop, I achieved a respectable rate of upward progress. Nevertheless, by the time I reached the half-way point, Tony and Bryan had disappeared over the brow of the hill, while the rest of the load-carrying party had appeared below me. Relentlessly they reduced the distance that separated us.

By now it was almost seven o'clock, and the sun had appeared from behind the ridge. As it climbed higher in the sky, the air warmed up, and it was not long before I had to remove my thick sweater and add it to my load.

After a further hour's steady climbing the top of the slope was just above me and I could see a flatter area ahead. Roger and John had already caught up with me, but Dharm Chand, to my slight surprise, was still struggling up the slope. I had expected him to acclimatise quickly, living as he did at six thousand feet, and his slow pace encouraged me. I allowed Roger and John to pass me and waited for D. C. to catch up. I would stay with him for the rest of the ascent.

Reaching the flatter ground at the top of the slope we could see Tony and Bryan ahead with Roger and John not far behind them. They had already crossed the snow-filled basin which was the next obstacle, and they were making their way up the left hand side of a snow spur which projected from the base of the ridge. Dharm Chand and I set off together across the basin.

He had been on the mountain before and he knew these lower slopes well. He suggested that we should follow a slightly different route.

"If we keep to the left side of the basin we will not lose so much height, Doctor Sahib. Although it is slightly further, there will be less climbing to do. It will be easier."

Anything which avoided even a few feet of the uphill slog found favour with me, and I swiftly agreed to his suggestion.

He continued to talk as we moved on, although where he found the breath from I do not know. Even my monosyllabic answers were a struggle.

"In a few weeks, when the snow has melted, down there will be a lake," he said, pointing at the snow basin below us. "Then we will all have to take this route."

I looked at the size of the basin. The melting snow from higher up would clearly form a substantial lake. I wondered how much the stream, which was currently hidden beneath the snow, would widen when it was in full spate.

"People say that a golden fish lives in the waters of the lake," continued D. C. "I used to believe them when I was a small boy, but now I think that it is just a story."

"Does it have a name?" I asked.

"The lake is called Chander Tal. I don't know about the fish."

D. C. gave me a wide grin. Our sirdar had a sense of humour.

We continued to rest at frequent intervals, but circling around the basin had made the going much easier and we were both moving better. The only discouraging thing was the deceptive landscape around us. The massive scale of the terrain continued to play subtle tricks with my perception of both height and distance. The ridge sometimes seemed to get closer, and then it would recede again as a different perspective opened up. The only positive evidence of progress was the ever-lengthening trail of boot-prints that stretched out behind us.

This distortion of scale, and consequent poor judgment, would continue throughout the expedition. What looked like a ten minute stroll would turn out to be a hard morning's slog. A snow slope would stretch endlessly upwards, the crest seeming to retreat tantalisingly as it was approached. I never got used to it.

When we reached the snow spur, which poked out from the ridge like a podgy, white finger, we could at last see the final part of the day's climb. It was a slightly depressing sight. The others had reached the proposed site of Advance Base Camp, but it was so far away that they looked like busy, black ants in the white distance. We still had a lot of ground to cover. The ridge now rose majestically above us, proclaiming its strength and sheer size. And yet this ridge was just a tiresome preliminary to the serious climbing which lay ahead, for my companions if not for myself. It was a sobering sight.

The snow underfoot was getting softer, as Tony had predicted, and my heavy boots were starting to break through the surface. At first this was no more than an irritating, ankle-deep stumble, but before very long I was disappearing up to my knees in soft snow. Had it been every step that collapsed it would perhaps have been tolerable. The strength-sapping aspect of the problem was that it occurred unpredictably, every third or fourth step. It was a very weary half-hour later that we found ourselves crossing the last snow gully and clambering up to where the other four were already clearing a site for a tent. It was right below the ridge, on a snow ramp which had formed itself into a flat shelf before falling away towards Chander Tal.

"Tired?" asked Bryan with a smile as Dharm Chand and I dumped our packs onto the snow and collapsed beside them.

He seemed quite unconcerned by the altitude, and was busily clearing snow away from the area where the tent was to be pitched. The base of the ridge was about two hundred yards away, and there was a slight depression between the shelf and the ridge which should catch any avalanches or falling ice. The judgment of my expert, climbing colleagues was that it was a safe place for a camp.

When I had recovered a little I gazed up at the ridge. How tall was it? Fifteen hundred feet? Probably more. I was already very suspicious of any attempt to estimate height and distance in these mountains, but of one thing I was certain. The ridge looked like a very tough climb.

To the left and right, it joined onto the other peaks and ridges which encircled the valley. High above us, to our left, I could see the leading edge of a hanging glacier. Numerous huge ice blocks, scattered on the floor of the valley below the glacier, bore witness to its ultimate fate. I was glad that we were well clear of it.

I felt better after a rest and began to assist with the erection of the tent in which Roger Brook and John Brazinton were planning to spend their first night on the mountain. On the way up they had decided that they were well enough acclimatised to start looking for a route up the ridge, for we could not afford to waste any of the present fine weather. There were no guarantees that it would continue.

The tent was a straightforward, triangular design and putting it up would normally have been a five minute job but, in the porridge-like snow, even the sturdy snow pegs would not take the strain of the guy ropes. Fortunately some long marker poles had been brought up as part of one load and, in the absence of any alternative, they were used as temporary tent pegs. Pushed deep into the snow, they seemed to be strong enough to hold the guy ropes in position.

Piled alongside the tent were the supplies which had been carried up. A couple of lengths of climbing rope, a primus stove, two cans of fuel and sufficient food for seven days should be enough to support Roger and John while they made a start on the ascent of the ridge.

They were already discussing the possibilities with Dharm Chand. With his previous experience to draw upon, he was strongly in favour of taking the most direct route, a narrow gully, or couloir, which bisected the face of the ridge directly above the camp. It led straight up to the lowest point on the ridge and, although far from easy, it looked like a reasonably straightforward climb. Tony and Bryan were not keen. Although they were fairly certain that the couloir could be climbed, they thought it looked like a natural avalanche channel. While the risk might be acceptable on a single ascent, it had to be borne in mind that the route would be used numerous times by climbers who were taking loads up to the higher camps.

Tony pointed to a long, snow slope on the far right hand end of the face, almost where it joined with the sides of the valley.

"I reckon that slope should be less of an avalanche risk. The fact that D. C. was able to use the couloir route safely last time he was on the mountain doesn't necessarily make it the best route for us this time. Last time you were here, it was the post-monsoon season, wasn't it D.C?

Dharm Chand nodded.

"The weather's colder then, so avalanches tend to be less of a hazard."

Roger and John insisted that they were both feeling really good, and they were keen to get to grips with their adversary. Despite a few half-hearted objections from me, as the guardian of their health, it was decided that they would take a look at the right hand route that same afternoon.

I was in an awkward position. I had no first-hand knowledge of altitude sickness. I had, of course, read all the available literature but there is no substitute, in medicine, for clinical experience. All the books in the world could not tell me how seriously to take the business of acclimatisation on this particular mountain and at this particular altitude. I was uneasy about the prospect of our two best acclimatised climbers doing too much and ascending too high, too soon, but I did not feel certain enough to veto their plans. They seemed to be fit and well, so I gave them the go-ahead, with the proviso that they should not climb for more than a couple of hours before returning to camp and resting.

The sun was now high in the sky. By the time the four of us who were returning to Base Camp started our journey down the hill, the ridge was bathed in the full glare of the sun and it looked more daunting than ever. The earlier shadows had created the illusion of a fairly easy gradient. Now, with features such as rocks and gullies merging into a single, shimmering whiteness, and the face of the ridge sweeping upwards in a great curve, it looked almost vertical. It seemed very unlikely that I would even get as far as Camp 1.

I pushed my dark goggles up onto my forehead to see if it made the ridge look any more promising, and immediately pulled them down over my eyes again as the brightness hit me with surprising force. An after-image of the dazzling, white ridge danced before my eyes as I screwed them up in an effort to retrieve my vision as I walked on down the slope. By the time my eyes had returned to normal the lone tent at Advance Base Camp was looking very small. Alongside it I could just make out Roger and John getting ready for their reconnaissance of the ridge. In the soft snow I found it an effort just to walk downhill, even without a loaded pack. I admired their energy and their enthusiasm. I just hoped they were not taking on too much.

John and Roger head for the first ridge *(JW)*

Eleven

A BRIEF SET-BACK

"Where on earth have they got to?"

There were just five of us at Base Camp, and we ate the supper which Tashi had prepared for us while all the time scanning the dark slopes outside the large tent, hoping to see a torch or some sort of movement.

"The snow'll have been like a soft blancmange this afternoon," said Geoff Arkless glumly. "I reckon they were mad to even think of doing a second carry. They didn't get away 'til three, and I wouldn't be surprised if it took them four or five hours just to get up there."

We had returned to Base Camp after doing the first carry to Advance Base and to our surprise, after having some lunch and saying that they felt fine, Tony and Bryan had announced that they each intended to take a second load up to Advance Base Camp that afternoon.

"Surely they'd have turned back if it started getting dark before they reached Advance Base?" I ventured.

"You don't know Bryan and Tony."

We sat in silence for a further ten minutes. Geoff was looking increasingly concerned.

"Do you think we should go and look for them? There may've been an accident."

"We'd never find them. It's pitch black out there now. It'd just end up with someone else getting into trouble."

Another five minutes passed. Then, suddenly, a figure loomed out of the darkness, moving towards the tent at a fast pace, almost a run. It was Tony.

He slumped, exhausted, onto a food box. Sitting there, with his breathing rapid and heavy and his lips slightly blue, he looked as though he was about to collapse.

"Where's Bryan?"

The question was in all our minds, but Geoff Arkless was the first to ask it.

Tony shook his head. He was still too breathless to speak.

"Is everything alright up there?"

Tony nodded. That, at least, was a relief.

We gave him some more time to catch his breath. He sat with his hands around a reviving mug of hot coffee which Tashi had almost immediately conjured up.

Finally he was able to speak.

"Phew. I reckoned I'd make it down before dark, but it was further than I thought. I almost ran the last bit. Well, as near to running as you can get on that soft stuff out there."

"Where's Bryan?"

"Don't worry. He's fine. We got to Advance Base alright with our loads, but Roger and John hadn't got back from the ridge, so we decided to wait for them to see how they'd got on.

I feared the worst.

"It was pretty late when they got back. About five o'clock, I think. They said it took them four and a half hours to reach the top."

Tony had still not explained why Bryan had stayed up at Advance Base Camp and I was now seriously concerned.

"What sort of condition were they in?"

"Not too good. Roger had one hell of a headache and felt pretty sick. John was just knackered. I think he'll be okay by tomorrow, though. They didn't think much of the right hand route so, if Roger is still feeling bad tomorrow, Bryan and John are going to have a go at the couloir that D.C. recommended."

I made a mental note that from now on acclimatisation was going to be taken seriously.

"If Roger's still feeling bad tomorrow he's coming down," I said.

"Okay. That's fine. You're the Doc," replied Tony.

It was some relief that he, at least, agreed with me.

"I've arranged a radio call for nine tonight so you can judge for yourself how he is, Doc. I've left my down boots and duvet up there with them so that Bryan can wear them tonight. It's not too cold at this altitude so he should hopefully be warm enough, even though he won't have a sleeping bag."

Happily Tony already seemed to be back to his usual self. He finished off the mug of coffee in one and handed it back to Tashi.

"Okay Tashi. Now what I need is some food. I'm starving."

Tashi got the message and set to work, warming up the remains of the rice and stew which he had prepared for the rest of us earlier.

= = = = = = = = = = = = = = =

"Advance Base to Base. Advance Base to Base. Are you there? Over."

The radio receiver crackled into life at exactly nine o'clock. The reception was not too good, but the accent was definitely New Zealand Welsh.

Tony took the microphone.

"Base Camp here. Receiving you okay, Bryan. How's things? Over."

"Rog seems to be a bit better. He's not been sick and the headache has eased off. He took two of the mild painkillers and a couple of sleeping tablets half an hour ago, and now he's asleep. Is Doc there? Over."

I took the receiver,

"Hello Bryan. A couple of questions. You say Roger's not been sick, and the headache's getting better? Was he short of breath or complaining of any chest pains before he went to sleep? Over"

"No. He seems be breathing fine. And he looks okay now, Doc. Over."

I gave Tony a thumbs up, and handed the receiver back to him.

"Great Bryan. Doc says that sounds okay about Roger. Call us again at six in the morning. If Rog is still not well Doc says he's got to come down though, until he's right. Anything else? Over."

"Nothing else Tony. John and I are both fine. We'll call you at six. Over and out."

There was a click, and then silence.

"He should be okay." I said to Tony. "Hopefully he's just overdone it a bit. We're going to have to be careful about acclimatisation in future though."

It was time to turn in for the night. Sitting in the big tent, waiting for the radio call, had done my feet no good at all. Despite the double boots they were numb with cold from the ankles down. I needed to get into a warm sleeping bag and massage some life back into them.

A late night inevitably meant a late start, and it was almost seven by the time we set off on our next carry to Advance Base Camp.

The news from higher up had been encouraging. A good night's sleep had refreshed Roger and he was feeling one hundred percent again. However he had agreed that, unless he was absolutely sure he was okay, he would wait at Advance Base Camp until I got up there and checked him out. We would then decide what he should do.

All except Tashi were involved in the carry. Both Geoffs were feeling a lot fitter after the extra day's rest and they had been determined to get on with some work. They had not travelled a quarter of the way round the world to sit doing nothing at Base Camp.

As on the previous day, the party became more and more strung out the higher and further we climbed. Geoff Tabbner was moving at my pace, and we stuck together all the way up to Advance Base. We arrived well ahead of Geoff Arkless who was struggling. I could not help thinking that it must have been galling for him to see me, a complete novice, outpacing him. I remembered how effortlessly he had tackled the hills back in Scotland, while I had battled to complete every pace. Now, through sheer physiological chance, I seemed to be acclimatising rather better than him. The altitude was certainly proving to be no respecter of experience.

When we got to Advance Base Camp it was deserted. Tony and D.C. had deposited their loads and were walking towards the ridge to get a closer look at the couloir. There was no sign of Roger.

Typically he must have decided that there was nothing wrong with him that a good climb would not cure, and gone off, up the couloir, with Bryan and John.

From the camp, Geoff and I could see no sign of any activity on the couloir. It stretched upwards towards a tooth-shaped rock which appeared, from where we stood, to mark the top. The three climbers must still be searching for a suitable site for Camp 1 on the far side of the ridge.

It was nine thirty in the morning. Alongside the camp there was a large boulder, the gently domed upper part of which poked about ten feet out of the surrounding snow. Once we had scrambled up to the top it made a very comfortable and dry vantage point, upon which we could lie and observe the couloir in relative comfort while soaking up some sun. A couple of days' extra exposure, plus a liberal coating of glacier cream to protect my nose and lips, had been enough to make some gentle sun-bathing a pleasure despite the extra strength of the ultra-violet rays at such an altitude.

By the time Geoff Arkless trudged into the camp, his face heavy with fatigue, we had stripped down to our shirtsleeves. He dumped his load and clambered wearily up to join us.

"It looks like Roger's gone up with Bryan and John," explained Geoff Tabbner. "We're just keeping an eye out for them coming down again."

I had carried some skis up with me and I was keen to try making use of them, preferably before the snow softened up too much. I was concerned that the short mountain skis would probably tend to stick in the snow more easily than the longer, more conventional type.

"If they don't appear soon I'm going to ski down. The snow's starting to get very soft. I'll give them another fifteen minutes or so. After that I'll assume that if Roger's fit enough to get up that ridge he probably doesn't need any medical attention from me."

Tony and Dharm Chand were on their way back down the slope towards us, half-walking and half-stumbling as the snow crust gave way beneath their feet.

"They're up on the couloir," shouted Tony once he was within earshot.

I looked up and could see nothing. There was no sign of anyone on the ridge. Geoff Tabbner shook his head. He could see no movement either.

Within a few minutes Tony and D.C. were standing on the snow beneath our boulder, and all three of us slid down from our rocky perch to join them. There were still no climbers visible on the ridge.

"There. Look." Tony pointed up at the couloir. "About a third of the way down. See. Three small dots."

And so there were. Three tiny black specs moving slowly down the white face. It was only by taking several looks, at intervals of a couple of minutes, that I could be certain that the dots were in fact moving, and that they were not stationary rocks, sticking through the snow.

The gigantic scale of these mountains was unbelievable. With no trees, or other objects of known size, to compare with, perception of scale went haywire. I stared at the small dots and realised that, judging by their size, the tooth-shaped rock at the top of the couloir must be enormous. Not fifteen or twenty feet high, as I had imagined, but the size of a city office block.

Two hours later we were all drinking tea together at the camp. Roger was fully recovered and the three of them had taken up a tent and two boxes of food which they had left at the top of the couloirs, ready to establish a camp. Everyone was well satisfied. It was just six days since we had left Johnson's Orchards and already the first ridge had been overcome. At the top of the couloir Bryan's altimeter had registered just over sixteen thousand feet. Things were looking good.

"It'll blow your mind when you get up there," said John. "The view is just incredible. I don't think you'd believe it, even if I could describe it to you. It's like seeing things clearly for the first time. Just amazing."

I sat there listening to him, and hoped that I would get the chance to see it for myself. The prospect of having my mind blown at sixteen thousand feet was curiously appealing.

Roger's recovery meant that Bryan, much to his disappointment, would have to return to the mundane load-carrying along with the rest of us. Although he would dearly have liked to stay out in front, we could not support three lead climbers at this stage. Once Camp 1 had been established it would take all our manpower to accumulate sufficient food and other equipment to keep two people up there.

The dramatic progress of the past two days, a height gain of two and a half thousand feet, would have to slow down a little. Tony had decided that we needed to have at least a week's reserve of food and fuel at every camp in case really severe weather closed in, and climbers at higher camps could not get down. Roger and John could continue route finding, while the rest of us worked to consolidate the gains we had already made. From my point of view such relatively slow progress was good, for it allowed plenty of time for proper acclimatisation.

We were all back at Base Camp by early afternoon. I had successfully managed to ski down the upper part of the route, but the softer snow and flatter terrain lower down had defeated me. I had been forced to join the others, and trudge down the final stretch on foot.

= = = = = = = = = = = = = = =

The morning of Friday 21st May provided a sharp reminder that we had to make the most of every day of good weather. The dawn sky, in stark contrast with the deep blue of previous days, was a dark, leaden grey. The crisp cold was gone, and replaced by an unpleasant damp chill. To the west we could see black clouds making their way up the valley towards us, to join the ominous collection that already hung over the camp. Some heavy snow was on the way.

We had been gone from Base Camp for less than five minutes, on the regular morning carry up to Advance Base, when the inevitable white flakes began to fall. They drifted past my face, floating gently to the ground in ones and twos at first, but very soon the snowfall became much heavier. Within half an hour semi-whiteout conditions prevailed, and visibility dropped to less than twenty yards.

I pulled my red, nylon cagoule out of my pack and put it on over my woollen pullover, only to take it off again after less than ten minutes as the accumulation of sweat inside the impervious material made me more uncomfortable than had been the case without its protection. The development of modern, semi-permeable waterproof material was still in its very early stages at that time, and we did not have the benefit of such sophisticated clothing.

The slow, uphill tramp was even more monotonous than before, as the surrounding landscape dissolved into a featureless, white haze. The route was familiar, and the snowfall was not heavy enough to obscure the trail of boot-prints ahead of us, so we pushed on despite the weather. With our increased fitness and better acclimatisation the journey took less than ninety minutes, a considerable improvement on the two and a half hours of just a couple of days earlier. We arrived at Advance Base Camp to find that John and Roger were already down from the couloir, and lamenting the fact that the tent at Advance Base seemed to be letting in almost as much snow as it was keeping out.

"Cheap New Zealand rubbish. I knew we shouldn't have brought it with us. Pooley can sleep in the thing. He must have known it was useless."

The tent in question belonged to Bryan, who had kindly loaned it to the expedition as a last minute stop-gap when it seemed that we might end up without enough of them. So he was at the receiving end of the complaints, albeit not entirely fairly.

The snowfall was getting heavier, and it was becoming increasingly obvious that we could not assume the bad weather would clear quickly. Something would have to be done to provide dry, warm accommodation at the camp. Bryan and D.C. were due to remain there overnight so that Roger and John could push higher up the mountain without having to ferry all their own supplies up the couloir to Camp 1.

Bryan, keen to make amends, suggested a snow cave. He had brought a snow saw up with him, in his pack, for emergencies, and he quickly began to cut blocks, three feet by two and about a foot thick, from the plentiful supply of snow beneath our feet. As he continued to saw away, we began to construct an igloo, the plan being that it would be built over the snow hole which Bryan was rapidly excavating. To save time we cheated a little and used the boulder, on which we had sunbathed the previous day, as one side of the structure. Four pairs of hands made for swift progress and, within an hour, the sides and roof were in place. All that remained was to dig down another couple of feet, to give some extra head-room, and the job was done.

I did not get the opportunity to experience the pleasures of sleeping in an igloo, for my first overnight stay at Advance Base Camp did not occur until after the structure had melted away, but those of the team who did use it commented that it was warm, relatively dry, and much more spacious than a tent. It survived for over a week and eased our critical tent shortage, as well as making Bryan feel better about the slight inadequacy of his tent.

The two Geoffs, Tony and myself all returned to Base Camp in steadily deteriorating weather. I had once again taken skis up with my load but, in the white-out conditions, there was no hope of skiing down safely so I left them at Advance Base for future use.

When we got back, Tashi was no longer alone. We entered the cook tent to find him engaged in earnest conversation with a stranger who turned towards us and thrust a scribbled note into Tony's hand.

'Please find new porter. Chamba Ladhaki. Good man. He will climb very hard I know. Also sack of fresh vegetables I have sent with him – 17 rupees. With sincere wishes. Wongdhi, Sirdar'

Chamba Ladhaki grinned a greeting and shook each of us by the hand. It was apparent that, like Tashi, he spoke no English. He must only just have arrived, for fresh snow still clung to his eyebrows and his bright orange, woollen hat. His clothes were soaked but, in the manner of all the local people, he did not seem to be too bothered and he would continue smiling through every adversity. He looked younger than Tashi. His slightly Tibetan features, together with the absence of any facial hair, made him very boyish in appearance but we were later to learn that, although he was born in Ladakh, near the border with Tibet, he was, in fact, married with four children and lived with his wife in Manali.

He wore a very ancient anorak, together with a pair of the standard grey, woollen trousers of the hill men. His trousers were tucked into knee-length climbing socks; and on his feet he had a pair of fairly new climbing boots, probably trophies from a previous expedition. His rucksack contained the rest of his climbing equipment, including an ice-axe and crampons. He seemed to be very adequately equipped.

We all exchanged names. That at least we could manage without an interpreter. More complex communication with our new arrival would have to wait until D.C. returned from the higher camp.

As Tashi started to brew up some tea, the combination of six bodies and a roaring primus stove soon warmed the tent up, despite the weather. We sat in our damp clothing and drank the welcome fluid. There would be no sun to sit in and dry our things out as we continued to wear them so, once we had finished drinking our tea, we piled our wet outer clothes on the floor of the big tent and changed into some dry kit. I was quite surprised how well the thick woollen sweater and breeches had kept the weather out. My inner layer of thermal clothing was hardly wet at all, so it was only necessary to pull on dry socks and breeches, and take my, as yet unused, down duvet from its protective nylon bag. As I was putting it on I found, in the pocket of the duvet, a diary in which I had scribbled some Hindi words a few weeks earlier. Perhaps I could manage some sort of conversation with Chamba after all?

SOME USEFUL HINDI WORDS

Tent ……………………Tamboo

Ford …………………... Khanna

Water ………………... Pani

Rice …………………... Chowell

Lentils ………………... Dahl

Rope …………………... Bashi

Man …………………... Admi

Hill ……………………. Pahar

Hillman ……………... Pahari

Festival .... *Mela (Kulu area only)*

Up .... *Uppa*

Cloud .... *Badel*

Rain .... *Badesh*

Sun .... *Suraj*

Here .... *Idra*

There .... *Udra*

Snow .... *Burf*

Come here .... *Idra Ao*

Give me water..... *Pani Lao*

To the great amusement of both Tashi and Chamba, I tried out a few phrases by stringing together several nouns, without any verbs at all. Despite their hilarity I managed to convey to Chamba that he would be sleeping in the big tent with Tashi that night, and I was just about to start finding out what he had brought up with him in the way of clothing and equipment when there was a shout from outside the tent.

We opened the flap to see Dharm Chand standing there, clad in a huge, red cagoule which covered him from head to foot and made him look like an abominable, red snowman. Behind him, peering through the snow, we could see the rest of the party we had left up at Advance Base just a few hours earlier.

As they crowded into the tent, Tony explained their unexpected appearance.

"It's hopeless up there. Even if the snow stops, the couloir isn't going to be safe for climbing tomorrow so we thought we might as well come down. There's no point in the four of us sitting there and eating all the food we've carried up. We might as well be in luxury with you lot down here."

Because of the avalanche risk in the couloirs it was obviously the right decision even though, less than an hour later, the clouds began to clear and the snow stopped falling. By late afternoon the only sign of the earlier, bad weather was the fresh, unmarked surface of the snow around the camp, and the drifts which had piled up against the windward side of each of the tents.

The swift improvement was typical of the unpredictability of high mountain weather, and it served to remind us all that a blissfully fine day in such mountains can deteriorate dramatically with equal swiftness.   We would have to be careful.

The plans that had been made for higher up on the mountain were put back by twenty four hours. Assuming there was no further snow it would, by then, be safe to return to the couloir. In the meantime, the unexpected extra numbers down at Base Camp would mean that additional loads of food and equipment could be carried up to Advance Base Camp next day.

Little time would have been wasted.   The climb was still on schedule.

Twelve

DOWN IN THE VALLEY

The days passed, and life began to fall into a fairly gentle and relaxed routine.

Each morning those of us who were at Base Camp, which essentially meant Tashi, myself, and any of the others who were not load-carrying higher up the mountain in support of the leaders, would take supplies up to Advance Base. Invariably I would ski down, and others such as the two Geoffs began to copy my idea, until the slopes around Base Camp became criss-crossed with the tracks of parallel skis, looking more like an Alpine resort in early spring than a Himalayan valley.

The weather had dropped into the expected pattern. The deep, blue sky of dawn would slowly cloud over as the morning progressed until, by two or three in the afternoon, it was completely overcast. Later in the day, as the temperature started to fall, the clouds would clear, often in time to reveal a spectacular sunset over the distant peaks far beyond Kulu.

It was very far from being the arduous existence that I had expected. Once the morning's load-carrying was over there was nothing to do other than lie in the sun and read, or sit idly upon a boulder and meditate upon the peaceful scene all around, breaking off only to consume the food and drink that was served at regular intervals by the invaluable Tashi. I had rarely before had so much time on my hands and I appreciated the luxury of being able to concentrate upon whatever I wished, in the certain knowledge that I would not be interrupted unless I chose to be. There were no urgent deadlines to keep and no trains to catch, or endless traffic jams to endure. Mobile and satellite phones had yet to be invented, so no ringing broke the silence. Looking back, it was a period of great peace and I savoured it to the full.

The only thing to worry about was the predictable, but disturbingly sudden, way in which the air temperature changed with the presence and absence of the sun. My daytime attire quite often consisted of nothing more than a tee-shirt and shorts, but when the warmth of the sun disappeared behind clouds I was forced to add two or three pullovers and thermal underwear to my garb, just to keep reasonably warm. At such moments I occasionally thought longingly about the central-heated luxury of a cosy, brick-built house or warm, city centre flat.

Such inactivity and relative idleness could not last, however. By Sunday 23rd May Tony had disappeared up to a higher camp, and I had been appointed logistic supremo. This was not because I was any great shakes at deciding how many pegs were needed here, or how much beef curry would be eaten at Camp 1 in six days, but because I was now the only member of the team who looked as though he would be in one place for any length of time; and it is much easier to see the bigger picture, and plan the logistics, from below.

Apart from the problem of keeping supplies moving to the right place, at the right time, I found that I had a medical problem to address. Geoff Tabbner had recovered from his slight acclimatisation difficulties, but Geoff Arkless was still far from well. His headaches and nausea had gone, only to be succeeded by persistent attacks of abdominal cramps which were associated with a disturbing loss of appetite. It was difficult to be certain whether he was still suffering from altitude effects, or whether he had picked up some sort of stomach bug. When after three days he had shown no sign of responding to the usual treatment for a stomach bug I was beginning to suspect that the altitude was the problem. According to the books the only effective cure for such persistent altitude problems is descent to a lower altitude. Maybe permanently.

This was the dilemma I had to resolve. Geoff would obviously be most unhappy at having to go down, and the chances of our enterprise being successful would be much reduced without his presence. I discussed the options with him and, as he did not seem to be getting any worse, and certainly did not want to return to Kulu, he had little difficulty in making up his mind what he wanted to do. I would have to keep a close eye upon him and see what happened. Fortunately, within a few days his symptoms started to improve and, although he was still not feeling one hundred percent, he was confident that he felt fit enough to start moving to the front when his turn to take the lead came.

= = = = = = = = = = = = = =

Eight days after our arrival at Base Camp the situation of the expedition was as follows.

Roger and John were up at sixteen thousand feet, having found a good site for Camp 1. They would stay in the lead for a further two days, trying to find a way up to the high plateau at eighteen thousand feet, after which they would return to Base Camp for a couple of days of rest and recuperation.

Bryan was climbing with Dharm Chand as his partner, and Tony with Chamba. The four of them were based at Advance Base Camp, below the first ridge, and each day they were taking loads up the couloir to Camp 1 in support of the two leaders. The rest of us, forming the lowest layer of the pyramid up which supplies were being passed, were making regular trips between Base Camp and Advance Base, carrying supplies with us.

The whole supply route was a human shuttle service which would become more and more stretched as the lead climbers moved higher up the mountain, and onto the West Ridge. I planned ahead, working towards the day when the back-breaking task of getting the food and equipment up to the plateau would be over. Everything that could possibly be needed for a successful climb would then be in place.

On that same eighth morning, those of us who were still at Base Camp woke to a most unexpected sight. Two hundred yards away from us, further down the valley, some more tents had appeared. There were three small ones, and a rather larger khaki ridge tent which looked very much as if it might belong to the military. There was no sign of life in them as we set out on the normal, early morning carry, but the implications were clear. Another expedition had arrived.

As we climbed up the long hill to Advance Base Camp I discussed the matter with Geoff Tabbner and Geoff Arkless. Was this new expedition intending to make an assault upon Indrasan as well? It was just this kind of situation that had forced the Nepalese Government to make attempts on the major peaks in their country 'by appointment only'. Everest, for example, was at that time fully booked up for five years in both the pre- and post-monsoon seasons, and it was expected that the number of people wanting to make attempts upon such well-known signature peaks would increase dramatically in the future.

Nobody though, back in 1971, could have imagined that, forty years later, people would be paying tens of thousands of pounds to commercial expedition organisers so that they could join a queue at twenty eight thousand feet, and take their turn to stand upon the summit of Everest.

We all agreed that the last thing our expedition needed was to get involved in a race up the West Ridge of Indrasan. The climbing ahead would be difficult enough without the added risk of competition.

We reached Advance Base Camp which was deserted. We decided that the four lead climbers must still be somewhere on the ridge which rose ahead of us. Keen to get back down and find out who the new arrivals were, and more importantly what their plans might be, we left a brief note for Tony and Bryan, explaining this latest development, and returned to Base Camp.

We could see signs of activity at the new camp when we arrived back at Base and, after a quick brew to recharge our energies, we wandered over to introduce ourselves and satisfy our curiosity.

From fifty yards away it was possible to identify the nationality of the men who were busily putting their camp in order. With the exception of three who looked like local porters, they were obviously all Japanese. The recognition was mutual for, before we had reached the camp proper, they were shouting greetings in English. It seemed there would be no awkward communication problems to overcome.

"Good morning. Our porters told us that you would be here. The news of your expedition was all over Manali when we were down there."

The English of the man who addressed us was excellent. We all shook hands and introduced ourselves.

"I'm John Winter, the expedition doctor. This is Geoff Tabbner. And Geoff Arkless."

"We are most pleased to meet you. We are all of the Ohta-ku Alpine Club of Tokyo."

Two others, who we had not previously seen, appeared from the large, army-style tent. They were obviously Indian and, judging by their clothes and general appearance, they were not local men. We were introduced.

"This is Dr Ravindren Nair, our medical officer, and Mr Sharma, our local liaison officer."

That was interesting. We had deliberately avoided engaging a local liaison officer, partly for financial reasons – their rate of pay is high – and partly because we had felt that we would be more relaxed and at ease without a stranger peering over our shoulders all the time, however well intentioned he was. The fact that the Japanese had employed such a person indicated that theirs was an officially-recognised climb which had the full authority of the local authorities. And it appeared they had an officially-appointed doctor as well. If it turned out that they were planning an assault upon Indrasan things could prove a little awkward, for to minimise the legendary red tape in India we had officially described ourselves as a trekking party. While we were not doing anything illegal in attempting the West Ridge, it would not be looked upon kindly if our activities interfered with the efforts of an official climbing party.

I decided to take the bull by the horns.

"Are you here to have a go at Indrasan?" I asked, attempting to disguise my obvious interest with an air of idle curiosity.

The man who had originally greeted us, and who I took to be the Japanese leader, laughed.

"Unfortunately, no. We were unable to get permission from the authorities. Indrasan is a very dangerous mountain with many crevasses and avalanches. They said we did not have the necessary experience. Anyway we are staying here for ten days only and there would not be time."

The liaison officer took up the tale.

"I could not leave my full-time job for longer than that, and no-one else was available in the area."

Geoff Tabbner and I looked at each other. We were both thinking the same thing. Perhaps it was fortunate that we had decided not to ask for official permission to attempt the West Ridge. Our request may have been turned down.

To my surprise Geoff then spoke.

"We are trying the West Ridge of Indrasan."

The liaison officer frowned.

"As my colleague has said, it is very, very difficult. I wish you luck. Our team will be making an attempt on Deo Tibba by way of the south-east glacier. Even that is a very challenging climb."

The Japanese leader smiled. He had obviously picked up on our concerns.

"It looks like we won't be getting in each other's way!"

We all walked over to the large khaki tent which turned out to be exactly what it had appeared to be – an Indian Army tent. The doctor was an officer serving in the Indian Army, and he had been engaged to assist the Japanese expedition. He told us that he was on his way to serve as an army surgeon in one of the mountain units, on the border between India and China.

The army tent was, by expedition standards, sumptuously equipped with two collapsible beds. Adjoining it there was what can best be described as an open ante-room, furnished with wooden boxes which presumably held food but which doubled up as a table and chairs. The doctor produced a bottle of rum from somewhere in the tent.

"Three rupees a bottle to the Indian Army," he announced happily, holding the bottle up for all to see. "Please join us for a drink."

The doctor clearly believed that climbing should be done in style as the rum was served in elegant, cut- glass tumblers and accompanied by a bowl of salted nuts. We each had several measures and, when we eventually took our leave, I was definitely feeling the effects. Either the rum was an exceptionally strong one, or the altitude had affected our ability to absorb alcohol, for my companions felt the same. The three of us made our way, a little unsteadily, back up the valley to a much needed curry lunch which Tashi had prepared in our absence.

The days passed, and the snow-covered valley in which we had pitched Base Camp was changing. The quantity of snow on the ground, three feet deep in places, had been a surprise to us when we had first arrived, for previous expeditions to the area who had pitched camp in the same valley had told us that we could expect a pleasant, green valley, completely free from snow by early May. The locals had told us, however, that this year the weather had been bad, with heavy snow-falls, and the snow-line was about a thousand feet lower than usual for the time of year.

By the end of May, however, the summer melt was well advanced and the deep, snow blanket was at last starting to disappear. The stream running down one side of the valley, which had been almost completely covered with ice and snow on our arrival, had doubled in size in a couple of days as thousands of gallons of fresh, melt water were carried past our camp and down into the Jagatsukh Nullah.

Here and there, on the floor of the valley, small patches of dark earth began to appear through the white snow, enlarging day by day until they merged into one large area. Within a few days young shoots were springing up everywhere, and in little more than a week a startling transformation had taken place. The lower reaches of the valley became predominantly green and grass-covered as the snow melted away in the increasingly temperate weather while higher up, en route to Advance Base Camp, the lake,

Chander Tal, was just starting to appear from beneath its covering of snow and ice.

The pattern of the weather continued as before, but the afternoon clouds were now bringing rain to Base Camp, rather than snow, except on rare colder days. Above Advance Base Camp, however, little had changed. Snow still lay on the ground, and the clouds sometimes brought with them an additional light covering.

As the melt in the valley progressed it became increasingly obvious that we had not chosen the best site for our tents. The camp had been pitched in a low-lying dip and it turned out that the cook tent was directly over the course of one of the main tributaries of the main stream. Our efforts to divert the flow of melt water became more futile each day, and eventually we were forced to move the whole camp to one of the snow-free areas on higher ground.

This enforced move in fact proved to be a blessing in disguise, for we were able to make a much better job of setting up the camp than we had managed to achieve in the poorly acclimatised and exhausted state which we were in when we first arrived. Some flat slabs from the surrounding moraine were collected to form a stone floor, and two or three conveniently sited boulders acted as seats inside the tent. The final result was almost luxurious, especially when compared with the cold, damp, snow-floored tent to which we had become accustomed.

Our afternoons were increasingly punctuated by sudden thunderous roars as the warmer weather caused the glaciers above us to release frozen blocks of ice and snow which would crash down into the valley. Less frequently a huge slab of the deep snow which had collected on the steep valley walls over the winter would break off and slide towards us in a spectacular avalanche. On each occasion, the initial roar would bring those of us in the camp rushing out of the tents, cameras at the ready, in time only to catch the last few blocks rolling gently to a halt or see a cloud of powdery snow particles settle slowly onto the valley floor. Such dramatic and unpredictable events are one of the commonest causes of injury and death in the Himalayas, and great care had been taken to place our tents a good distance from the edge of the valley. Even the largest of the avalanches came to a halt well before there was any risk of it engulfing our little encampment.

As more and more of the area between Base Camp and Advance Base became snow-free, my daily journeys up to the ridge were made more interesting, albeit less pristine and beautiful. Each day's melt would reveal evidence of earlier camps in the valley, mostly in the form of scattered, rusting tins and half-decayed wooden and cardboard boxes.

No other team had, as far as we knew, approached Indrasan by way of Jagatsukh, and it was therefore likely that most of the debris that was appearing was from long abandoned camps which had been used to attempt Deo Tibba. Indeed, the most noticeable accumulations of rubbish were situated immediately below the south-east glacier of Deo Tibba, the most commonly-used approach route, and the one which the members of the Japanese team were using.

The Himalayas at that time were beginning to resemble The Alps at the end of the nineteenth century. All the major peaks had been climbed, and adventurers were turning their attention to the numerous, less well-known mountains. Eventually, as happened in the Alps in the early decades of the twentieth century, more and more climbers will be attracted to the area with the development of the Indian economy and the increasing ease of travel over long distances. Ski resorts may even start to appear. It was sad to see the debris that such activity tends to leave behind it before the necessary infra-structure for removing it is in place. I hoped, as I looked at the little pockets of rubbish, that these lovely valleys would not become irreparably spoilt. As India becomes more affluent, and increasing numbers of people inevitably want to visit these incredibly beautiful mountains, the Kulu Valley, with its relative ease of accessibility, is likely to be one of the first areas to be developed as a major tourist destination.

= = = = = = = = = = = = = =

"That ridge is just incredible."

The speaker was John Brazinton. He and Roger had returned to Base Camp after nine days out in front. They had achieved a remarkable amount in that short time.

Since I had last seen them, the two of them had firmly established Camp 1 at 16,000 ft. The next target had been the De Graaff couloir, the recommended route up to the top-most plateau. They had found, however, that the only way to reach the bottom of the De Graaff couloir had been to cross the Malana Glacier, descending five hundred feet in the process. This had not seemed a very logical thing to do, and so they had started looking for an alternative route.

About half a mile west of the De Graaff route was another couloir, just under two thousand feet in height, and offering a possible route directly from the head of the Malana Glacier up to the plateau at eighteen thousand feet. It had many attractions, not the least of which was that if a route could be found up it there was the possibility of saving a camp. Without the long traverse across the glacier to delay a climber, the top plateau would be reachable from Camp 1 in a single day. There would be no need for an intermediate camp at the bottom of the couloir, as had been envisaged in the original assault plan. Taking into account the amount of equipment that had to be carried between camps day after day, the total saving in terms of time would be as much as three or four days.

On Monday 24th May Roger and John had set out to attempt the new couloir. As they had got closer it had towered above them, an unbroken expanse of white snow and ice. Carrying only a tent, a few hundred feet of rope, and assorted pegs and ice screws, they had started up. The top seemed to get further away as the hours passed but the two of them had forced themselves on, despite not knowing for certain whether, even if they were successful in reaching the top of the couloir, it would prove to be a feasible route to the West Ridge.

Eventually, after several hours of climbing, they had put the worst behind them and the plateau was ahead but, just as they reached the top, the inevitable afternoon cloud and mist closed in. They had been forced to retrace their steps down the couloir in snow and hail, having had no real opportunity to see the west ridge properly or make the vital reconnaissance at the top.

I sat drinking coffee with them at Base Camp and listened to the rest of their story.

"It was really sickening. We got to the top of the couloir and just got a glimpse of the ridge through the clouds before they closed in completely. It was pretty hairy going down. We left all the equipment we had carried up at the top. No point in climbing all that way with it and then taking it all down again. But that meant we had no screws or anything to use as belays on the couloir, and we lost our way a bit. Instead of going down the right side, as we had done on the way up, we found ourselves somewhere out in the middle of a massive sheet of steep ice. That was when we decided to put our crampons on!"

John continued the tale.

"As we were taking a rest and putting our crampons on it started to snow and hail pretty heavily. The hailstones were piling up in mounds between us and the slope. It was quite weird. Anyway, we carried on down the ice; a bit anxious because we'd seen these ice cliffs on the way up and we weren't keen on slipping over them. Luckily we got to the bottom without any serious mishaps and set off across the head of the glacier towards Camp I. It was still snowing and the whole area was covered in snow and hailstones. We couldn't see properly and Rog went up to his chest in a hidden crevasse; just to round the day off with a bang!"

"We got back to the camp at about six, so we'd been out for nearly twelve hours in all. Tony was waiting for us, having just about given us up for lost."

I did a quick mental calculation.

"That must have been three or four days ago. What have you been up to since then?"

"Tony thought we should take a rest after that little epic," grinned Roger, "so we spent the whole of the next day just sitting around at Camp I. Then we went back up the same couloir. The weather was much better and we could see the tracks we had left on the ice where we'd come down in the mist. We were very lucky, I reckon. Without realising it we'd moved right out into the middle of the couloir, and there's a large bergschrund at the bottom of the slope which we'd crossed on a wide, snow bridge without even noticing it. The good thing is we managed to fix quite a lot of rope on the right-hand side of the couloir second time round, and Bryan and Tony, who've had a look at it, are pretty chuffed with it as a route. When it's completely roped it'll be pretty easy to carry loads up and down, and it should save us several days."

"The view when you get to the top is unbelievable. The West Ridge sticks up on the far side of the plateau, all on its own. There's hardly any snow on it apart from the summit cone. It's just too steep for the snow to hold, and the granite rock is exposed all the way along the ridge. There are huge pinnacles and gendarmes of dull, red rock, and it just goes on and on. It's easy to see why the Derbyshire Expedition couldn't crack it with an Alpine assault. It's far too long and tough. And even if you get past all those obstacles there's still a massive, vertical buttress to get up before you're anywhere near the summit. It looked completely smooth from where we were seeing it, so we'll just have to hope there's some sort of crack on the side we couldn't see. If there isn't, we could be in trouble."

= = = = = = = = = =

There were just the three of us, and Tashi, at Base Camp that night. Geoff Tabbner and Geoff Arkless were at Camp I, making their way up to the ridge from where they would take over the lead from Tony and Bryan. Geoff Arkless seemed to be much improved and, although he was still not fully fit, he was able to do his share of the lead climbing. Dharm Chand and Chamba, who were both extremely fit and strong, and capable of carrying far heavier loads than any of us could manage, were spending most of their time moving equipment between Advance Base Camp and the plateau. It had already been decided that they would not go up onto the ridge as they would be much more useful to the team as load carriers. The difficult, technical rock climbing on the West Ridge was best left to those who were most experienced on such extreme terrain.

Nobody yet knew who might be involved in the final push for the summit. It was far too early to say. At that stage of the climb it was simply a matter of each climbing pair taking their turn at the front, and then falling back for a rest when they became tired. The tough climbing at twenty thousand feet and above would take its toll on the climbers' stamina, and fresh leaders would need to move to the front every couple of days.

In the evening Tashi cooked yet another excellent curry for us. It was a sumptuous dish which I took for granted, but John and Roger, who had been living on a more frugal diet higher up the mountain, went into raptures over it. Tashi was delighted by the reception which they gave to his cooking and disappeared outside the tent, returning a few minutes later with some dried vegetation which he offered round.

"What's this?" asked Roger.

I shrugged my shoulders.

Tashi waved his hands excitedly, pointing at the grass.

"What for, Tashi? What for?"

He put his fingers to his lips and made a sucking noise.

"I reckon he wants us to smoke it," said John. "Has he given this stuff to you before, Doc?"

"No way," I replied, shaking my head.

"Maybe he brought it up with him from Manali?" suggested Roger. "There's loads of hashish growing wild lower down That's why Kulu is getting so popular with the hippies."

"I don't think so" I said, thinking of how Tashi had been disappearing each morning and returning laden with green-leaved plants which he would spread out to dry in the sun behind the tent. "I think he's been collecting it up here in the valley since the melt."

"I assumed it was some sort of herb" I added. "It never occurred to me that he might be planning to smoke it. He's got some roots as well from somewhere. D.C. said they're called radu roots, or something like that. Apparently the shopkeepers in Manali will pay two rupees a kilo for them. They dry them and grind them up into a powder which they sell as a cure for anything from headaches and rheumatism to an upset stomach. There's usually some truth behind such folk remedies, so they probably contain a natural pain-killer of some sort."

"Yes, but what about the grass? It can't be anything like hash. It'd never grow this high up. It's too cold and wet."

"Maybe old Tash just fancies a smoke," said John.

Whatever the dried leaves were, Tashi seemed determined to smoke them. He rummaged around in a rucksack and pulled out some thin paper which he fashioned into a tube before stuffing some dried grass into it. The end product was a thick, cigar-like object which he proceeded to light up. He inhaled deeply and then blew out a cloud of foul, acrid smoke which filled the tent. After two more such inhalations he collapsed in a fit of violent coughing which made his eyes water. We could not be persuaded to join him.

Once he had recovered, the three of us laughed at him. He just smiled back at us serenely. Whatever he was smoking, he was clearly enjoying it.

Right in the middle of this performance, three members of the Japanese expedition appeared to take coffee with us. John and Roger had not met them before and, after the introductions, we sent Tashi outside and closed the tent flap to retain some warmth while we sat down for a chat.

"Tomorrow we must go," said the leader sadly. "It has not been good for us. We were unable to beat Deo Tibba. We wish you better luck with your climb. You have more time."

Indeed things had not gone well for them. The whole team had suffered badly from altitude sickness, so much so that two of their members had been forced to return to Manali to recover. Their badly depleted, small team had tried to continue with the climb but, on the previous day, they had finally abandoned their attempt. We discovered with some surprise that, restricted by their annual holiday entitlement from work, the ten days they had allowed themselves for the ascent included the march to and from the Kulu Valley. They had been left with hardly any time on the mountain proper. With no time to acclimatise properly it was hardly surprising that some of the team had succumbed to the altitude, and I could not help wondering if they felt it had been worth travelling all the way from Japan for such a brief skirmish.

"In four days we shall be back in Tokyo. We fly out from Kulu Airstrip on the first of June."

"And then next day back to work," one of his colleagues added ruefully.

"What about all your equipment?" I asked.

"Most of it we will send back by sea. The ropes we have left on the mountain, and we have brought some spare food over to give to you. We cannot take it back with us, so you might as well make use of it."

Two of them went outside and returned with a neat, wooden packing case filled with packet soups, dried noodles, and other delicacies the like of which we had not seen for some weeks. They really had been climbing in style. With a doctor and interpreter to pay for, as well as air fares and freight, their short stay must have been very expensive for them.

"I hope you have enjoyed your climbing," I said, trying to be positive.

The leader smiled ruefully and shrugged his shoulders in reply.

They would have no summit photographs to show to their families and friends back at home. Would our luck, I wondered, turn out to be better?

We thanked them for the extra food, and wished them a good journey home. When we woke the following morning their little group of tents had disappeared. We were on our own again.

Thirteen

A STORMY NIGHT

Roger and John had been down at Base Camp for a day and a half, resting after their efforts in trying to reach the plateau. They were due to return to the fray the following morning and I decided it was high time I did a bit more than oscillate between Base Camp and Advance Base Camp as I had been doing for the past thirteen days. I wanted to see for myself what lay beyond the ridge. The two of them were fairly easily persuaded that my presence higher up the mountain might not be such a handicap, and might even help to move the equipment up to the plateau faster. They agreed to take me up with them.

It was decided that we might as well make use of the empty tent at Advance Base as an overnight stopping place. It would make the long journey to the plateau slightly less arduous, for an ascent of almost five thousand feet in a single day would involve a very exhausting climb on soft snow later in the day. The snow in the couloir would be crisp and much easier to ascend in the early morning.

We spent the rest of the day playing the usual card games and drinking gallons of the tea and coffee which Tashi would regularly provide. By three o'clock I was ready to go. Looking down the valley I could see the usual afternoon clouds making their way towards us. They seemed to be thicker and blacker than usual, billowing and merging together as they got nearer. Roger and John were unconcerned but, being a bit more particular about staying dry if possible, I decided to set off for Advance Base Camp before the seemingly inevitable snowstorm broke. My companions, who were just at a very critical phase in a game of chess, said they would follow me later.

When I left, the sun was still shining. The massed clouds were hanging just below Seri at the head of the Jagatsukh Nullah, but it could not be long before they spilled over into the Base Camp valley. Within ten minutes, and sweating profusely, I was at the beginning of the steeper section. The melt of the past two weeks had exposed a lot of the underlying, rocky moraine, and the stream running out of Chandar Tal now swept past boulders and rocks amongst which were dotted patches of grass and numerous tiny, alpine flowers that had survived the long winter beneath the snows. A few thicker patches of snow that had not yet melted were all that remained of the previously solid, white blanket.

As I climbed higher, and nearer to Advance Base Camp, the snow covering was unbroken and still thick underfoot. At this slightly higher altitude the melt was having much less of an effect.

Now that I was fitter the going was easy, but the exercise still made me hot and I was not sorry when the gathering clouds finally covered the sun. Within minutes of the sun's disappearance a thick mist surrounded me, enveloping and obscuring both earth and sky. The visibility and the temperature dropped and I soon began to feel chilly in my perspiration-soaked clothes. This place was at one moment far too hot, and then, in such a short time, far too damp and cold.

I trudged on around the lake, thunder now echoing from peak to peak. It was still distant, but the swirling mist made it seem louder, the deep notes reverberating around the encircling ridges. I thought of the glaciers hanging high above me, hidden away where my eyes could no longer penetrate and revealing their presence only by the rumble of an avalanche as yet another huge ice block broke away from the leading edge and tumbled into the valley. I pressed on, half expecting the small tent with its sentinel posts to appear through the mist at any second. It had begun to snow but there was little chance of my getting lost. The trail of boot-prints which I was following was worn deep into the snow by the constant load-carrying, and it would have to be quite a storm to obliterate them completely.

The tent at last appeared, a dull yellow shape in the mist, and it was with great relief that I finally deposited my pack alongside it. Snow had been falling for the past half hour or so, and it was already collecting on the tent roof which was partially collapsed. I peered inside the flapping doorway and saw a scribbled note which had been left by the two Geoffs.

27TH MAY. GONE UP TO CAMP 1. TWO FOOD TINS AND PARAFFIN TAKEN WITH US.

The date on the note indicated that the tent had not been used for a day or two. I spent a couple of minutes adjusting the guy ropes, which had worked their way loose, to make it more stable before placing my personal gear inside and making a start on pumping up the primus. I was, by this time, resigned to a night on my own, for I did not expect Roger and John to follow in such weather conditions. I wanted to get supper over before darkness fell for, even if they did arrive, they would probably have eaten before leaving Base Camp.

As the light faded, with large, feathery snowflakes diving at me like white moths from the grey sky, I sat outside the tent and sipped my evening meal. I had heated up one of the dehydrated curries in some melted snow, and then thrown in a couple of handfuls of potato powder to make a mixture which was the consistency of thin custard. It was certainly not haute cuisine, but at high altitudes it becomes increasingly difficult to digest solid food. Watery stews and curries start to be increasingly appetising and palatable. Most of the others were experiencing the same digestive problems, and they had been telling me that higher up on the ridge things tended to get worse.

The previous, semi-collapsed state of the tent had reduced the efficiency of the waterproofing, and the sewn-in groundsheet was soaking wet. I was glad I had with me a spare, lightweight, exposure blanket which I spread out on the floor of the tent to act as a make-shift, waterproof layer. The thin, metal-foil blanket was designed primarily for mountain rescue work, and to combat exposure, but in the absence of anything better it would at least keep my precious sleeping-bag relatively dry and warm.

By 7.30 p.m. there was no sign of Roger and John, so I decided to turn in. The snow was still falling steadily, and loud claps of thunder would occasionally break the otherwise complete silence. Hopefully the storm would have passed by morning. Having set my alarm clock for six fifteen, I wormed my way into the warm sleeping-bag and closed my eyes to try to get some sleep. After what seemed like an age I drifted off into a light doze.

A tremendous clap of thunder woke me up with a start. Everything was blackness, and the terrifying noise seemed to bounce back at me, time after time, as it rolled around the ridges at the head of the valley. The luminous dial on my alarm clock indicated that it was just before two o'clock in the morning. I tried to get back to sleep again but every few minutes I was aware of flashes of lightening, even through my tightly closed eyes, and almost simultaneously there would be another of those tremendous thunderclaps. The centre of the storm was very close.

Thunderstorms had never bothered me in the past, but this was no ordinary storm. I lay on my back with my eyes wide open, having given up all attempts at sleep. It felt as though the tent must be very close to the source of the lightening, and I was uncomfortably aware of the amount of metal which surrounded me in the camp.

I kept looking at the clock. 2.30 a.m., 3.30 a.m., 4 a.m.. The time dragged by until, at long last, the thunder became a little quieter, and the lightning flashes seemed to be less bright and more distant. In a half-awake state, I lay there and listened to the groaning and creaking of the snow beneath me. My semi-conscious mind imagined a crevasse suddenly opening up beneath me and swallowing the tent up. As the night wore slowly on, the inside of the tent seemed to become increasingly cramped and claustrophobic and I was glad that there were not three of us inside it. Pulling my arm out of the sleeping-bag and reaching out in the darkness I could feel the roof of the tent only a foot or so above my face. The guy ropes must have slipped, but I could not be bothered to crawl out and fix them as it was just after five in the morning, and very cold. I must have drifted off to sleep again, for I was woken by the noisy jangling of the alarm.

For 6.15 a.m. it seemed unusually dark. I rolled onto my back with some difficulty, for the roof of the tent was now just a few inches from my face. Further towards the middle it actually sagged down to touch my sleeping-bag. I pushed the offending canvas away. It felt damp and heavy and I suddenly realised what must have happened. Instead of sliding off, the overnight snowfall had been so heavy that it had collected around the tent and covered the sloping roof.

I punched hard on the canvas above me, and was rewarded by a satisfying, swishing sound as some of the accumulated snow slid clear. Immediately more light entered the tent and I could see, looking around, that one of the two aluminium tent-poles had given way under the weight of snow and was now bent at a crazy angle. For the sake of lightness the poles appeared to have been manufactured from a grade of tubing that was too weak for such extreme conditions, and I was grateful that the two tent poles had not collapsed completely and encased me in a cocoon of snow.

A couple of hefty kicks, with my feet still inside the sleeping-bag, cleared sufficient snow for me to be able to crawl out and survey the scene outside. It was still snowing but the snowflakes were now very fine and dry, giving almost the impression of a mist as I looked into the distance. Visibility was perhaps one hundred yards, and I could see neither the ridge above me nor the Base Camp valley below. The only breaks in the complete whiteness were the few bare, granite boulders that fell within my immediate field of vision. Without experienced companions an ascent of the ridge via the couloir was completely out of the question and, with a big dump of fresh snow lying on the steep slope, it could presumably avalanche at any time.

The snow which had not been cleared with my kicks still lay in slabs, several inches thick, on the roof of the tent. The area immediately surrounding the camp, which the previous evening had been littered with discarded plastic bags and other refuse, looked clean and fresh with its new, white covering.

Because of the mist there were no distant mountains to be seen, but the all-embracing whiteness had a solitary beauty all of its own. It was one of those rare moments when it is possible fully to appreciate the preciousness of life. The air was still, and my exhaled breath gathered around me in icy clouds as I contemplated the tranquillity that such isolation brings. To be given time to stand completely alone, hands in pockets against the cold, and think such thoughts was a joy in itself.

Before very long, having lost the extra insulation of my sleeping bag, I was starting to feel cold and I hastened to brew a warming mug of tea. Not feeling like anything to eat, I was soon on my way and, at just after 9.30 a.m., I was walking back into Base Camp to find that the others had taken advantage of the poor weather to have a lie in. The walk down had given me an appetite and we breakfasted together.

It had been an interesting experience and, as I had made the decision to leave all my climbing gear at Advance Base, my journey had not been completely wasted. On my next trip up I would be able to carry a full equipment load.

It was two full days before the weather started to improve. The long night in the storm, plus the intermittent, but fairly heavy, snowfalls, had dampened some of the enthusiasm I had been feeling to achieve greater things and I decided that, until the weather showed definite sign of improvement, I would settle for the relative comfort of Base Camp.

Roger and John returned to Camp 1 without me on the day after the storm.

Fourteen

TOWARDS THE PEAKS

While I remained a fixture at Base Camp, there were various comings and goings. The day after John and Roger had left, Bryan Pooley and Tony came down from the ridge for their break. Camp III was well established at the foot of the West Ridge, below the final 2,500ft climb to the summit. Bryan and Tony had made a start on the process of fixing ropes along the crest of the massive ridge, and had descended from Camp III once the two Geoffs had arrived to continue the work.

On June 2nd, D.C. and Chamba returned after a carry across the plateau with further news. Despite the fact that the weather was not too good higher up, the leading climbers were continuing to break new ground on the ridge each day and would soon reach the buttress.

Tony was pleased. Everything was going to schedule. He was confident that, somehow, a route up the buttress would be found, and then the final barrier to the summit would have fallen. If we were fortunate with the weather, it now seemed to be only a matter of time before the West Ridge would be conquered.

But the weather remained stubbornly against us, and it was not until the morning of June 6th that the good weather, which we had grown accustomed to early in the expedition, returned. Dharm Chand and Chamba were due to return to the plateau that same morning and, seeing the improvement in the weather, I decided to join them. I quickly packed a food load which I would take as far as the Advance Base dump, from where I would pick up the equipment I had left there.

We were away by six: a long climb lay ahead of us. The tent at Advance Base Camp, fitted out with a new pole, had been taken up to the ridge by Bryan and Tony. Empty food boxes, surrounded by discarded tins and wrappers were all that remained of the camp. The absence of a tent meant a climb right up to Camp I in a single day, and I was glad that my sojourn at Base had not been long enough to lose my hard-won fitness.

We made excellent time to Advance Base. At last I approached the long awaited couloir. Standing at the camp, the couloir seemed to be right above us, but in fact, as was so often the case in the high mountains, appearances were deceptive. An aching and seemingly endless climb up a shallow snow fan had to be endured before we started up the couloir proper.

It was not as steep as I had expected. Protected by rock and snow walls on each side from the wind, and climbing in the full glare of the early morning sun, the temperature rocketed. Every spare protrusion on my pack frame was soon festooned with wind-proofs and woollens as I tried to keep cool.

There was curiously little sensation of height. Even when the pile of debris at Advance Base Camp had shrunk to the point when I could no longer distinguish the camp from the surrounding boulders, there was none of the limb-stiffening fear that I had felt on some of my climbs in Scotland. Was the whole Himalayan mystique a myth perpetuated by climbers, or was I just getting a little more used to heights? Who knows? Certainly the absence of objects of known size in my field of vision as I looked down helped to create an illusion of less distance to fall, and thus minimise the feeling of exposure.

Dharm Chand and Chamba, fitter and better acclimatised than I, kept going relentlessly, stopping only occasionally for rests. Although I found the steeper slope less tiring than the long trudges through softer snow which I had got used to, it was an effort to keep up with them. We were climbing without ropes, and the two of them gradually pulled ahead of me. Probably oblivious to many of the potential hazards, I followed the steps they left behind them. Unconscious of the drop beneath us, I began to move with what in retrospect was a probably dangerous confidence, feeling more like I was ascending a gigantic staircase than a high altitude, Himalayan snow gully.

After an hour and a half of almost non-stop ascent the two porters, who were some sixty or seventy feet above me and moving with increasing speed, had almost reached what appeared to be the top of the couloir. I envied the extra distance they had climbed, for the closeness of the top made me suddenly very aware of the tiredness that was starting to overtake my limbs.

I stopped for a rest as they finally disappeared from sight up a small defile to the right which I supposed must form the route out of the main gully. The tooth-shaped rock at the very top of the couloir, which I had noticed many times when gazing at the ridge from Advance Base Camp, had now assumed its true perspective. The very first time I saw it I had judged its height at maybe twenty or thirty feet until I had compared it with the size of my three colleagues as they descended the couloir. Standing right beneath it, I could now see for myself that it was indeed a gigantic granite block, at least one hundred and fifty feet in height. Not for the first time I was astonished at the tricks that perspective and distance played in the clear air and massive scale of the highest mountains.

I drove my ice-axe up to the hilt in the still crisp, snow crust of the couloir and, having scooped out a large step, I sat down to survey the scene before me. The wide valley wandered westwards into the distance, towards Jagatsukh, and finally merged into the slurry of clouds and peaks that lay beyond Kulu. Looking down into the basin I expected Base Camp to be visible, even if only as a few dots, but I could see nothing on the floor of the valley. I was now too high up and too far away to make out even the large, blue cook-tent against the green of the valley floor.

The rest rejuvenated me and I made good time over the last fifty feet or so. Within ten minutes I was ploughing my way up the exit gully to join Dharm Chand and Chamba. The snow was getting softer in the increasing warmth of the sun and to my annoyance the last few feet took a lot out of me. The crusty surface collapsed as soon as I put any weight upon it but I forced myself to complete the journey, dragging myself off the snow and onto a loose, stony scree before flopping down beside the two porters who were sitting in the shelter of the tooth-shaped rock. I was totally exhausted.

Chamba watched me gasping to regain my breath with a wide grin which threatened to bisect his weathered brown face.

"Okay Doctor Sahib," he shouted gleefully. "Okay?"

This was followed by an outburst in his native Hindi, which ended in a great laugh. Evidently he and D.C. were amused at my complete collapse, but were nevertheless glad to see me arrive in one piece!

When I had recovered sufficiently to care, an incredible sight met my eyes; an extravaganza of peaks that seemed to stretch away to infinity. Having been confined in the valley for so long, with just the encircling ridges to look at, I was unprepared for such a sight and could only gaze, and gaze again, speechless. This, I thought, this is what it is all about.

The crest of the ridge fell away slightly in front of where we sat, and then swept away as a huge snowfield, mile after mile of untouched whiteness, before finally breaking up into a wrinkled, crevassed tongue which curved away between the mountains to the south. From the map I knew this to be the Malana Glacier. Beyond the snowfield lay further myriad peaks. Snow spires and granite fortresses of every conceivable shape and size, they were far too numerous to count; too numerous even to properly comprehend. It was like standing on the threshold of another world, and words are inadequate to describe the emotions that crowded in on me. It was simply unbelievable. As John Brazinton had rightly commented, it was mind-blowing.

"It is very beautiful," said Dharm Chand simply.

I nodded quietly. "Yes. Yes, it is very, very beautiful."

I now understood John's excitement when he had tried to describe the scene to the rest of us after he and Roger had reached this place for the first time.

We sat and looked for five or ten minutes, Dharm Chand pointing out the peaks whose names he knew. There to the south-east was

Ali Ratni Tibba, 18,000ft high, with the Malana Glacier disappearing behind its eastern flank. In front of us rose the 17,000 ft ridge beyond which lay the valley of Dos Nullah; and beyond that again, more nameless peaks and ridges, rising and falling like waves upon a sea of rock and snow that stretched to the horizon.

Immediately to our left, a vast, snow-covered ridge completely blocked our view to the north. It seemed to tower above us, and Dharm Chand confirmed what I thought. The ascent of this huge ridge was our next objective.

"The plateau and the West Ridge are beyond," he said, his arm pointing to the top of the high barrier. "Tomorrow we shall climb up to the plateau. From here we cannot see the route which we will follow, but I will show you when we reach the camp. It is not too far now."

It was time to move on, for I was tired and anxious to complete the long journey. The two thousand five hundred foot ascent had affected me more than I had expected and, now that the initial, heady exhilaration of the panorama before us was wearing off, I was starting to notice the distinctly thinner atmosphere.

We followed the rocky scree for a hundred yards or so, and then the route dipped gently down towards the snowy neve. We negotiated a long, slow curve around a buttress and, as we did so, the tiny, orange tent which marked Camp I came into sight.

When we got closer I could see that it was perched upon a ledge of rocks and smaller stones. Above it a dark red, granite cliff rose steeply, overhanging the ledge and providing protection from possible rock falls. Sitting a little above the cold, damp snow the rocky platform was dry and well insulated. It was an excellent site for a camp.

Unfortunately, as we got nearer to the camp, the view was somewhat marred by a proliferation of litter. The snow beneath the ledge was dotted with empty meat tins and other discarded packaging of various sorts. I suppose it was inevitable. In such a hostile environment, with all available energy being conserved for climbing, it was quite simply too much of an effort to keep the surroundings of the camp tidy. Apart from ourselves there was, for now at least, nobody to object to the mess. And the litter, together with all other evidence of our brief visit, would very soon be buried by the next monsoon snows and disappear, eventually to be carried away, buried deep within the glacier for tens or even hundreds of years.

Suddenly D.C. gave a shout.

"Doctor Sahib. Doctor Sahib. Look. Over there. See."

He was pointing urgently with his right hand.

"Snow leopard. Over there. On that ledge."

I stared in the direction of his hand. He was pointing at a distant, rocky ledge. It was at least two or three hundred yards away across the glacier, but I could just make out the shape of what seemed to be a large cat.

"Can you see him?"

I strained my eyes, but it was difficult to make things out clearly at such a distance.

"Look   Now he is starting to move."

D.C. was right.   The creature was making its way along the ledge onto a snow slope.   Once it was outlined against the snow I could see that its body was a pale brown colour which had previously merged into the rocky background.   There were black markings scattered all over its head, body and legs, and stretching out behind there was a similarly marked, and thickly furred, tail.

The three of us watched as it made its way across the slope and disappeared from view behind some more rocks. If it was indeed a snow leopard, and both D.C. and Chamba seemed quite certain that it was, it was a privilege to have caught even such a brief glimpse of what is a rare and beautiful animal.   D.C. told me that he had seen one in this area before.   We were at the right altitude for such a sighting, and snow leopards tend to hunt for their food in the early morning and late afternoon.   Forgetting my tiredness I kept watch for a few more minutes, but sadly it did not reappear.

I pulled myself up the sloping rock that led to the ledge and thankfully dropped my heavy pack alongside the other items of equipment and food that lay scattered around, where they had been dumped by my fellow climbers. Exhausted, I stretched out on a conveniently flat and comfortable part of the ledge in order to rest.

It was just after three o'clock in the afternoon and the flat rock was still warm.   The overhanging cliff and the platform formed a sheltered sun-trap at this time of day although, within an hour or so, the sun's passage through the sky would take it behind the ridge and the camp would be cast into shadow.   Past experience had told me how quickly the temperature would fall when the sun's rays disappeared and I made the most of the comforting warmth while I could.

Chamba, true to form, had immediately occupied himself with cooking a meal which the three of us sat and ate greedily as we watched the sun dip lower in the sky, causing the shadow of the cliff to sweep towards us. All too soon we were enveloped in its icy grip. My two companions, who seemed to be relatively unaffected by either cold or heat, made no move but within a few minutes the rapidly increasing chill in the air caused me to pull on an extra jumper and a windproof jacket.

Now, although it was only late afternoon, there was nothing for it but to unroll our sleeping bags inside the tent and retire before it got too cold to linger outside. After the exertions of a long day, and a very early start, I had little difficulty in dropping off to a deep sleep, despite the unaccustomed altitude.

Aiming High – Overland to the Himalayas 1971

Ascending the lower couloir at dawn *(JW)*

Dharm Chand and the Malana Glacier - Camp I *(JW)*

Fifteen

INDRASAN AT LAST

After an uninterrupted sleep I woke at five-thirty. Dharm Chand was still asleep alongside me in the cramped little tent, but Chamba was already up. I could hear him outside, singing away quietly to himself while the primus stove hissed away beneath the saucepan in which he was melting snow for our morning brew.

I crawled out of the tent and onto the ledge. It was a dry, chill morning and the air temperature was still well below freezing. The orange colour of the tent was almost hidden, stiff beneath a thick layer of hoar frost that had coated it, both inside and out. The entrance flap crackled, like a dry, frozen leaf on a winter morning, as my shoulder brushed against it. The sun was yet to rise and the distant peaks, which had looked so magnificent the previous day, were almost invisible in the misty, half-light of the dawn.

Dharm Chand followed me out of the tent and the three of us busied ourselves with preparations for the ascent to the plateau as we waited for the primus to do its work. It seemed to take an age, and the saying that a watched pot never boils is certainly true when it comes to melting snow at high altitude.

Breakfast consisted of three cream crackers, with a large blob of very cold, and almost solid, syrup upon each of them, washed down by a lukewarm liquid that was meant to be tea but which could have been anything. The boiling point of water drops lower and lower as one ascends higher so, even though Chamba had boiled the snow melt, the teabags had been brewing at much less than the normal 100 degrees. I would have appreciated some margarine on my crackers as well as the syrup, but the 'easy-spread' brand we had carried up with us was frozen completely solid.

Thus fortified we set off towards the huge ridge to the north which barred the way to the plateau. Dharm Chand had already pointed out the route which we would be taking; a wide open couloir which rose almost vertically between some towering, granite cliffs. The fixed ropes which we would be using to assist us on the ascent, for we were carrying quite heavy loads, were pegged to the granite rock on the right-hand side of the couloirs but they were not yet visible to us. At the very top of the climb I could see tall, ice cliffs which hung ominously over the couloir. Long grooves, gouged deep into the snow, marked where huge blocks of ice, some of them the size of a small house, had fallen from the cliffs above and tumbled down alongside our route. It was altogether a much more forbidding prospect than the previous day's climb.

Our journey initially followed the northern edge of the Malana Glacier itself. This part of the route consisted of a long slog up a snow slope that was mercifully firm and crisp in the cold of the early morning but which was just steep enough to make it hard going in the thin air at 16,500 feet. Even so, I soon dropped into the regular routine of putting one foot in front of the other that was becoming second nature to me. Every now and then the route we were following would dip down a little as we came to a crevasse and there would be a moment's respite from the upward slog as we moved down, and then crossed the bottomless chasm by means of a snow bridge. These crossing points, left behind by the deep, winter snow which had previously covered the crevasses completely, were now starting to melt away. They would soon be of varying thickness and safety.

I was never completely happy when traversing these bridges since, a few yards along the same crevasse, there would often be two snow parapets, with a yawning gap between them, marking the point where a snow bridge had melted and collapsed into the crevasse below. I had been reassured that such unpredictable collapses usually take place in the late afternoon, when the snow has been softened by the sun, but I was unable to place total faith in such assurances when an icy slit of unknown depth lay beneath me, waiting to swallow me up. I invariably found a bit of extra energy, and quickened my pace, when negotiating such obstacles.

We trudged slowly, onwards and upwards, as the sun rose from behind the distant mountains. The slope began to steepen and the gigantic couloir, now getting ever closer, dwarfed our puny figures as it leapt skywards. It was at once a magnificent and an awesome sight. I looked up and my eyes sought the tell-tale strands of colour against the white background which would mark the beginning of the fixed ropes. I could see nothing and it seemed they were still some way above us. Dharm Chand indicated that we had another three or four hundred feet of steep slope to negotiate before we would reach the rocky cliffs at the side of the couloir where the ropes began.

Our route now wound its way between large lumps of solid snow and ice, the debris from the avalanches which had hurtled down the snow face from the ice cliffs at the very top. The staggering size of the remains which lay, broken up, all around us made me wonder at the enormity of the blocks that had begun their two thousand foot tumble to destruction. It was as if the forces of nature were master-minding the destruction of some monolithic, ice temple that had once stood upon the mountain plateau, a tribute to some long-forgotten god, leaving only the scattered and broken building blocks as evidence of its past existence.

Chamba and D.C. had moved ahead of me over this last stretch, and I was relieved when I saw them come to a halt beside one of the smaller blocks and begin to slip off their hefty packs. Within a couple of minutes I had caught up with them, and I joined them in taking off my pack and taking a much needed rest.

The route ahead, from where we were resting, steepened considerably. Looking upwards I could see smooth, glassy areas on the slope where the underlying, glacial ice was starting to show itself beneath the thinning snow. With the relative safety of the fixed ropes still a long way above us it was time to put some crampons on to improve our grip. As we strapped the twelve-pronged spikes to the soles of our boots, each crampon also having two, forward-pointing spikes which could be kicked into the ice on steeper sections, Dharm Chand talked me through the climb ahead.

"The first part is not too steep, but it is very icy so we must be careful. We keep to the right side of the snow slope until we reach the fixed rope because we must cross a wide crevasse which is very, very deep. But it is not so wide if we keep to the right, so that is safer. Then we reach the fixed rope and it is easy. A long climb from there to the top, but not too hard for you, I think, Doctor Sahib."

"Okay. Okaay?" Chamba grinned encouragement and gave the universal thumbs-up sign. He had not understood any of Dharm Chand's explanation, but he knew the route and he clearly wanted to offer me his own assurance that all would be well.

I grinned back at him and returned his thumbs-up gesture, well aware that I was very fortunate to have such patient and agreeable companions.

We were ready to go. I swung the hefty pack-frame onto my shoulders and secured the waist strap tightly for extra safety. I certainly did not want the pack slipping, and its weight would need to be distributed as evenly as possible across my back during the long climb ahead.

The surface of the snow was still firm and we made fast progress. The steep, icy stretches that we crossed took the leading points of our crampons well and did not slow us down too much, although every now and then Dharm Chand would indicate that we should traverse sideways to avoid a particularly treacherous patch. The wide couloir was considerably steeper than the one we had climbed the previous day and I was glad when, with the wide crevasse safely behind us, I was able to clip my ascendeur onto the lowest of the fixed ropes.

We were now some four hundred feet above the glacier and, securely attached to the rope, I was able to take stock of my surroundings. I looked down on our route across the snow from Camp I. We had traversed the upper section of the Malana Glacier which moved, a few centimetres each day, on its remorseless journey down the valley, the great ice sheets being pushed across the bedrock by the weight of the accumulated snowfalls.

A thousand feet below me, and slightly to the right, I could just make out an orange dot which marked the tent we had left several hours earlier at Camp I. The bare crest of the ridge which overlooked Advance Base Camp had the appearance of a row of dark, granite teeth which seemed to be biting into the expanse of clean, white snow. The sea of peaks which stretched as far as the eye could see to the east shone like jewels, brilliant in the clear light of the sun.

To gaze out over them was every bit as exciting as when I had first viewed them the previous day and it seemed unfair that such mighty and majestic Himalayan mountains, each one of which would have dominated almost any other range on earth, did not, in most cases, have even the dignity of a name.

I could have spent much longer taking in the magnificent panorama before me but, with over a thousand feet still to climb, it was time to push on. Dharm Chand and Chamba, who had not wasted time staring at the view, were already a hundred feet above me and I could delay no longer.

I started to climb but my ascendeur, a ratchet device which is designed to prevent a fall by sliding up the rope and then gripping it tightly when a downward pull is exerted upon it, did not seem to be functioning too well. The fixed ropes had iced up as they lay on the snow overnight and the teeth of the ascendeur were becoming clogged up with ice. Removing the device from the rope in order to shake it free of ice became an irritatingly frequent, and slightly hazardous, necessity which delayed my progress. Fortunately this problem resolved itself when I reached the cliffs, where the route was less exposed to the elements and the fixed ropes were therefore less prone to icing. The ascendeur began to work better and I was able to increase my pace.

I once again found the steep climb less exhausting than the slog across the snow field and I soon reduced the distance between myself and my fellow climbers to no more than twenty or thirty feet. The security of the fixed ropes bred confidence and, with my ascendeur firmly attached by a strap to my waist belt, the occasional slip did not worry me too much. Even so, each sudden jerk as the ascendeur gripped the rope and the slack was taken up to arrest my fall caused me to stop for a few moments to recover my breath.

As we climbed higher I was conscious of a definite increase in the rate and depth of my breathing as my respiratory system tried to compensate for the thinner atmosphere but, apart from this, the lower oxygen levels and barometric pressure did not seem to be affecting me too much. A further hour passed. Up and up we went, like spiders on a great white wall, but the top of the couloir did not seem to be getting any closer, and the giddy drop beneath my feet did not seem to be increasing. The Himalayan perspectives were once again playing their tricks and, even though I was sure we were making good progress, the lack of obvious evidence was discouraging. The fixed rope, which snaked down below us and finally disappeared into the void, was the only definite sign that we had achieved any significant upward movement at all.

Another hour of climbing, and then, suddenly, a spur of rock which had been blocking my view was immediately above me. I rounded it with some difficulty, the heavy pack threatening to topple me backwards as I leaned out to negotiate a particularly difficult stretch, and I was very grateful for the added security of the fixed rope.

I fought my way past the rock and realised that the previously steep and icy cliff face was beginning to mellow into a relatively gentle snow slope. The end of the climb, was at long last in sight and an overwhelming tiredness began to hit me as I pulled myself up the last fifty feet of fixed rope to reach the 'dead man', a snow anchor which dug into the snow at the top of the couloir and made a secure fixing point for the top of the rope.

I was totally exhausted but once again the sight which greeted me made the long climb worth every step. Camp II, a single orange tent with the words INDRASAN WEST RIDGE emblazoned in black across the canvas, was some thirty yards away from me, nestling in a shallow basin which afforded a little protection from the wind. Beyond the tent stretched the highest plateau, an unbroken expanse of whiteness that undulated gently like the sands of a desert. And beyond the plateau, dominating the entire scene, was Indrasan. The brown granite of the West Ridge stretched across my field of vision, rising slowly from left to right in a series of rock spires and mighty buttresses until, at over twenty thousand feet, the crest of the ridge met the triangular summit snow-field. The mountain, in all its motionless grandeur and fierce beauty, seemed like a monstrous, prehistoric creature which had been caught in a moment of slumber. As it lay there I could not help thinking that at any moment it might wake, and brush us off its flanks like so many flies. Behind the ridge was a sky of the deepest blue which had the depth and intensity of the heavens on a clear night, but with the strange absence of stars.

I stood and stared for what must have been five minutes, my aching legs and the heavy pack upon my shoulders forgotten. I felt deeply privileged to have been granted the opportunity to gaze upon such a sight. I took my camera from its case and routinely held it to my eye to record the moment for posterity but, as I did so, I knew that no photograph could ever do full justice to the scene I was witnessing. How could a photograph even begin to capture the atmosphere, the almost religious, total silence, which made me feel as if I was standing in a vast cathedral with the domed and infinite universe stretched out above my head. It was suddenly very easy to understand those climbers who say that they feel nearer to God in the highest of mountains. For those few moments I certainly had that feeling.

I walked slowly towards the camp, crossing what looked like the beginnings of a crevasse, and climbing a gentle slope which took me up to the level of the plateau proper. As I did so another peak, which had been hidden by the slight slope, came into view. I had seen no photographs of it, but I assumed that it must be Deo Tibba.

Quite different from Indrasan, it spread itself along the western edge of the plateau, a rounded hump of snow with very little rock showing through the surface layers of the relatively gentle slopes. Large quantities of snow had accumulated on the nearest face, and I could see that great blocks had broken off and avalanched down to the plateau, leaving snow cliffs several hundred feet in height. On the mountain's southern flank, which was just visible from where I stood, the accumulated snows divided into several smaller tongues before spilling down in the direction of Base Camp, above which they formed the hanging glaciers which were visible from the valley below.

Deo Tibba looked a much less formidable adversary than Indrasan, and it was easy to see why it had suffered some thirty successful ascents over the years since De Graaff first stood on its summit nineteen years earlier.

Dharm Chand and Chamba were sitting on two food boxes in front of the tent when I finally arrived. They were munching jam-covered cream crackers and gazing over the plateau towards the West Ridge, screwing up their eyes against the glare of the sun despite their dark goggles.

I pulled an empty box up for myself and sat down to join them. Breakfast seemed a very long time ago, and I looked at my watch. Half past eleven. The ascent had taken five and a half hours. Jam and crackers did not appeal to me much, and I hunted through a half-empty food box to find a pack of Mars Bars which the three of us demolished in a couple of minutes. We would have liked some tea or coffee but, having struggled up the couloir with the precious supply of paraffin for the primus stove, it seemed senseless to use it up at the top. The brew would have to wait until we were back down at Camp I where fuel was less valuable.

For half an hour we sat motionless in the sun, all of us recovering our energy. I continued to stare out across the snow, unable to tear my eyes away from that incredible ridge. Then, all too soon, it was time to start down the long couloir once again. The sun was climbing progressively higher in the sky, and each minute spent up on the plateau meant an increasingly unpleasant and tiring return journey through the ever softening snow. Reluctantly I shouldered my empty pack-frame and turned my back on Indrasan. More supplies waited at Camp I to be carried up the couloir. I was confident that I would return.

= = = = = = = = = = = = = =

Safely down at Camp I again I lay on a rock, basking like a lizard in the heat of the sun. This was a pleasant and relaxing occupation now that my skin had become accustomed to the strong ultra-violet radiation. I had just dropped off into a quiet doze when I was woken by a tap on my shoulder. It was Dharm Chand, looking much more serious than usual.

"Chamba says he will not climb the couloir again. It is too dangerous and he is afraid after coming down today."

The announcement did not come as a complete surprise. Chamba had not hidden his dislike of the couloir on the descent. We had taken a slightly different route on the way down, and had crossed some very slippery sheets of ice just above the large bergschrund. Chamba in particular, who had about as much experience with crampons as myself and whose crampons were less modern and efficient than mine, found the ice especially difficult. Without the security of the fixed rope to assist him he had slipped on several occasions, and only the swift use of his ice axe as a brake had prevented an uncontrollable slide into the gaping void. Had the slips occurred on the ascent, burdened with a half-hundred-weight pack, he might well have been unable to stop himself. I could not help but sympathise with him. My spikes had luckily held firm in the ice, but I knew that even one such slip would have destroyed my nerve completely.

"What about yourself, D.C.?" I asked.

He shrugged his shoulders. "It is not good climbing, and there are no fixed ropes to help us on the lower part of the couloir. Chamba, he is not so experienced, so he is right I think. It is not good for him, but I am paid as head porter, so if you wish it I will go up again."

"Does Chamba want to give up altogether and go back to Base?"

"No. He says he is happy to work as much as he can, carrying loads between Base Camp and here, but not up the big couloir again. He wants to stay with the expedition because the pay is very good, and his wife will be unhappy if he gives up. He wants the money, but he will not risk his life anymore."

I nodded in understanding. D.C. had put his finger on the difference between the porters and ourselves. Unlike us, the porters climb because they are paid for doing so, and Chamba quite simply did not feel that the money he was earning justified the risks he was being asked to take higher up on the mountain.

"Would he climb if we arranged for more rope to be used on the bottom part of the couloir to make it safer?" I asked.

"I have asked him that already," replied D.C., "I think that would help him, but there is no more rope. It is all with the others up on the ridge. There is none to spare."

He was quite right. The supplies of rope we had brought with us were already stretched to the very limit. Only a day or two earlier, at Base Camp, Tony had been toying with the idea of removing three hundred feet of the fixed rope on the couloir for use on the ridge, so he would hardly be enthusiastic about putting more valuable rope on the couloir to please Chamba.

There remained one unexplored possibility. Chamba had spent one afternoon on his own a few days earlier, removing some rope which the Japanese expedition had left behind them on the south-eastern side of Deo Tibba. It was by rights his property, but maybe he would lend it to us for use on the couloir. I put the idea to Dharm Chand.

"We could borrow it from him, and either replace it with a length of better quality rope or pay him for it when we get down to Manali. What do you think"?

Chamba was sitting with his back to us, boiling up more tea on the primus. Dharm Chand shouted a question to him and received a grunted reply. Chamba knew we were discussing him and, despite the fact that he could not follow the conversation, he clearly felt embarrassed and ashamed about the whole business.

"He says it is at Base Camp."

"Okay. If we bring it up here, can we use it?" I asked.

Another rapid exchange of words and Dharm Chand announced that Chamba was agreeable and that he would continue to climb the couloir if there was fixed rope down to below the large crevasse. The Japanese ropes, several hundred feet of twisted hemp, would just about do the job.

A couple of hours later, I found myself trudging wearily back into Base Camp to join the two Geoffs, who were taking their two day break away from the ridge.

"We've got a problem up there," I announced and told them all the details. "Chamba is coming down to Advance Base tomorrow morning. I'll meet him there with the rope and he can take it up so that D.C. can fix it on the couloir. Another problem is that we haven't got any ice-screws to spare. Do you think D.C. could just tie the Japanese ropes onto the end of the kernmantle, and let it hang in one length down to the crevasse? It'll be a bit unwieldy to use, but at least it might make the couloir a bit safer. The ice is lethal at the moment."

Geoff Tabbner and Geoff Arkless were both slightly unhappy about making use of a rope whose reliability could not be guaranteed, but the number one priority was to get Chamba climbing again and this seemed about the only way to do it.

= = = = = = = = = = = = = =

I met Chamba at 8 a.m., as arranged. Eager to show his keenness he told me by means of sign language that he had been waiting for over an hour. It was obvious that the previous day's experience, with the constant slips, had terrified him out of his wits. It had been the final straw that had forced him to release the fears that he had been bottling up every time he went up to the plateau.

I wanted to tell him that it was not unusual, and actually very sensible, to be frightened, and that it would not diminish the real friendship that had been built up between all of us during the weeks together. Unfortunately such messages are not easily translatable into sign language and I could only shake him warmly by the hand as we parted company and hope he understood. His crestfallen expression when we first met was evidence enough that Dharm Chand had probably been a little brusque with him, and I was pleased to see a bit of the old grin return as he left me to climb back up to Camp I. I wandered back to Base, intending to join D.C. and Chamba again the following day.

That evening, the two Geoffs and I were enjoying a piping hot, Tashi-style curry, when we were interrupted by a shout from down the valley towards Jagatsukh. We rushed out of the tent to see a figure standing on the far side of the stream which was by now swollen to a fast flowing river by the melting snows. As we appeared he started to wave his arms and shout once again.

"Ay! Ay! Tashi! Tashi! Ayay!"

Tashi, as easily excited as a small boy, jumped up and down grinning from ear to ear as he heard his name.

As we watched, the figure moved towards the river and plunged into the freezing waters which immediately engulfed him up to his waist. Steadying himself with a long pole, which he used to probe the river bed ahead of him, the man waded into the middle of the torrent. The swift water rose like a skirt above his waist, reaching in icy rivulets towards his arms which he now held out to assist his balance. All the time the powerful current tugged at him, threatening to sweep him away at any moment. Then, miraculously, he was out of the water and scrambling up the near bank.

We all walked towards the river to greet him and, as he got closer, I recognised him as one of the porters who had carried a load as far as Base Camp three and a half weeks earlier. Geoff Tabbner also remembered him and said that he was one of the few porters who had been able to speak any English. Wongdhi must have sent him up to us with a message, and maybe some mail.

He walked up to us, soaking wet and breathing deeply, and handed over a waterproof, oilskin bag which contained a few letters. As he did so, he complained volubly in a mixture of Hindi and English about the state of the rivers which he had been obliged to cross on his way up the valley from Manali. He was most bitter about the way his clothes had suffered on the journey and I could see that his precious woollen suit was indeed torn in several places.

Pleased to have news from the world outside, and ignoring the possibility that his suit may well have been rather less than perfect before he left Manali, we furnished him with a spare pair of bright yellow long-johns to put on beneath his wet outer clothing and sat him down to eat some warming curry while we read our letters.

Geoff Arkless opened the letter he had been waiting for since the start of the expedition. Back home, far away in Wales, he was expecting an addition to his family. The news was as he had hoped. A bouncing, baby boy, and both mother and child were doing well.

In the absence of any alcohol we celebrated with tea. The news was a comforting indication that, away from our isolated existence, life was carrying on much as usual.

Sixteen

UP WITH THE LEADERS

I finally joined Dharm Chand and Chamba at Camp I a day later than I had anticipated. With the two Geoffs wanting to stop at Camp I en route to the West Ridge, and with the two porters already being up at the camp, it would have been distinctly crowded if I had gone up at the same time. Even fitting four men into one small tent was a little too much of a squeeze for comfort. Five would have been foolish.

I was perfectly happy to remain at Base Camp for one extra day, and I arrived at Camp I just before eleven thirty in the morning. Having had a comfortable night's sleep, I had left Base Camp at six thirty. I was feeling very fit and well, and my times between camps were definitely improving. I was eager to have another go at the big couloir.

As I sat and sipped at the tea which had been brewed for me, Dharm Chand pointed up at a tiny black dot which was just visible on the right hand side of the couloir, between the bergschrund and the rock cliffs.

"I think that is Geoff," he announced. "It is not good. He left here at six o'clock. Chamba and I have been watching him for more than an hour now and he has hardly moved."

It was indeed not good, for the small dot was not even half-way up the couloir, and if D.C.'s timing was right he had been climbing for over four hours and he should have been much higher."

"Are you sure it's Geoff?" I asked him.

"We are very sure, Doctor Sahib. Young Geoff went up to the plateau last night because he said he was feeling very good and he wanted to get on with things. Old Geoff waited here with me and Chamba, so it must be him. He was very tired last night."

I watched intently as the black speck inched its agonisingly slow way up the snow face. At times it stopped moving for what seemed like an age, and each time the three of us wondered if he would be able to carry on. Concerned that he may be suffering from the altitude again I wanted to go straight up after him, taking D.C. with me, but I knew that, having just ascended from Base Camp, I was too tired to attempt an ascent of the couloir as well, despite the fact that I was feeling very fit. The snow surface would be getting soft and the surface of the icy stretches would be dangerously wet and slippery. Unless Geoff stopped climbing altogether I would never catch up with him.

We decided to watch and wait, and keep any thought of an immediate ascent in reserve. D.C. and I would go up only if Geoff seemed to stop altogether.

We kept an eye on him as he moved very slowly upwards. By two o'clock he had nearly reached the top and I felt very relieved. As we waited for him to complete the last few feet the afternoon clouds rolled in up the Malana Glacier and within minutes the whole scene was lost in a thick, white mist.

As I tried in vain to catch another glimpse of him, I could not help thinking about the tales I had read of the last sightings of Mallory and Irvine, high up on Everest, in the nineteen twenties. They, too, had disappeared from sight in mist and cloud, never to be seen again. Although Mallory's body was found many years later, there was no evidence to show how high he had climbed, and it remains a mystery as to whether he and Irvine succeeded in reaching the summit almost thirty years before Hillary and Tenzing made their famous ascent.

I hoped that Geoff would be alright. As he was one of the UK's top mountain guides, and very experienced, I felt fairly confident that as he had only a short distance left to climb he would safely reach Camp II. Nevertheless D.C. and I decided that we would leave at first light next day in order to get up to the plateau as early as possible and make sure he was okay.

= = = = = = = = = = = = =

We woke to find that the couloir was still lost in clouds, but D.C. and I stuck to our plan. We made the ascent in worsening weather and, when we reached the top, a very different scene met our eyes. As soon as we emerged from the shelter of the couloir, cold, swirling gusts of wind, carrying mist and fine powder snow, swept towards us across the plateau, reducing visibility to a few yards. The West Ridge was nowhere to be seen. From where we stood, bent forwards to shield ourselves from the howling wind, even the vivid orange tent with its distinctive lettering was completely invisible. It was an unexpected and intimidating change from my first visit, and a more inhospitable place I could not imagine.

We hastily made our way to the snow basin in which we knew the tent lay, but the camp was deserted. Looking inside the tent D.C. found a karabiner and a set of ice pegs which Geoff had taken up with him from Camp I the previous day. It was an indication that he had definitely made it to the camp, and his absence meant that he had presumably felt well enough, after an overnight rest, to carry on across the plateau despite the weather. It was an encouraging sign.

Feeling much happier, the two of us dumped our loads and hurried back to the relative shelter of the couloir. The biting winds made the plateau no place to hang about without good reason.

The clouds were thickening and the snow was getting heavier by the minute. We thankfully retraced our steps back to Camp I where Chamba, who had been down to Advance Base Camp for more food and fuel, was awaiting our return.

I removed my outer woollen garments, which had become wet as the heat of my body melted the snow which had accumulated on them, and pulled on the only spare clothing I had with me before retiring to the tent. The damp pullovers which I had removed lay on the ledge outside the tent. They would be frozen solid by morning.

Dharm Chand seemed to have no such problems. Adapting, as always, to the adverse conditions he had worn a large, billowing cagoule on the climb down and his clothing beneath had remained completely dry. I had tried a similar solution but, as I had found before, the accumulation of perspiration inside the impervious, nylon cagoule caused more discomfort than allowing a relatively waterproof layer of frozen snow to gather on the outside of my woollen pullover.

I lay inside my sleeping bag, huddled up with a torch and a book, and luxuriated in the welcome warmth which gradually built up within. The time was just after midday but the dark clouds, combined with our very early start, made it feel like late evening. Having vowed that I would remain within the cramped sleeping bag and tent until the weather improved, I did not venture outside again that day. It was not long before D.C. and Chamba joined me and the three of us lay together inside the frail tent, feeling irrationally protected from the wild elements which were on the loose just a few inches away from us on the other side of the thin layer of nylon.

= = = = = = = = = = = = = =

Unpredictable as ever, the weather cleared during the night and we ate the meagre rations that made up our breakfast while looking out at another perfect and unforgettable dawn. Only the snow, which lay banked up against the exposed side of the tent, reminded us that it had ever been otherwise.

Even so, it was becoming plain that the patches of bad weather were starting to fall into a regular and uncomfortable pattern. Time was getting short. It was June 11th and the weather was starting to break. The monsoon proper, with its heavy and persistent snowfalls, could be upon us at any time. Mid-June would be very early, especially as we were in the western part of the Himalayas, but it had been an unusual year in the Himalayan range as a whole and, even as we left Jagatsukh at the start of our walk-in, the locals were uttering gloomy predictions of an early and severe monsoon.

I wondered how the leaders were faring on the ridge. Had the previous day's storms been as bad at twenty thousand feet? Or, as can happen, were they safely above the worst of the weather high on the ridge? Would today's good weather hold? Eager to know and be involved I made up my mind to go up and join them at Camp III below the West Ridge. Another couple of food boxes would help to ensure a sufficient supply on the plateau, even in the event of a fairly prolonged spell of inclement weather. I could do a carry up the couloir with Dharm Chand and Chamba, and we could continue across the plateau. I would then hope to be able to stay up at Camp III for a few days and experience the excitement of what would hopefully be the final days of a successful climb.

Carrying the heavy loads of food made it a long, hot climb, a marked change from the miserable conditions which had prevailed just twenty four hours earlier. By the time I reached Camp II I had fallen quite a way behind my two companions who were mere dots half-way across the plateau as I gazed at them from my vantage point amidst the debris of the camp. The West Ridge of Indrasan, clearly visible once again in the bright weather, rose beyond them at the far edge of the plateau. It had lost none of its magnificence and grandeur, and this second view of it served only to reinforce the impression it had left upon my visual memory.

Exhausted, and breathing heavily in the thin air, but still anxious to reach Camp III, I decided to leave some of my load at Camp II and cross the plateau with the minimum of personal equipment. If necessary I could retrieve the food box later. Despite this significant saving in weight my pack remained heavy. The minimum of personal equipment which is needed for safety in the Himalayas still amounts to quite a hefty collection of items.

I set off across the plateau, following the usual routine of laboriously counting my steps to keep myself going. The thin snow crust collapsed unpredictably every few steps, wearying my tired legs even more. It was all becoming very familiar after several weeks in these high mountains and even the majestic scenery all around me failed to lessen the feeling of weariness that soon spread from my legs and penetrated every fibre of my body. It was only by cutting myself off from the increasingly urgent messages that were flowing into my brain, telling me to stop, that I was able to keep my legs moving. I was moving mechanically, like a robot, and making every effort to place my boots in the foot-prints left by Dharm Chand and Chamba as they moved ahead of me. I hoped that the snow crust which had been compressed by their passage would be less likely to collapse under my weight but, because my companions were so much smaller and lighter than myself, my hopes were in vain. My large boots continued to break through the crust and my exhaustion became such that, on occasions, I was not quick enough to adjust my balance and a collapsing step would tumble me in an ungainly heap upon the snow.

I lost all sense of time and it was a great surprise when, about three quarters of the way across the plateau, I saw D.C. and Chamba walking towards me. They must already have deposited their loads at Camp III, I thought to myself. They appeared over a slight rise in the otherwise flat terrain, grinning all over their brown faces, and almost ran to greet me, floundering as they ploughed knee-deep through the powder snow.

"Doctor Sahib! Doctor Sahib! It is climbed."

I was lost for words. The news was so completely unexpected. I only remember Chamba, dancing ecstatically from one foot to the other, sinking ever deeper into the snow as we all shook hands. They were truly over the moon. For the two Indians it was a great fillip. The success of the expedition would be big news in the Kulu Valley. The 'unclimbable' west ridge of Indrasan had been climbed, and their part in the achievement would help to ensure work for them in the future. Their personal reputations as climbers would be greatly enhanced, and they might be able to negotiate a higher rate of pay from Wongdhi in the future. They were well pleased.

We stood together for several minutes, three small figures in the vastness of the plateau, exchanging more handshakes and mutual pats on the back, before the two news-bearers continued on their happy way.

What did it mean to me? Satisfaction, certainly, that we would not return to England empty-handed and that the risks and hard work of the past weeks and months would not be left unrewarded. But there was no uncontrollable elation. No unconfined joy. The overwhelming feeling was of pleasure on behalf of the others in the team who had done most of the hardest work while I had been fortunate to trail along in their wake. They would, I was sure, find ample happiness and satisfaction in their achievement.

I wandered slowly on across the flatness, lost in my thoughts, my tiredness forgotten for a few minutes.

The desire to achieve the summit of a mountain is a strange passion. The rocks and snow are there as a challenge and a barrier, but if victory is finally achieved the conquest is not of the mountain at all. Indeed the mountain itself has never entered the competition. The victory is over one's own doubts and fears. Looking back, I think the real gift that the high mountains gave to me was the opportunity to test myself against them. Mountains are dangerous, emotionless and implacable foes that can never be beaten, but with respect, fortitude, and a little good fortune, it is possible sometimes to engage with them for a short while. I knew that I would miss them, and I was sure that I would one day have to return.

While mulling upon such thoughts I seemed to cover the ground quickly despite my tiredness. Quite soon, looking ahead, I could see that the route crossed a snow bridge which spanned a small crevasse. And a mere hundred yards or so beyond it was a group of tents which I knew must be my destination.

The tents of Camp III were erected in a tight semi-circle around a central food and equipment dump. The camp nestled in the shadow of the West Ridge which reared up from the flatness of the plateau some quarter of a mile behind the tents, dwarfing everything beneath it. The area surrounding the camp was the usual scene of disarray, with used food boxes, tins and other items thrown here and there out of the way of the tents. The equipment dump was a mess of skis, sticks, straps, ropes and odd items of clothing, much of it partially hidden beneath a recent snowfall. The snow immediately around the tents looked dirty and trodden down in comparison with the pristine whiteness elsewhere. A wide track led away from the camp towards the West Ridge, while other narrower tracks led in the direction of what I presumed must be latrines.

Tony, Bryan and Roger stood by one of the tents. Otherwise the camp appeared to be deserted. I trudged towards them. They had not seen me and, as I moved closer, I wondered how they would expect me to react to the news of their success. They would realise that I must have encountered D.C. and Chamba en route.

"Well done lads!"

The three of them turned towards me as I shouted my congratulations from a distance of about fifty yards. Almost immediately John Brazinton's head popped out of the furthest tent.

"Hi Doc. Good to see you up here!" Bryan Pooley was the first to shout a reply as they moved to meet me.

Another session of hand-shaking, back-slapping and general celebrations followed. Their obvious enthusiasm and delight was infectious and I found myself being swept up in the palpable sense of achievement and victory.

I learnt from them that Geoff Arkless had successfully reached Camp III the previous day. According to Tony he had seemed to be fine, and the others were surprised when I described my concern at his slow ascent of the big couloir. Their view was that he was must have been taking it slowly so that he could enjoy the climb, for he had gone up onto the ridge that morning with Geoff Tabbner to make a second attempt upon the summit, and he had said he was feeling one hundred percent.

This was good news, and we sat and talked late into the afternoon. When the sun finally dipped down behind the slopes of Deo Tibba in the west, we all crowded into one of the tents to continue the saga of the summit assault over tea and biscuits.

Five of us were crammed into a tent designed for three. Two primus stoves roared away in the entrance, melting snow for further brews and keeping out the cold at the same time. As darkness fell, the atmosphere of muggy, convivial celebration was strangely like that in any sports club back home after a victory in the Saturday match in mid-winter.

We continued our celebrations as the temperature outside fell far below freezing and a light wind whipped the powder snow from the surface of the plateau, sending it snaking beyond the cosy warmth of our stoves and away into the dark, cold night.

A small figure climbs the icy surface of the couloir above the bergschrund which would swallow him up in the event of a fall
(JW)

The deep bergschrund below the upper couloir *(JW)*

Ascending the upper couloir

The steep and icy upper couloir – early morning

Mountain peaks extend to the far horizon beyond the Malana Glacier with its numerous crevasses *(JW)*

Aiming High – Overland to the Himalayas 1971

18,000 ft - afternoon clouds gather behind Dharm Chand

Camp II - the magnificent West Ridge of Indrasan looks intimidating set against the deep blue of a high-altitude sky

Seventeen

THE WEST RIDGE

I never set foot upon the West Ridge itself but, having listened late into the night to the tale of the final ascent, I feel qualified to retell it here. The story would not seem complete without it.

On May 30th, while I was still down at Base Camp, Tony Johnson and Bryan Pooley crossed the plateau for the first time and pitched camp beneath the West Ridge, getting their first close look at the task ahead of them. They had used one of the two sledges to drag a seventy pound load across the snow with them in addition to the loads which they were both carrying on their backs. They were thus in a position to make a start on the ridge climb without needing to worry too much about a shortage of equipment or food.

At five o'clock the following morning they headed towards a snow fan which looked as though it promised a route from the plateau to the crest of the ridge. As they approached closer they were every bit as impressed as Dennis Gray had been some ten years earlier. Pinnacles of red granite like miniature aiguilles were interspersed with ice-filled gullies and steep snow slopes. They made good progress, fixing nine hundred feet of rope before retreating to Base Camp for a couple of days' rest.

Geoff Arkless and Geoff Tabbner then took over the lead, staying on the ridge for three days and progressing slowly but surely towards the summit. Most of the climbing was done on the north side of the ridge, each lead climber inching his way out over a drop, almost sheer, of nine thousand feet to a glaciated moraine far below. Those following behind with loads would make use of the ropes which the lead climber had fixed, dangling like spiders over the abyss.

The weather was kind and each day, having retreated to Camp III overnight, they would quickly reach the previous day's high point by use of the fixed ropes before starting to break new ground. Progress was good but, as the supply lines down to Camp III became more and more stretched, it was clear to them that a summit attempt from the plateau was not going to be feasible. A site had to be found, somewhere along the precipitous and knife-sharp ridge, to pitch some kind of tent or bivouac. A miniature tent had been carried up to Camp III for just this eventuality. The only question that remained was where to put it.

As expected, the route to the summit was blocked by the massive rock tower which had been seen from the plateau and which formed a steep step in the otherwise continuous sharp crest of the ridge. The rock tower was smooth and vertical, extending to some five hundred feet in height, and it presented a serious challenge at such an altitude. Overcoming it would take time, even with ropes in place, and any camp from which a summit assault could realistically be mounted would have to be placed right at the base of the huge vertical step, or time would be too short to push on and reach the top of the mountain.

The two Geoffs, having completed their stint on the West Ridge, had returned to Base Camp to recuperate. Geoff Arkless was over his illness and climbing as well as anyone else, but the thin air was a hard task-master when such testing and technical rock and ice climbing was being carried out. After three days they were due for a well-earned rest.

June 8th saw the other four climbers, Tony Johnson, Bryan Pooley, Roger Brook and John Brazinton, on the West Ridge together, transporting heavy loads from the plateau to the base of the rock tower. The route was varied and difficult with the unwieldy back packs increasing the hazards considerably. One moment they would be crawling on hands and knees along a narrow ice ledge; and the next they would be manhandling their loads up overhanging rock pitches with that giddy north face falling away, sheer, beneath them. At one point Bryan dropped a large ice-screw as he was trying to fix it in place and he swears that it touched the face just three times as it fell, before disappearing from view into the void below.

The sort of lucky break which can often be the difference between success and failure occurred when they finally reached the tower. Tucked in at its base, between the vertical granite face and one of the numerous smaller pinnacles, was a small ledge. It was not really wide enough to pitch even the tiny tent properly, but it was sufficient to offer a secure site for the tent and, most importantly, it would provide a reasonably sheltered, overnight stopping place from which the final push for the summit could be made.

While Tony and Bryan used the remaining daylight to make a start on the assault of the tower, Roger and John spent some time clearing the ledge of as much ice and snow as possible and making a space in which an attempt could be made to erect the tent. The four of them would have to squeeze inside it for the night, in sitting positions if lying down proved impossible. So every inch which could be stolen from the mountain to enlarge the camp site was important.

Eventually the tent was in position and they spent a long and uncomfortable night, crammed together like sardines, while outside there was a relatively light, but persistent snowfall. There was no room to put up the flysheet and, very early on in the night, the inside of the tent became damp with a combination of wetness from the snowfall and condensation from the breath of the four occupants.

Half lying and half hanging over the edge of their small platform they were grateful for the presence of the sewn-in groundsheet, but even so they managed little more than a few hours of fitful sleep before it was time to melt snow for a quick brew and make a start. By six in the morning they were on their way.

The knowledge that this was it, that this was the day when they might be able to crown all the long months of single-minded endeavour with success, removed all trace of tiredness and hunger after their night-long ordeal. The adrenaline was flowing, and they set about completing the ascent of the granite tower which seemed to be the last major obstacle between them and the summit. Many thousands of feet of rope had been transported to the mountain, and now just four hundred and fifty feet were left. A one hundred and fifty foot length would be utilised as a fixed rope on the rock face. The other two lengths would be needed to make the final assault in pairs. The margins could not have been finer.

By eleven o'clock the towering buttress had fallen. Five hours of the toughest rock climbing which they had ever experienced lay behind them, and the way to the summit seemed clear.

The route now consisted of hard rock pitches, alternating with snow slopes and sharp arêtes. Progress was steady. John Brazinton lead a particularly treacherous and steep ice pitch, slippery and as brittle as glass, on which the following climbers were very glad to be able to make use of the rope which he had fixed in place. At last, by three in the afternoon, the summit cone was in sight.

All morning they had been climbing in reasonably clear weather, but as the afternoon wore on the clouds began to gather and close in, threatening to defeat them at the eleventh hour. It was to be now or never.

Leaving the two lengths of rope which they had been climbing with on the final rock spire, the four men began to ascend the summit snowfield. Unprotected by a rope, Bryan Pooley lost his footing and slipped, a lapse of concentration that might have proved fatal, but he managed to arrest his fall using his ice-axe. A mistake so close to the top would have been the ultimate tragedy, and they all took extra care as they made their way up the final few feet.

Roger Brook was the first to stand upon the summit. The time was 3.10 p.m. The others quickly joined him, and the four climbers stood together, oblivious to the sleet and snow which had begun to swirl around the lofty peak, driven by a biting wind. They had been going for just over nine hours and the West Ridge of Indrasan, a mountain which is technically far harder than Everest, and a route which Wongdhi with all his experience thought was impossible, had been climbed.

They had not noticed the cold during the final heady moments of the climb, but the weather was deteriorating and, now that victory was theirs, it suddenly became very important to get down safely.

At around four in the afternoon they started the long descent. It was clear that it would be late in the evening, and pitch dark, before they could hope to reach the comparative safety of the miniature tent and the tiny ledge. In the blanketing mist and gathering darkness they retraced their steps. A layer of fresh snow now lay upon the icy stretches, making them even more treacherous. As the gloom increased and darkness fell they made their way back down the ridge, sharing a single torch between them. They were determined to reach the tent in safety and not repeat the experience of the Japanese men who, nine years earlier in 1962, had been the only others ever to stand upon the summit they had just left. They had to keep going. Darkness or no darkness there was no question of an overnight bivouac in the open at such an altitude. As the Japanese had discovered, the loss of fingers and toes through frostbite would be almost inevitable, and a slow death from exposure to the bitter cold would not be impossible.

They descended the granite tower successfully and reached the start of the fixed ropes. The tent was getting nearer. On one of the last pitches a peg came loose and Roger, who was descending on the rope, dropped twenty feet. Fortunately he was uninjured and carried on unperturbed.

At 10.45 p.m. they arrived at the camp. They had been climbing for sixteen and three quarter hours. It was time for Mars Bars, lukewarm soup, and as much fluid as they could manage to melt. But, after such an epic, there was very little sleep.

Aiming High – Overland to the Himalayas 1971

Roger Brook tackling the West Ridge

Early morning - West Ridge

Dawn at Camp III with Deo Tibba in the background. The north-west arête is outlined against the sky on the right-hand side.

Eighteen

DEO TIBBA

Bryan Pooley was lying on his sleeping bag in the orange Annapurna tent. It was the afternoon after my arrival at Camp III and all morning I had been eyeing the soft contours of Deo Tibba, sitting upon the western edge of the plateau like a huge meringue. My imagination had been fired by the exploits of the others on the West Ridge and I suddenly had a burning desire to climb a peak myself. Deo Tibba, nearly twenty thousand feet in height and already ascended a number of times, seemed a natural target for my ambition.

I crawled in alongside Bryan.

"Do you fancy having a go at Deo Tibba tomorrow?"

He rolled onto his back for a few moments, his hands behind his head, as he considered my proposal.

"Yeah, great. If the weather holds, why not?"

An expedition was born.

The two of us asked around for a third person to join us on our climb. Roger seemed vaguely interested.

"Where's the route up?" he queried.

I pointed out a fairly shallow snow slope which appeared to offer an uninterrupted route to the top, winding between the numerous crevasses that ran jaggedly across the lower slopes of the mountain. He was not enthusiastic. Crossing so many crevasses would be fraught with danger and far too risky.

He and Bryan stood alongside the tent and considered the peak. I watched them with interest as they considered, and then for various reasons rejected, several possible routes. Perhaps the effort they had put in to overcome the enormous challenges of the West Ridge had left them feeling too tired to summon up much enthusiasm for what, if successful, would be the thirty first ascent of Deo Tibba? If so, I could hardly blame them.

"Has that arête ever been climbed?" asked Bryan, pointing out a steeply angled snow ridge on the north-west face of the mountain.

Suddenly Roger was interested.

Tony was called over to join us and he confirmed that, as far as he knew, all previous ascents of Deo Tibba had been from the south following a route up one of the large glaciers.

"If we can crack that arête and get to the top we could try and get down via the south face which should get us back onto the plateau somewhere near Camp II."

Roger was now very definitely interested, and he agreed to join us. It would be a long climb, but an ascent of the north-west arête would be a new route up the mountain and descending the south face would mean we had achieved the first ever traverse of the mountain from north to south. It would be foolish to claim that I had no doubts at all about my ability to complete such a challenge, but the two professionals seemed happy to take me along and I was certainly not going to miss out on such an opportunity. A spell of good weather seemed to have settled in and, if it continued, Deo Tibba would be our goal the following morning.

There was fortunately no pressure to abandon the camp and start our retreat from the mountain because Geoff Arkless and Geoff Tabbner were still up on the West Ridge trying for a second ascent.

= = = = = = = = = = = = = =

Next morning I woke at 4.45 a.m. I had commandeered a small one man tent which had previously been utilised as an equipment store, and I was feeling the benefit of good night's sleep. It was still very cold outside and my breath froze as soon as it came into contact with the semi-circular roof of the tent. I lay there for a few minutes, comfortable and warm in my down sleeping bag, before summoning the courage to lift myself up on one elbow. This movement allowed some of the freezing air to find its way into the sleeping bag and I shivered involuntarily despite the several layers of clothing which I now habitually wore overnight. Gingerly I pulled at the draw-cord which held the circular tent entrance closed, trying not to dislodge the frosty particles which hung above my head. The knot which held the cord in place was frozen solid, and the necessary sharp tug to loosen it resulted in the icy cascade, which I had been hoping to avoid, descending upon my bare face and neck. I brushed the frost off my skin. It would do for a wash.

I put my eye to the small opening I had made. Outside the stars shone from a deep, clear sky. The thinness of the air meant that their light was almost constant, with almost none of the twinkling that characterises starlight at lower altitudes. There was an eerie silence and the snow of the plateau, frozen hard overnight, stretched out a dull, putty white. The sun was yet to rise and make the surface shine. It was as if I was gazing out onto another world from a tiny, frail spacecraft.

I curled up in my bag again to steal a few more minutes of warmth before summoning up the courage to endure the daily chore of pulling on cold breeches, extra socks and pullovers, and finally the double boots with their endless laces. This daily routine was made even more awkward in the confines of the small tent, despite the fact that I had learnt to keep my outer boots close to the warmth of my sleeping bag to avoid them becoming frozen. By five I was outside the tent with just my breeches to pull on over my boots. The physical contortions required to get them on while still inside the small tent had proved to be beyond me.

It was cold and very still. All was quiet.

I wandered over to the Annapurna, the soles of my boots making a gentle squeaking noise on the tightly packed snow. I unzipped the entrance of the tent.

"Beautiful day for Deo Tibba."

I pulled hard on the two sleeping bags within.

"Knock it off you lunatic and get back to sleep," muttered an angry, sleepy voice.

I retreated along one of the tracks which led to a deep hole in the snow, well away from the camp. I had often in the past wondered how the great adventurers had coped with the basic necessities of life in the frozen wastes. Somehow the subject never seems to crop up in their accounts. The plain answer is that nothing really changes. The whole process is just a little more inconvenient. And a great deal colder.

By the time I returned to camp Bryan was crawling out of the tent. He looked up approvingly at the cloudless sky and gave Roger, who was sharing the tent with him, a good shake as he exited. Roger, a notoriously good sleeper in even the most uncomfortable of situations, soon joined us and we pumped up the primus to prepare the morning brew. The necessary equipment for our climb had been prepared the previous evening so it was merely a question of waiting for the snow to melt and boil, while dividing a tin of half-frozen Spam between the three of us.

And then we were off.

The snow crust glistened as dawn approached, shimmering in the early morning light as though millions of tiny sequins had been scattered at random overnight. As we moved closer to Deo Tibba the eastern flank of the mountain took on a glorious, golden-yellow hue as it caught the first rays of the rising sun.

We maintained a fairly brisk pace, making straight for the north-west arête where it met the edge of the plateau. The air was still cold to breathe, but the altitude did not seem to be causing me any difficulty. My companions, of course, were well acclimatised after their stay on the West Ridge. After the crumbling afternoon snow that I had experienced the previous day, the crisp surface was a delight to walk upon and I was able to raise myself on the front welts of my boots as I walked, almost as if I was on terra firma. It was nice to be able to take decent-sized strides for a change.

We reached the arête much more quickly than we had expected and, as the first rays of the sun started to warm the plateau where we stood, we roped up, Alpine style.

Bryan was to take the first lead, a traverse across a small crevasse which would take him out onto the crest of the arête. He set off, cutting huge steps with his ice axe as he went. The snow slope was firm.

"New Zealand buckets!" shouted Roger.

Pausing only to lift two gloved fingers in Roger's direction, Bryan carried on cutting his steps. New Zealand or not, I was grateful. The large steps were probably for my benefit. Slowly, with Roger and myself belaying him as he went, he crossed a rather frail-looking snow bridge and reached the crest. For the first time he could see over onto the western side of the mountain.

"Hey!" he shouted. "Wait 'til you get out here. The view's just like on the ridge. I can see right down to the valley. It's all green."

With that he moved further onto the western face and out of our sight. We could judge his progress only by the rope we were paying out as he moved slowly upwards. Some rapid mental arithmetic on my part had already worked out that the drop down to that green valley must be eight or nine thousand feet. It would be a long way to fall.

"Another ten feet, Bryan."

I shouted to the invisible New Zealander, to warn him that he had almost reached the end of the one hundred and fifty foot rope.

"Okay.   I'll cut a good, big step and belay right here."

His voice drifted down to us over the crest of the arête.

"Okay. I'm belayed.   Come on up."

It was my turn. A few steps and I had reached the snow bridge. A couple of tugs on the rope and I felt Bryan take up the slack. I was still out of his sight. I stepped onto the bridge.   The crevasse was more of a slit than a yawning chasm and I could see the icy walls coming together beneath me. Over time this slit would widen, and the frozen snow slope onto which I was about to step would detach itself from the mountain and hurtle down towards the green valley far below. Our route assumed that such an event was most likely to occur many months in the future rather than today, and I fervently hoped our judgment was right.   A dozen more steps, making full use of Bryan's buckets, took me to the crest of the arête.

The view was breathtaking.   Far from being a true arête, the ridge which we had chosen overlooked the leading edge of a hanging glacier. This was one of the places where the accumulated snows of the plateau, succumbing to the relentless pressure from behind, reluctantly broke away and tumbled off the precipitous edge into the abyss.

How many veteran climbers, I wondered, would have given anything for the opportunity to stand in my place on this perfect white ridge, which seemed to reach out for the sky, with the whole world stretched out far below. There must be hundreds whose dreams I was fulfilling, and I hoped that I was appreciating the full richness of the experience.

I straddled the crest of the ridge and moved out onto the west face. I was now shielded from the sun and the snow slope was ice-hard. A trail of New Zealand buckets, slightly smaller because of the harder surface but still more than adequate to give me confidence, led up to where Bryan was perched.

Alongside him I hacked out a platform for myself and plunged the handle of my ice-axe as deep as possible into the slope, hitching to it the rope which trailed down from my waist belt to where Roger was waiting. In the very unlikely event of Roger slipping as he followed me, my size eleven boot would push the axe-head into the snow and provide an efficient friction brake. This type of belay, much used in the New Zealand Alps according to Bryan, was his preferred method of minimising risk and maximising safety.

Roger was soon up with us and he then carried on past our position to lead the second pitch of the day. I continued to belay him as he climbed upwards having coiled up the excess rope so that I could pay it out to him as he ascended.

It was 6.45 a.m. The first one hundred and fifty feet of the arête had taken us just over an hour.

"We'll have to move faster than this if we're going to get to the top and complete the traverse. We won't have time to cut steps all the way."

Roger made his point as he stopped for breath after cutting about a dozen small footholds.

"And it's seriously tiring at this altitude."

Chunks of ice and snow slithered and skipped past Bryan and I as he started off again. I was not entirely sure whether the steps were just for my benefit as there is a tradition in New Zealand mountaineering which applauds good step cutting, and Bryan was certainly adept at it.

"Don't bother with steps just for me if you don't think they're necessary," I shouted up to Roger. I had climbed the couloir without steps, so why not this arête? "I'm perfectly happy using my crampons and kicking steps provided I'm belayed."

"Okay then, Doc. Let's go for it."

Roger immediately set off upwards at a greatly increased pace, kicking step after step with his hefty, double boots. Within a few minutes he had exhausted the rope and I followed him, before belaying Bryan as he came up last.

We continued in this fashion, Bryan and Roger alternating the lead and keeping me safely tied between them like a toddler in its first walking harness. I appreciated the solid confidence that their experience and obvious ability gave me.

The pace had increased now that steps were no longer being cut. The kicks in the snow provided no more than toe-holds but, with the spiked crampons to reinforce the grip of my boots, I never felt in any serious danger. The main hazard was of loss of concentration, for the fast progress was making all three of us tired. My own tiredness was exacerbated by the unaccustomed altitude, for we were now at around nineteen thousand feet, while the long and arduous climb of the West Ridge must surely have sapped the energy reserves of my two companions.

By seven thirty we had passed the halfway point on our climb. Moving nearer to the crest we could see Indrasan to our left and, tucked up against the foot of the West Ridge, the tiny, coloured tents of Camp III. We stopped to take a breather and shoot some pictures with the still awesome West Ridge of Indrasan in the background.

"Bet it'd make a great telephoto picture from down there, the three of us silhouetted against the sky on this ridge," said Bryan. But there was no sign of activity in the camp far below us.

"Let's wake the lazy buggers up."

We shouted in unison, our outlandish calls disappearing towards the plateau far below. A couple of minutes passed before two black dots emerged from one of the tents.

"Get some pictures you idle sods."

They waved up at us.

"Get your cameras out!"

We yelled in vain, receiving only further waves and unintelligible shouts in reply.

"Dim pair," grinned Roger. "They don't really function all that well on the oxygen that's available at sea level. So there's not much hope of getting any sense out of them at this sort of altitude."

We gave up and pushed on.

After another few hundred feet we noticed that the slope was becoming less steep and we soon found ourselves looking at a long, shallow incline that led towards the summit. The north-west arête was behind us. All that remained was to negotiate any crevasses that barred the way to the final snowfield. Would that be possible? Nobody had ever been this way before so we could only cross our fingers and trust to luck that that we did not come up against an impassable barrier in this final section of the climb.

As we trudged up the gentle slope I was able to turn and look back at the way we had come. The green valley that had been visible throughout our ascent was starting to disappear from view beneath a solid cumulo-nimbus cloud formation that was gathering several thousand feet below our lofty station. The west face of Deo Tibba dropped steeply away to our right, a shimmering expanse of icy snow that was as yet untouched by the day's sun. This snow face extended for several thousand feet, but we could just make out some jagged rocks, part of the underlying skeleton of the mountain, breaking through the white surface as the slope became steeper and the snow found it more difficult to maintain a hold.

We walked on, placing one foot in front of the other in a steady and regular rhythm. The thin air was beginning to bite and I found myself gulping in great lungfuls of cold air to try and satisfy my body's oxygen requirements. My respiratory rate increased, and I found that I was breathing entirely through my mouth. I wondered how on earth anyone could think of climbing at twenty-four or twenty-five thousand feet without supplementary oxygen, and I could only marvel at the confidence of the early Everest pioneers who had contemplated reaching the summit of that mighty mountain without using any such artificial aids.

If someone had suggested that, just seven years later in 1978, two men might climb to the very roof of the world without using any oxygen at all, I would have come up with a hundred and one very sound physiological reasons why it could not possibly ever happen.

I could only speculate that, in the case of the early Everest pioneers, slow and careful acclimatisation had allowed them to climb so high into the thin air. The alternative theory was one that had been put forward to me by Dharm Chand as we were chatting one afternoon at Camp I. He told me that the locals believe that altitude effects vary in different parts of the Himalayas. In areas like Nepal, he explained seriously, where even the valley floors are at nine or ten thousand feet, the air higher up is thicker and contains more oxygen. It was an interesting theory, but one that my training in physiology would not allow me to accept. D.C., however, was adamant that the Italian expedition to Parbati had more trouble with altitude sickness at 21,700 feet than any of the climbers on Everest have experienced at 25,000 feet or more.

Such interesting thoughts helped my brain to block out the tiredness I was feeling. My thighs ached, and my calf muscles were tightening up with cramp. I longed to stop as we ploughed on, up the long slope which seemed to continue endlessly. We crossed several crevasses, which happily presented no problem at all, while all the time the route seemed to be taking us further round onto the western side of the peak. Then, quite suddenly, we were there. On all sides the ground dropped away and the three of us stood upon a summit that was more like a football field than the traditional cone which I was expecting. Flat or not, it was my first Himalayan summit, and it was a heady moment for me despite the fact that there would be no dramatic pictures of the brave mountaineers with one foot on the summit, celebrating victory, to show to the folks back home.

We removed our ropes and took the obligatory photographs to celebrate this 31st ascent of Deo Tibba, The Peak of The Gods. We had successfully completed the first part of what would hopefully turn out to the very first, full traverse of the summit from north to south.

We spent some fifteen minutes on the summit, eating the chocolate which we had brought with us while all the time scanning the white cone which marked the highest point on Indrasan, clearly visible a couple of miles away across the plateau. We hoped that we might see two small figures moving up the snow, which would indicate that Geoff Arkless and Geoff Tabbner had achieved a successful second ascent, but there was no movement to be seen.

"I suppose they could've got a really early start," mused Bryan. "If they did, they'd be on their way down by now. We might have missed them."

That was true so, having decided that there was little hope of getting a glimpse of the two Geoffs, we sat and gathered our energy for the long descent which lay ahead. My feelings, as we sat there, were mainly of great satisfaction. 19,687 feet (6001 metres) was not bad for a first peak, but I was not overjoyed. The main thing I felt was a very matter-of-fact, sort of, 'Right, we've done it. Now let's try and get back down in one piece.' My strongest emotion was quite certainly a deep longing for a refreshing cup of English Breakfast Tea, but a celebratory brew in the camp far below us was still several hours away.

Roger was the first to set off, heading towards the south-east glacier. Bryan and I followed, only to come across him a few moments later looking down our proposed route. It was decidedly steep and uninviting. The snow was soft and uneven, with loose chunks here and there hanging in seemingly impossible positions. It appeared to have been changed many times, the whole of the south face of Deo Tibba being much more exposed to the melting action of the sun each day, which would be followed by the vicious, nightly freeze. These extreme variations of heat and cold had twisted and cracked the surface into the strange and unfamiliar formations which we were now seeing.

"I think we're going to have to rope up." Roger announced. "It'll slow us down a bit, unfortunately, but it looks decidedly dodgy down there."

Bryan agreed and, once more in a rope of three, we began our descent. Roger took the first pitch, a narrow snow ridge which ended in a steep drop into a small couloir. At the end of the ridge he unclipped a long, hollow ice-screw from the bunch of pegs on his belt and began seeking a secure placement for it. The ice was soft and he had three tries before it was fixed to his satisfaction.

"I'm going to abseil down into the couloir," he shouted up to us. "Belay me with the other rope in case this screw comes out. The snow's rotten."

I tossed the other length of rope down to him, after securing it with the shaft of my ice axe, and prepared to belay him. The ice screw held, and within a couple of minutes he was standing on a snow shelf down in the couloir. Bryan and I followed him, both of us abseiling off the screw. It jiggled ominously as I came to use it, but thankfully it did not come away.

I pulled the doubled rope through the eye of the screw, which was now high above me. Once the rope was free there was no way of retrieving the screw so we left it as evidence of our passage. It was one of the very few pieces of equipment which we abandoned anywhere in the mountains. Our expedition was funded on a shoestring and we could afford to leave nothing behind, unlike the

Japanese who had quite happily left several hundred feet of rope in place after their own unsuccessful attempt on Deo Tibba, for Chamba gratefully to retrieve on his afternoon off.

After a couple of similar pitches we found ourselves in a gully from which the route to the plateau looked fairly obvious and straightforward, even if not entirely safe. Nevertheless it was certainly safer to continue down than to try and retrace our steps, so we pushed on. We descended a snow ramp beneath some ice cliffs, from the top edge of which ice showers and miniature avalanches fell continuously. Another abseil, this time down a rocky cliff and across a series of small crevasses, led us to a wide bergschrund, beyond which was the plateau.

The only way we could cross the bergschrund was by sliding down the slope above it and then launching ourselves over it to reach the far side. Happily the far side was lower than our jumping off point, otherwise none of us would have cleared it. We were back on the plateau. The first ever north to south traverse of Deo Tibba was complete.

The descent had taken a couple of hours, and I had found it much more testing and hazardous than the ascent of the arête. It was well into the afternoon and, tired as we were, we still had to walk a couple of miles across the softening snow of the plateau to reach our camp.

Roger, amazingly, seemed full of beans but I felt that Bryan was almost as tired as I was. I prayed that my judgment was right, otherwise I would be left trailing far behind the other two as we made our way back across the plateau.

The hard crust, which had been such a pleasure to walk upon in the early morning, had degenerated in the hot sun and it was once again the consistency of firm porridge. Each step was a terrible drain upon my dwindling reserves of energy. I had volunteered to take the number three position, for it meant that the snow was made slightly firmer by two pairs of feet ahead of mine, but the benefit was marginal and the surface still gave way at almost every step. The journey across the plateau seemed never-ending and before very long Roger and Bryan began to count their steps to keep themselves going. I watched them, counting the steps they took. Twenty tortured steps, then a rest to recover. I followed their example and began to count my steps too - in fours.

At long last the snow bridge came into sight and with agonizing slowness I approached it. My rest stops were getting longer and longer as I gasped for air, like a fish out of water. I crossed the bridge just as slowly, still stopping for rests, for I had reached that dangerous stage of exhausted demoralisation when the collapse of the bridge, and the consequent final plunge into the depths beneath, would have been no more than a merciful release.

Happily, or unhappily, the snow bridge showed no sign of weakness, and I forced myself up the slope on the far side, making for the tall pole which marked the last section of the route. Three hundred yards away was the camp, a conglomeration of windswept tents and debris, but a very welcome and beautiful sight.

Bryan, who had pulled ahead of me, had already reached the tents and had stopped for breath while Roger, showing little sign of any ill-effects, had wandered past the tents and seemed to be heading for the West Ridge. Where he got the energy from I had no idea.

Count four steps; pause for breath; another four steps; another breather. I continued with the routine that had been going on for the past mile.

As the tents drew nearer I forced myself to increase my paces to ten. There were fifty yards to go; three lots of twenty paces? Or perhaps four lots? And then I was there, collapsing with relief onto the nearest food box, head in hands and elbows on knees. My lungs ached and my head felt as though it was about to burst. The pulses on both my temples throbbed wildly. The last three hundred yards had taken me fifteen minutes.

Tea and soup were already on the boil, the preparations having been started by Tony and John as soon as the three of us had been sighted. A couple of minutes after I reached the camp the mug of tea which I had longed for on the summit was sitting in my hands, and the life-giving fluid was gratefully being lapped up.

It was exactly three o'clock. We had been out for almost ten hours.

As Bryan and I sat there, recovering our energy, John Brazinton broke the silence.

"There's been no sign of life up on the West Ridge."

Tony shook his head.

"The weather's been ideal. They must have had a go at the summit today unless something's gone wrong."

"We were looking out for them from up on Deo Tibba," I added, "and we didn't see anything either."

"It's very strange," continued Tony, sounding not a little concerned. "We've been shouting up to the ridge camp all day, on and off, without getting any joy. They must have heard us."

None of us could believe that they had not tried for the summit. Days as clear and perfect as the one that was now drawing to a close are not so frequent that they can be wasted. Were they perhaps still on their way down? The others had not returned to camp until late at night after all. Even so, it was difficult to understand why there had been no sign of them on the summit. On such a clear day it would have been hard to miss them against that white snowfield. All we could do was hope and pray that nothing had gone seriously wrong.

"Well," said Tony. "They'll have to give it a go tomorrow or not at all. This good weather's not going to last, and it's time we were getting out of here."

Roger had by this time returned from his extra walk.

"Anyone fancy an Alpine assault on the east ridge? We could meet them at the top and give them a surprise."

Whether he was being serious or not was uncertain, but knowing Roger his question may not have been entirely frivolous.

The talk continued as dusk fell, and soon another freezing, but clear, night was upon us. After a quickly-eaten stew I was more than ready to repair to my tent, slip off my outer boots and wind-proofs, and lose myself in the warm luxury of my sleeping bag. With no dawn starts planned I could drift off into a deep and well-earned sleep in anticipation of the quiet and relaxing day which lay ahead.

The author on the north-west arête. The sheer, nine thousand foot drop to the valley below is half-hidden in shade *(RB)*

Aiming High – Overland to the Himalayas 1971

Nearing the summit of the north-west arête *(BP)*

Bryan Pooley and John Winter on the summit of Deo Tibba. The West Ridge and summit of Indrasan are in the background *(RB)*

Nineteen

A LAZY DAY

An ice-cold droplet fell upon my face and caused me to wake. The sun was up and the frosty layer which once again coated the tent roof was melting. I looked at my watch. The time was six thirty and it was immediately clear that the icy drops were likely to increase, rather than decrease, in number and frequency. It was time to get up.

Roger and John were already sitting beside a roaring primus, sipping their morning tea. I wandered over to join them.

"Morning Doc. Lovely day again."

"It is indeed."

"Seems a shame to waste it," continued John. "We've got to hang around anyway 'til the two of them come down from the ridge."

I knew it was only a matter of time before one or other of them suggested a climb. Everyone on the mountain seemed to have an uncontrollable urge to try and climb anything which departed from the horizontal. And the nearer to the vertical it was, the better.

Roger pointed at two pyramids of granite which rose from the western edge of the plateau.

"What about those rock peaks over there?"

Here we go, I thought, as I settled back to enjoy the lazy, idle day that I had already planned.

The sides of two peaks were so steep and precipitous that little or no snow had collected upon them to obscure the colour of the rock.

"Why don't we wander over and take a closer look at them?" replied John. "There's probably some pretty interesting routes on that granite."

No more words were spoken, but it was decided. I watched as they hunted around in the mess of equipment and ropes that lay around the camp looking for all the paraphernalia of the dedicated rock climber. Pitons, slings and karabiners (affectionately known as 'crabs') were all identified and collected together. A couple of lengths of climbing rope completed their requirements.

I continued to sip my tea slowly, making the most of the first leisurely breakfast for several days and soaking up the gently warming rays of the rising sun.

"Coming with us, Doc?"

I looked at John, amazed. There I was, still in my inner boots, in the lap of relative luxury, having a quiet sunbathe, and he was asking me to go climbing again.

I shook my head.

"I don't think so, no thanks, I fancy a quiet day."

"I thought the bug might have got to you after yesterday," he answered, laughing.

"Well, maybe slightly. It was a great day. But I think it'd be better if I stop while I'm winning."

I was content to sit on my laurels. There was no point in tempting fate.

"Anyway, I'd hold you up too much."

It was an unnecessary, and potentially fatal, extra few words.

"No you wouldn't. You managed fine yesterday," said Roger, "And John said the Grade 5 when he took you climbing at Helsby didn't seem to worry you too much."

Helsby. It was only a few months ago, but how distant and totally unconnected to my present situation it now seemed.

I gave it a few minutes' thought.

"Okay then. I don't fancy doing any climbing, but I might as well wander over there with you. There's nothing doing here, and it'll be a nice walk at this time of day."

The snow that stretched out towards the two peaks looked firm and inviting. A brisk walk would be a pleasant start to an otherwise sedentary day.

I finished my remaining tea in one swig and went over to my tent to don my outer boots. It was already warm in the sun, almost shirt-sleeves weather but, mindful of how rapidly mountain weather can change, I packed an extra sweater and a windproof to take with me. In a few minutes I was ready and, shouldering one of the two ropes, I set of with the other two across the snow. The tiredness of the previous day had completely disappeared.

"They look straightforward enough," I found myself saying as we walked along. "Maybe I might give it a go."

One summit; and now I wanted more.

The two rocky outcrops towards which we were walking were directly to the east of us, almost in line with the rising sun, so it was initially difficult to see any detail on the steep granite. As we got closer, however, we could see that the left-hand peak was a tall pyramid which seemed to have large, well-broken sections leading up to a fine, pointed summit. It looked much more inviting and less formidable than its neighbour, which was a smaller, squat structure, the sides of which were exceedingly precipitous. Its western side, which we were now approaching, dropped vertically towards to the surface of the plateau; and as we got closer it seemed to get ever steeper and higher.

I prevailed upon my companions to try the easier, left-hand peak first. Reaching towards the heavens like a crumbling church spire, the sun glinting on patches of ice and snow which lay in cracks and gullies between the dull, red-brown granite blocks, it looked like a worthy objective.

Half an hour later we stood at the bottom of what was to be our route. A snowy col ran between the peak and the eastern ridge of Indrasan, and John and Roger had decided that we should mount our assault from where that col merged into a well broken ridge on the northern edge of the pyramid.

A short, but tiring, climb took the three of us up the already softening snow slope leading to the col. We then headed along the crest to the point where we would leave all our equipment except the ropes, and other items such as pitons and slings, which would be needed for the climb.

As we sorted our gear out and started to rope up there was an opportunity to survey the spectacular vista to our left. The far side of the col fell away giddily, as I had come to expect, to another green-floored valley. A narrow ribbon of palest blue, just visible to the naked eye, was a river which ran the length of the valley taking the glacier melt-water down to the plains of India. All the waters from many such small valleys would eventually combine together to form the mighty Indus, traversing the plains as it made its way to the Arabian Sea. We were standing on the backbone, one of the watersheds, of the continent of Asia and, from far above, we were witnessing the birth of one of the world's great rivers.

On the far side of the valley, stretching out in the direction of Lahul, the Hampta Pass, and beyond towards China, were more mountains. Burke's Fortress and White Skull were named and recognised. There were so many others, all without names and lying in the region behind India's Inner Line, where no foreign nationals are permitted. The narrow col which we were standing on marked the Inner Line. We had ventured as far as we were allowed to go.

I had been tying the rope around my climbing belt as I gazed around me and I was ready for the business of the day. The route from where we stood looked easy enough and I did not feel the need to concentrate too hard. I found myself day-dreaming about the life to which I would return after this great adventure. What could I possibly do in the future to match such an experience?

"Watch yourself, Doc!"

Roger was above me and he had dislodged a few small rocks which whizzed past my head as John shouted out the warning. I swiftly returned to the here and now, and resolved to remain there, giving my full attention to the climb. Otherwise there might be no future to contemplate.

The falling stones had come from a rock chimney, perhaps forty feet in height, which led out onto a gentle snow and rock scree. Half an hour more of scrambling up fairly easy rock steps with nice positive hand and foot holds on the rough granite and the top was within reach. We clambered up a final steep gully and we were there.

It was nine thirty exactly. We stood, two at a time for there was not room for three, upon a very satisfying summit. I was glad that I had joined them.

From our perch we had a wonderful view of the east ridge of Indrasan. Roger and John both agreed that it would never fall to an Alpine assault. There were some nasty-looking ice-cliffs just below the summit snowfield, with no obvious route around them. Climbing those cliffs would, just by themselves, be a very good day's work. They continued to discuss its possibilities as we munched sweets, while we also kept an eye out for any sign of the two Geoffs. The altitude was affecting my appetite and I was unable to finish all my mints, so I left two of them in a niche behind the summit boulder along with some butterscotch. I hoped that the mountain gods would enjoy them. If not, they will still be there for whoever makes the second ascent to that remote place.

As the novice I led the way down, safely roped in case of any slips. Some two hundred feet below the summit I took the wrong route and found myself going down a rather more awkward chimney than the one we had ascended. My length of leg allowed me to negotiate it successfully, while the considerably better technique of my two companions meant that they hardly noticed the unintended change of route. I cannot name the manoeuvres they employed, but their descent looked effortless. A traverse along a wide ledge took us back to our original route, and five or ten minutes of sliding and scrambling down easy slabs then saw the three of us back on the col. It was twenty five past ten and I decided it was time to call it a day.

Leaving me to take a short rest, Roger and John set off towards their second peak. They had been gone some ten minutes when I realised that they had left a rope and quite a lot of hardware behind. They would surely need these items for their climb.

Hurriedly I gathered the stuff together and followed their fast disappearing figures across the softening snow. By the time I caught up with them they had already reached the foot of the massive granite wall and were studying it intently, seeking out a worthwhile and possible route. The rock face was made up of many overlapping and adjoining slabs with narrow ledges running across the upper edge of each individual slab. The slabs themselves were almost vertical and devoid of any cracks or holds as far as I could see, It was going to be a much more difficult and challenging climb.

"Great isn't it," enthused Roger. "Fancy it, Doc?"

"Thank you, but I think not. To be quite honest it looks impossible to me, and I've done enough climbing for today. I just came over with this gear you left on the col."

"Go on. Give it a go. That climb before was nothing. This'll be much more fun."

"That's exactly what I was afraid of," I replied. Roger laughed, but already I felt myself wavering. It looked like it would be a really good climb, and I was unlikely to get the chance to climb with such experts again.

"Okay then. It does look as though it'll be a pretty interesting climb. I'll come with you."

I could hardly believe what I was saying, but it seemed I was back on board.

The route was soon decided. A narrow snow gully would allow us to reach a ledge. From there an easy traverse along a broken crack would lead to the lower part of a thin vertical crack which looked as though it would take us up towards the summit, but we would have to review the route when we were higher up and could see it better.

The three of us walked towards the snow gully, an inverted 'Y' which pointed up to the rock face proper. John led the way up to the first ledge. He made it look like an easy scramble up the slightly inclined slab but when I tried to follow I found that the holds which he had used so effortlessly were in fact rather small and awkward. The rock was worn smooth by countless years of snow and wind and my grip was not helped by the fact that I had put on some fingerless mitts to help keep my hands warm in the cold wind.

With no little assistance from the rope which John was using to belay me I managed to scramble onto the ledge alongside him. I then belayed Roger as he joined us.

From this vantage point we could see that there was already some mist creeping over the far edge of the plateau between Deo Tibba and Indrasan. I glanced at my watch. It was barely eleven thirty. The afternoon clouds were rolling in early. It looked as though it might be a cool afternoon.

Roger took the next lead, making his way swiftly across an easy horizontal pitch which led to a ledge from which he could gain access to the proposed summit route. The next hour or so saw us doing some relatively straightforward rock climbing with nothing more dramatic than stops for a few action photographs on a couple of the more hairy sections.

We reached the halfway point and things suddenly got trickier. Roger, who was in the lead, reached the end of a very narrow ledge on the upper border of a slab. The slab, at this point, merged in with the rest of the rock face. Bracing himself in a ludicrously awkward position, supported only by two minute toe-holds and a small protrusion which he gripped with his left hand, he leant outwards slightly to get a better look at the rock face above him.

I turned away to recheck my belay, which would need to hold him if he came off. My rope was looped behind a sliver of rock which had wedged itself between two of the large, granite slabs. I had tested it with my own weight and it seemed secure. I just hoped that my judgment would prove to be right should the belay be needed.

Roger maintained his gravity-defying posture for what seemed like several minutes as he studied the rock above him.

"How many pegs and crabs have you two got left on your belts?" he shouted as he returned to a more relaxed pose. "There's a crack which seems to disappear about a hundred foot up. There are a few, small holds, higher up, that I can see, and maybe a couple of cracks, but not much else. We'll need a lot of pegs, and even then we might not be able to make it."

I had four crabs, while John had three plus an assorted bunch of perhaps half a dozen pegs.

"Don't think it'll be enough," announced Roger when we gave him the numbers. "I think we'd be better trying to find a different route rather than wasting a couple of hours on this. I don't honestly think it's going to go."

John looked at me.

"What time is it, Doc?"

His own watch, one of the specially prepared, sporting models which had been supplied to the expedition by an optimistic manufacturer to test their durability, had long since succumbed to the merciless battering which it had been subjected to on the West Ridge.

"Just after quarter to two."

The clouds were getting thicker and, given that we had only a couple of hours of climbing left, all three of us were agreed that our only sensible option was to try and identify an alternative route to the summit. We had already wasted over an hour.

With renewed energy we headed left up a broken gully which led towards a crest on the northern side of the summit. Once we were on the north ridge there would hopefully be a way to the top.

We were climbing Alpine-style with John leading and Roger bringing up the rear. As on Deo Tibba, I was roped in the middle. We pushed on, quite tough stretches being interspersed with easier scrambles as the ridge got nearer. Then, after a wriggle up a more than usually awkward chimney, I found myself alongside John. He was firmly braced across the top of the chimney, part-sitting on a ledge which was just below the crest of the rock face.

"It looks fairly straightforward to the top from here," he said as I came up to him. "You might as well go on while I stay here and belay Roger."

Two or three minutes later I found myself peering out over the far side of the ridge from where, but for the swirling mist, I could have looked down again upon the peaks and valleys beyond the Inner Line. Ahead of me was the summit, an enormous square granite block the vertical sides of which were ten or fifteen feet high. I was soon at its base, seeking a route up the smooth rock. Only a couple of tiny holds presented themselves. It was like one of those boulder problems which rock climbers back in England practice upon, the only difference being that this particular, square boulder was perched over an uninterrupted drop of several thousand feet to a valley far below. Mercifully, the precipitous fall was hidden from my view.

Roger and John were close behind me but I desperately wanted to be the first on top. I reached up for two of the hand-holds I had picked out. My height helped me for, by pulling myself up on them, I was already almost halfway up the block. What next? A lovely crack was there for the asking within range of my left foot, but that meant moving further out over the awful drop. A moment's hesitation, then I committed myself to the move. The welt of my left boot slipped into the crack and I was able to place my right boot upon a rough granite knob. At full stretch I found that I could get my right hand up and grasp the top edge of the block.

I rested in this relatively stable position and gathered my strength for the last pull. I was still roped to the other two but they were below me. It was not difficult to work out how far I could fall. The answer was twice the thirty feet or so that separated us; probably not fatal, but quite enough to break a bone or two. And I was the doctor.

I tensed my muscles. In my mind's eye I could see the move that was required. Taking my weight with my right hand I would need to move my left boot a little further into the crack and then mantel-shelf myself up onto the flat summit. It was now or never. It took a supreme effort, but suddenly I found myself scrambling onto the top of the block. I was on the summit.

I carefully pulled myself upright and realised that I was almost certainly standing where no human being had ever stood before. I was lost in amazement when, suddenly, I remembered that my two companions were about to start on the final pitch themselves, and I had to be ready to belay them.

"Not much of a view is it," said John as he pulled himself up beside me effortlessly. Roger quickly followed.

"Glad you came with us, Doc?" he asked, as we stood for the obligatory photo-call in the swirling mist.

There was no view to admire so we did not linger for long. My watch said twenty past four and, once a few pictures had been taken, it was time to start the descent. As first onto the summit is was my privilege to be the last off and, with no rope to protect me, the move down to the ledge seemed even less inviting than it had been on the way up. But I negotiated it safely and then we scrambled back down the route we had used for the ascent.

To save time we made for a wide ledge which John had noticed on the way up. From the ledge we should be able to abseil straight down to the plateau without using the snow slope. John reckoned it was save at least half an hour. A peg was hammered into a suitable crack on the ledge, and twin hundred and fifty foot lengths of rope then snaked down the rock face. The drop to the plateau had been judged to a nicety and the bottom six feet or so of the two ropes lay upon the white snow. The mist had lifted slightly and visibility had increased to about three hundred yards

With a final sharp tug on the ropes, to test the security of the peg, Roger launched himself into space. He descended in great leaps and was quickly on the plateau. I followed, rather more cautiously, and we both clicked away with our cameras as John bounded down in what was a remarkable imitation of Errol Flynn at his most piratical. The ropes pulled easily through the eye of the peg, eventually collapsing in coils around our feet.

Once we had retrieved the rest of our equipment from the bottom of the gully where we had left it, there remained only the long trudge back to the distant tents of Camp III, still hidden in the mist.

Looking across the plateau towards the first rock peak *(JW)*

Roger Brook leads the way - second rock peak (JW)

Looking for a route up the vertical slabs – second rock peak *(JW)*

Twenty

RETURN TO BASE

It was six o'clock, and snowing quite hard, by the time we finally got back to Camp III. Having stopped en route to take some pictures of the two conquered peaks I was once again the last to reach the camp. Bryan Pooley told us that Tony and Dharm Chand had left at midday to head back to Base Camp. Tony had developed a troublesome cough overnight and he was getting a bit of pain in his chest, so he had wisely decided to retreat to a lower altitude.

Bryan's other news was that the two Geoffs had been sighted on the summit of Indrasan at ten thirty that morning in perfect conditions. The sighting had come as something of a relief, and knowing they were safe had made it easier for Tony to leave. Nothing had been heard from them since the sighting, shouts up to the ridge having brought no response, but Bryan thought they were probably moving down slowly, removing fixed ropes as they went. He confidently expected them to be down from the ridge the following morning, together with as much equipment as they could manage. Before they went up, Tony had given instructions that all the fixed ropes were to be removed from the ridge, together with the tents and other hardware. Any remaining food and fuel would be left up there, which seemed wasteful, but the cost in man-hours and expended energy did not justify lugging such perishable and expendable items back down the mountain.

While Bryan and John took shelter in one of the tents, Roger and I braved the worsening weather conditions in order to raid the remaining food boxes and remove luxury items such as Mars Bars, chocolate bars and the inevitable Kendal Mint Cake. There was no point in hanging on to them so, back inside the tent, they were consumed in one gigantic, and highly enjoyable, feast. When we finally retired to our tents, a good deal later than usual, I shared the Arctic Guinea with John, as Tony and D.C. had taken the smaller tent down with them.

My plan for the following day was to head straight down to Base Camp to ensure that Tony was alright. Climbers who have pushed themselves hard at high altitude can very easily develop lung problems such as pleurisy and pneumonia, as well as more dangerous conditions such as blood clots, or emboli, within the lungs. I needed to check him over. As long as any overnight snow was not too heavy I reckoned that I should be able to make it, although it would be a long day.

I woke feeling fit and refreshed. The skies were clear and, after a quick, fluid breakfast, I set off with a fifty pound pack on my shoulders. Along with my personal gear I had with me the irreplaceable 35 mm Kodachrome photographic films, each film secure in its screw-top metal container. What precious memories those pictures would trigger in the future. To make a decent-sized load I had grabbed a couple of ropes, and assorted metal pegs and karabiners, and thrown them into the pack as well.

It was nine o'clock exactly as I crossed the snow bridge leading away from camp. The storm had covered the plateau in a fresh, white blanket and, even with the darkest lenses in my goggles, I had to screw my eyes up against the glare. In view of the hefty load I was carrying I had picked out a couple of ski-sticks to improve my balance, and hopefully take some of the weight, but they provided only marginal help. The fresh snow crust continued to give way with almost every step I took and the long journey across the plateau took almost three hours.

Camp II was deserted. The tent and all the equipment had disappeared, apart from a single oxygen bottle which lay, half-buried in snow, alongside an abandoned food box which still had a few items left inside it. Tony and Dharm Chand must have taken everything else down. I added the oxygen bottle to my pack before rifling through the food box. I found a couple of packs of fruit sweets, one of which I consumed, slipping the other into my pocket for later.

As I sat and rested, gathering my energy for the descent of the big couloir, I took one last, long look at the mountains which had been the focus of attention over the past weeks. Deo Tibba and the twin granite peaks had been very special for me, but the ascent of the West Ridge of Indrasan was the ultimate achievement. It would mark our expedition with the badge of success, and hopefully open new doors for all of us in the future.

The peaks looked magnificent. I knew that I would have the photographs to look back upon to remind me of what it had been like, but even the best of pictures is unable fully to capture and do justice to such magnificence. With the passage of time I would gradually find it harder and harder to recall what I had actually seen. Only the pictures would remain; and over the years the pictures themselves would gradually become the memory.

It was with a sad heart that I finally shouldered my pack and turned away for the last time.

= = = = = = = = = = = = = = =

True to form the weather deteriorated in the early part of the afternoon and I arrived at Camp I in driving snow and a bitterly cold wind. The descent of the big couloir had taken longer than usual. A combination of fatigue and the weight of my pack had hampered my ability to abseil effectively down the fixed ropes and I had been forced to climb down the steep slope, step by laborious step. The snow bridge over the bergschrund at the bottom remained firm but the crevasses on the upper reaches of the Malana Glacier seemed to have opened up significantly since my last crossing. The whole route had been icy and slippery. It felt much more dangerous than a few days earlier, and I was heartily glad to be off it for the last time.

The tent was still there at Camp I, perched upon its rocky shelf. I deposited my heavy load in the snow basin below the tent and climbed up to fix myself a much-needed brew. I had been on the move for six and a half hours. As I sat in the increasingly heavy snow I toyed with the idea of remaining at the camp overnight. I knew that I was very tired, and that tiredness breeds mistakes in the later parts of any climb, but I badly wanted to get down to Base Camp, not least to see Tony, so I decided upon a compromise. I would leave the heavy ropes and pegs at the camp and descend with just my personal things. My pack would be lighter and easier to manage, so it seemed a sensible move.

I finished my tea and returned to my pack. As quickly as possible I unpacked and re-arranged the load, tying all my personal items back onto the light, aluminium carrying-frame with a length of rope. Being too exhausted to carry the wet climbing ropes up to the tent I left them where they lay. If the snow buried them overnight, it would be just too bad. It was time to leave.

Tony and D.C.'s boot tracks, which marked my route across the snow to the top of the next couloir, were already half-hidden beneath a rapidly-thickening layer of fresh snow, but I was confident that the visibility was still good enough for me to find the couloir which was only about four hundred yards away.

My reserves of energy were fast being depleted but the top of the couloir soon loomed out of the mist and I started on the long descent. As I climbed ever lower the increasing amount of oxygen in the air seemed to recharge me and once I got below sixteen thousand feet the difference was very noticeable. I started to feel increasingly confident that I would make it. I began to move easily and quickly, each downward step taking me nearer to one of Tashi's magnificent curries. The prospect was so alluring that I could almost taste it in my mouth.

Then, disaster. The weight on my back was suddenly no longer there. I turned quickly and looked down just in time to see my sleeping bag and duvet, together with the rest of my personal belongings, bouncing and tumbling down the couloir into the gathering mist and gloom. I watched, horrified, as they gradually disappeared from sight. The down sleeping bag and the duvet, protected only by their lightweight nylon covers, would surely be ripped to pieces on the rocks below, and the rest of my belongings would be scattered far and wide over the slopes below me. I hurried down after them, looking left and right as I went, but everything seemed to have vanished completely.

As I continued down I wondered what on earth had happened. I remembered stowing the sleeping bag, plus most of my personal gear, in a large polythene bag to keep them dry in the snow. After re-arranging my pack I had roped everything onto the aluminium frame at Camp I. The only possible explanation was that, thanks to fatigue and the need to hurry and not waste time, I must have failed to tie everything on securely. The knots must have worked their way loose as I descended the couloir. I cursed my tiredness and my carelessness.

A hundred feet further down I found the polythene bag, but it was empty apart from a rag and two small tins of Wet-Pruf boot polish. The partly-torn bag had lodged itself in a little gully, and the last of the day's snow-melt was pouring into and past it. Where had all my equipment gone? My main concern was still the loss of my sleeping bag, and the possibility of having to endure some rather cold nights if it could not be found. Then an awful realisation suddenly struck me like a thunderbolt. My films!! All those irreplaceable little canisters had been in the bag. I had been carrying my precious memories down the mountain, and now they were gone.

I stood in the falling snow and shook my head in dejected misery. All those pictures, lost through one moment of carelessness. I was in a daze of depression and utter exhaustion. What could I do now?

Already the light was starting to fade. The darkness would soon be closing in and I knew that remaining on the couloir would achieve nothing. I would have to carry on down and pray that the snow would not cover everything without trace. In the morning I would return and carry out a proper search and hope that at least some of my possessions could be found.

I quickly reached the rock shelf at the bottom of the couloir and slipped and slithered down it. Small waterfalls of melting snow were running down the exposed rock, but I was already soaked through and did not really care.

The slope was gentler below the shelf and I was able to walk down, instead of descending using both hands and feet. Straining my eyes I stared through the gloom for any flash of bright red which might be my sleeping bag or duvet, but there was nothing.

I trudged on towards Advance Base Camp sinking up to my knees in the sugary snow at every step. In a final expression of anger and sheer frustration I strung together every blasphemy I could think of into one savage sentence and hurled it out across the barren wastes. Faintly, and mockingly, the words bounced off the surrounding ridges and echoed back at me.

As I continued down the slope I was still on the lookout for my red sleeping bag and duvet, which I thought might stand out against the snow, but I reached the flat area around Advance Base Camp without seeing them. The green tent was gone. Perhaps Chamba had trekked up from Base Camp to collect it, or maybe Tony and D.C. had decided to take it down with them.

I looked at my watch. It was just after six in the evening.

Getting down to a lower altitude had boosted my energy levels and I decided I could afford to spend about an hour searching below the couloir in the hope of finding at least my sleeping bag. I had a small pocket torch which would allow me to find my way back to Base Camp even in pitch darkness. I had done the route enough times.

I turned back towards the ridge, trying to work out, in the gathering dusk, where an object rolling out of the couloir would be most likely to finish up. I had just descended what seemed to be the left flank of a fan of avalanche debris which spread out from the bottom of the couloir. It therefore seemed sensible to start my search further to the right. I decided to make my way back towards the couloir, working across to the right as I went, and then come down again along the right-hand side of the avalanche fan.

Going back up the hill again was desperate, despite the extra oxygen in the air, and only the thought of a freezing night without a sleeping bag kept me going. I was almost back at the rock shelf when something red caught my eye about thirty feet to my right. I could hardly believe my luck. I clambered across the slope. It was my sleeping bag! The nylon outer sack was ripped from top to bottom and the sleeping bag spewed out from the gaping hole. The sleeping bag itself, though, seemed to be undamaged.

I carried my precious trophy down the slope. The duvet could wait until morning. I felt a little happier, and my disposition improved even more when, about seventy feet below where the sleeping bag had been lying, I found my duvet, its bag completely intact. It was unbelievable. Two fragile nylon bags had bumped and rolled their way down almost fifteen hundred feet of ice, rock and snow, and emerged virtually unscathed. The sleeping bag must have hit one rocky outcrop, but it appeared that the duvet had bounced clean over the sharp rock shelf at the bottom without touching it. I was very lucky.

The snow had abated somewhat and, with a very firmly tied pack, I set off for Base Camp. Darkness had fallen and I was glad of my torch, for the snow melt had exposed a lot of small rocks and boulders on the moraine above the valley floor. Without a torch to pick them out it would definitely have been ankle-breaking territory.

After what seemed only a few minutes I was down in the lower valley and walking on firm, springy grass. Just one more shallow slope to climb and the lights of Base Camp should be visible. I reached the crest of the hill, but ahead there was only darkness. For a brief, and slightly anxious, moment I wondered whether I had somehow stumbled down into the wrong valley, such had been my tiredness, but a few minutes consideration convinced me that there could be no other, and I carried on. A further ten minutes passed and there, at last, was the faint glow of a Tilley lamp shining through the blue canvas of the large cook tent.

I quickened my pace.

The flaps of the tent were closed and zipped up when I reached it. It was twenty to eight and late-night visitors were obviously not expected. Dramatically I pulled up one of the zips and stepped inside.

Tashi jumped to his feet as I entered, looking alarmed.

"Doctor Sahib! It is you."

His face broke into a smile of recognition and relief. He must have thought at first that his unexpected visitor was one of the many, and not always friendly, gods who are said to roam the remote Himalayan valleys at night.

There was another porter in the tent whose face was unknown to me. He did not speak and remained seated. Tashi made no attempt to introduce him and I assumed he must be another of Wongdhi's mail runners from Manali. There was no sign of Tony, or of the two high altitude porters.

"Tony? Chamba? Dharm Chand?" I queried. Tashi pointed in the direction of a smaller tent which was in darkness to one side the cook tent and held both hands together, flat against his cheek, in the universal sign for sleep.

I nodded to indicate that I understood. The others had obviously got down to Base Camp safely, and they had already retired for a well-earned rest.

"Chai, Sahib?"

I nodded again, gratefully, and within a couple of minutes I was sipping the very welcome, and much needed, mug of hot tea which Tashi thrust into my hands.

I sat down and began to remove my soaking wet clothing while I was still warm from my exertions. My spare clothes were stored in the big tent, and it was a great pleasure to be able to change into clean and dry clothing.

As soon as I had finished my tea I climbed into the sleeping bag which I had so fortuitously recovered. I was keen to cocoon myself in its warm embrace before my body heat had dropped too much.

I was badly in need of some sleep, so the hot curry which I had dreamt about on the way down would have to wait for another day. I set my alarm for five and drifted off to forget about my troubles. An early start would be needed if I was to have any chance of finding those missing films.

Twenty-One

THE FINAL DAYS

Tony came into the big tent at five o'clock, just as my alarm went off.

"Morning John. Didn't expect to see you down here so soon. Is everything alright up on the plateau?"

"Yes, everything's okay," I replied as I shook myself awake. "The two Geoffs were still on their way down from the ridge when I left Camp III. I heard you were suffering a bit so I just came down to make sure you were okay."

"That's good of you. I didn't know you cared."

"I don't," I retorted, smiling. "It's the nurses that do the T.L.C., not doctors. We just diagnose and prescribe So if you don't mind I'll have a quick listen to your chest and prescribe something if necessary. But first let's have a bite to eat. I'm starving."

After a welcome breakfast I put my stethoscope to work.

"The cough's got a lot better since I came down here," Tony told me, after I had listened to his chest. "I think it was probably just the colder air up on the plateau."

"What about pains in your chest?"

He shrugged his shoulders. "They seem to have gone completely."

Through my stethoscope I had heard a few crackles as he took deep breaths, but nothing that sounded too sinister. Nevertheless I decided to put him on a course of antibiotics as a precaution. I didn't want him going down with pneumonia so near the end of the expedition.

Dharm Chand was going up to Camp II to help with the final carry of all the equipment off the mountain. After seeing to Tony, and agreeing that it'd be best if he stayed at Base Camp for at least twenty four hours, I set off with D.C. I had briefly told both of them the story of my lost pack and my intention to carry out a search in daylight. D.C. was very sympathetic and said he would keep an eye out for my things on his way up the couloir.

At Advance Base Camp we split up. D.C. had a long climb ahead of him, while I wanted to make a start on my search. I was starting to feel the after-effects of the previous day's eleven hour slog, and first of all I needed a rest.

The air was clear and from where I sat, resting, most of the slope below the lower couloir was easily visible. I scanned it and was disappointed that there appeared to be no sign of any loose objects. It was strange and difficult to understand. Items of clothing such as the bright red anorak should have been very obvious against the white background, and there had not been enough snow overnight to cover anything up.

It was time for a closer look. I moved systematically over the slopes for about an hour but found nothing. Despondently I started up the couloir. Fortunately it was good, firm snow after the overnight freeze and the going was easy. I had borrowed half a dozen rolls of film from Tony, and I was shooting pictures off every couple of minutes to try and replace at least some of my lost collection. I was becoming increasingly certain that I had seen the last of the originals.

Half-way up the couloir, and still there was nothing. I decided to climb right back up to Camp I to take some pictures from there too but, much as I wanted to, I knew I did not have the energy to make it all the way back to the plateau again. I would just have to settle for copies of other people's pictures.

I had nearly reached the scene of the previous evening's disaster when I suddenly saw, jammed against a rock on the edge of the couloir, a white kit-bag. I remembered immediately that I had, of course, packed all my belongings in a kit-bag for convenience. They had not been loose inside the polythene bag at all. I found myself laughing, both at my stupidity and with great relief. In my exhaustion and confusion the previous evening I must have passed within a few feet of the kit-bag without noticing it in the snow and gloom. Maybe I was totally pre-occupied with looking for small, bright objects, or perhaps my tired and confused brain had simply not registered its presence.

I moved across to the side of the couloir and grabbed the kit-bag tightly, before driving my ice-axe deep into the snow crust to act as an anchor. I tied a length of rope around the haft of the axe and clipped both myself and the precious bag to it with a karabiner. I was not going to lose my gear for a second time. Anxiously I fumbled with the half-frozen cord around the neck of the kit-bag.

One vital question had to be answered before I could even think of going back down. Were my film canisters in there? Or had I left them loose?

The knot came undone and I pulled the sack open to find the precious, metal canisters lying right on top, safe in their own waterproof bag. I did not bother about anything else. Pulling the cord closed, and knotting it tightly, I roped the kit-bag very securely to the metal frame and swung it onto my back before heading down the couloir. The weather was closing in again and, stopping en route only to add the small amount of equipment which still remained at Advance Base Camp to my load, I was back at Base Camp in time for lunch. As a treat, and to celebrate the retrieval of my gear, Tashi agreed to rustle up the hot curry which I had promised myself a day earlier.

Another huge thunderstorm struck in the early afternoon and at about six o'clock Dharm Chand returned empty-handed. He told us he had reached a point about two-thirds of the way up the big couloir, heading for the plateau, when he was forced back by the ferocious storm. He had not been able to make contact with the others.

The storm continued without a break for two days. In the valley the rain was torrential. The four of us who were left at Base Camp, Wongdhi's runner having returned to Manali, could only sit there and imagine how much worse things must be higher up.

On the morning of the third day, the weather having finally improved slightly, Dharm Chand set off once more. Hopefully the rest of the team would be on their way down in the improved conditions and he would be able to meet up with them in order to assist with the equipment they would be lugging down. Tony was, by this time, anxious to get everything, and most importantly everybody, off the mountain as soon as possible. The last couple of days had strengthened our feeling that the monsoon was imminent.

As if to confirm our fears, the improvement in the weather lasted only a few hours. By midday it had clouded over and the temperature dropped. A mixture of sleet and snow, rather than rain, started to fall. Tony and I sat in the big tent, watching the weather, and waited.

At four-thirty in the afternoon, six figures appeared out of the sleet and mist. They were soaking wet and their faces and clothes were encrusted with icy droplets.

As they refreshed themselves with hot tea and biscuits they told us that, using the two sledges, they had managed to move all the equipment across the plateau and down the big couloir. Everything had gone well until they reached the lower section of the couloir when Dharm Chand, who had just linked up with them, was asked to hold one of the sledges for a moment while the load was adjusted. Unfortunately he had taken hold of the wrong rope and the fully loaded sledge had hurtled down the precipitous snow-face into the bergschrund at the bottom, embedding itself into the soft snow on the far side of the crevasse some fifteen feet down. Miraculously the load had stayed on, and a couple of the team had managed to reach it before it dislodged itself. Climbing ropes were used to secure it and, after a long and exhausting struggle, the sledge and its precious load had been hauled out. Everyone was already exhausted, and the effort of retrieving the sledge had been the last straw. Both of the fully-loaded sledges were left on the upper slopes of the Malana Glacier, near the bottom of the couloir, for later retrieval.

The return of the rest of the team to Base Camp heralded the first, and only, major row of the expedition. In our mentally and physically exhausted state, and living in such close proximity to each other for so long, it was frankly surprising that personalities and tempers had not clashed earlier. Tony and myself were accused of idleness, sitting out the storm at Base Camp while everyone else was working, while poor Dharm Chand was branded both idle and incompetent after the episode with the sledge.

The rights and wrongs of the arguments were unimportant. Given the extreme pressure and the difficult conditions under which we had all been living, such a break-down was almost inevitable at some stage. Paradoxically, it was probably the very success of the expedition that gave us the feeling that disagreements within the team no longer mattered, and that we could, in those final days, afford to be brutally honest with each other.

We all blew our tops, and then slowly simmered down. Everyone was involved, and nobody was really to blame. By the morning we were all friends again.

= = = = = = = = = = = = = = =

The loaded sledges still had to be got down off the mountain. The members of the high altitude team were sorely in need of a good rest, so Dharm Chand and I volunteered to go up. Tony insisted on accompanying us, arguing that three people could get all the remaining gear off the mountain to Base Camp once and for all. After three days on antibiotics his chest sounded fine, and I persuaded myself that he should be alright.

The morning dawned bright and clear. By six we were away. Little of the previous day's sleet and snow had stuck so we made good time across the green valley. Countless tiny alpine flowers, red, blue violet and yellow, now lined our path and dotted the valley floor. They glistened with icy dew, sparkling in the early morning sunshine.

The spell at altitude, and a couple of days' rest at Base Camp, seemed to have done me good for I hardly felt tired. Tony, too, seemed to be moving well and we arrived at Advance Base Camp in less than seventy minutes, easily my fastest time. As we started to climb the lower couloir, though, Tony started to flag and he began to cough. His chest problems were back and he admitted that he was not feeling too good. I told him that I thought it would be best if he returned to Advance Base Camp. I suggested he should rest there until he felt well enough to carry on down to Base. He did not argue. He well knew that he was not capable of doing any significant load carrying. D.C. and I would retrieve the gear.

Dharm Chand and I pressed on alone. By quarter to ten we had reached Camp I and we stopped for a much-needed brew. Since the perishables and the fuel were not going down with us we felt we might as well make use of them. There was no need for economy any more.

As we sat there drinking some welcome tea Dharm Chand, who appeared to have taken the criticisms of the previous evening very much to heart, spoke dejectedly.

"Will Tony give a bad report about me to Wongdhi now?"

It was very important to him. Despite the success of the expedition, his next job also depended upon a favourable assessment of his climbing abilities and enthusiasm.

I did my best to explain to him that I felt the whole episode was simply down to tiredness, and that we all had a very high regard for his willingness to work hard and his undoubted contribution to the success of the climb. I told him that I would make certain that the report to Wongdhi was a good one. He seemed to be reassured by my words and, as we made our way over to where the sledges had been left, he was smiling again and in much better spirits.

The first sledge had two cans of fuel on it in addition to all the other gear. With the two cans abandoned, which saved fourteen pounds, we felt the two of us might be able to manhandle the two sledges on our own. It was worth a try anyway.

With as much gear as possible securely roped to the pack-frames on our backs we heaved the loaded sledges, one at a time, across the steep slope at the top of the Malana Glacier. Our plan was to reach a spot from where we could hopefully point them down the slope and let them run on their own into the snow basin below Camp I.

The sledges had not been designed for such heavy and awkward loads and, although we had devised an intricate system of guiding ropes to try and control them, they kept turning over onto their sides. Despite this difficulty we successfully managed to get the first sledge across the slope. We secured it, using my ice-axe, at a point from where we calculated that we could safely let it go. All that remained was to get the second sledge to the same position.

We were half-way across the slope with the second sledge when, suddenly, I slipped. I was in charge of the rear end of the sledge and, as I slithered down the slope out of control, the rope I was still hanging on to, pulled the back end of the sledge around so it was facing straight down the hill. Dharm Chand reacted immediately to my instinctive shout, but he had no time to belay himself. He was dragged off the slope and slid downwards, pulled by the combined weight of myself and the loaded sledge.

The next few seconds were a blur. Having used it to secure the first sledge, I had no ice-axe with which to slow my fall, while D.C. was frantically using his ice-axe to try and brake the two of us as well as the heavy sledge. I arched my back and dug my heels in as I had learnt to do in Scotland but, without an ice-axe to augment the braking action, it had little effect. I had slid down about a hundred feet when I felt the snow crust give way beneath me. My headlong fall came to a sudden stop as I plunged up to my waist in soft snow. The sledge thumped into the small of my back and skewed past me. I had broken through a layer of snow which was covering a crevasse.

Dharm Chand, showing remarkable presence of mind, stopped braking and shot past me, following the sledge over the crevasse and down the snow slope. The rope that tied us both to the sledge snaked out its full length upon the snow, and I felt a violent tug upon my waist as D.C. and the sledge both jerked to a halt. My body, wedged into the soft snow, was now acting as an anchor for both the sledge and Dharm Chand.

"Are you okay?" he shouted as he plunged the handle of his axe into the snow to secure us should I break through the frail crust which supported me.

"Yes. I think so," I called back. I ached in various places, but I was thankful just to be in one piece.

Seeing that he was safely belayed I carefully wormed my way out of my precarious position, pulling on the rope which still joined us. Once free I untied the rope from my waist and, using my crampons, inched my way back up the slope towards the sledge we had left behind. Dharm Chand sensibly remained where he was, holding onto the first sledge with a rope and still securely attached to his ice-axe belay.

I retrieved my own ice-axe and let the second sledge go, watching carefully as it passed D.C. and picked up speed. If our calculations were wrong we would have a long walk ahead of us. Should it miss the basin below Camp I, the sledge would carry on down the long slope towards Dos Nullah on the far side of the glacier. Happily it remained upright and slid gracefully to a halt on the uphill slope of the basin, right below the camp. Dharm Chand, having watched the progress of my sledge, then released the one he was holding. Taking a slightly different route it finished up on its side about thirty yards away from mine.

I carefully edged my way down to D.C., and we roped up again before making our way down to join the two sledges. We added what was left at Camp I to the two sleds and arrived at the top of the lower couloir, utterly spent. The whole procedure, from when we first reached the sledges, had taken just under four hours.

The little disaster of a few days earlier, when my pack had come loose, had convinced me that the least energy-sapping method of getting unbreakable equipment down to Advance Base from Camp I was to let it roll down the couloir, suitably protected. On our way up we had deposited four strong, hessian sacks at the top of the couloir for just that purpose. We loaded one of the sacks up with rope and tied its neck securely. This was the experimental one. We launched it into space and watched as it rolled down the centre of the gully, picking up speed as it went. It was soon hurtling along, assuming strange shapes as the ropes within the sack pushed against the hessian sides like struggling snakes. It leapt high into the air as it hit uneven stretches, and finally cleared the rock step at the bottom in one great bound before disappearing from our sight.

The method seemed to work, so more ropes and tents, together with various other odds and ends, went down the same way in the other three sacks. Only the two sledges, and items such as pegs and karabiners which we dared not drop for fear of fracturing them, were left to be manhandled down the couloir in a more conventional way. We descended the couloir for the final time, finding two of the sacks just above the rock ledge. These we pushed and kicked down to join the other two on the slopes below. We left them all where they lay. They were safely in the valley from where they could be collected very easily the next day, no matter what the weather was like.

It was seven-fifteen in the evening when we finally dragged our weary way into Base Camp. The news that all the equipment was safely down to Advance Base was greeted with considerable enthusiasm and relief.

Dharm Chand was happy. The report to Wongdhi would now be fine, and we had both more than made up for any earlier laziness.

Aiming High – Overland to the Himalayas 1971

Team photograph at Base Camp at the end of the climb

The snow has all melted away, and monsoon clouds are gathering

Tashi   Geoff Tabbner   Dharm Chand   Roger Brook   Tony Johnson   John Winter

Geoff Arkless

John Brazinton   Bryan Pooley

Twenty-Two

BACK TO KULU

"Anyone for a haircut?"

Tony was trying to drum up business for Tashi who had produced a pair of scissors from somewhere and was proudly displaying the short back and sides he had fashioned for Dharm Chand.

Base Camp was crowded with people and equipment, the last few loads having been carried down from Advance Base that morning but, despite the crowds, nobody else could be coaxed into the barber's chair. Not to be beaten, Tashi propped a small mirror up on a boulder outside the tent and set about his own hair with gusto.

Chamba had already been sent down to Manali with a message for Wongdhi, telling him that the West Ridge of Indrasan was climbed and asking him to send eighteen porters up to Base Camp. Tony had requested that the porters should arrive in time to start the trek down on 21st June, so we had two days to get things organised.

There was plenty to do. The gear had to be arranged in loads for the porters but, before that could be done, the tents and ropes from the higher camps would need to be dried out. There was quite enough weight to get down to Kulu without the added burden of rainwater.

The morning of June 20th dawned sunny and bright but as we sat around eating a leisurely breakfast I was not altogether sorry to be leaving. I would miss the mountains but the discomforts, and the relative isolation, were starting to make me think longingly of the luxuries and benefits of life back at home. I was quite pleased, therefore, when Tony, who was feeling his normal self again, suggested that he and I should leave a little ahead of the main party so that we could push on and reach the Kulu Valley in time to arrange transport from Jagatsukh, where the porters would be leaving all our equipment.

The weather at Base Camp stayed fine until late in the afternoon, allowing us to spread the ropes and tents out across the grass to dry in the hot sun. Hundreds of feet of climbing rope soon lay across the grass, like multi-coloured spaghetti, along with flattened out tents. Once all the equipment was completely dry it was split up into loads which were stacked inside the big tent in case of further rain. We had no weighing scales with us, so Dharm Chand was allotted the task of ensuring that the loads were all roughly equal. No sack was sewn up and placed in the tent until he had passed it. The expectation was that most, if not all, of the porters would hail from his home village of Vashisht, so if disputes arose over the weights to be carried, D.C. would be responsible for sorting them out.

By early evening we had assembled sixteen fairly compact loads which D.C. judged were fair and manageable. Items which we had been unable to fit in one of the loads were then piled up together. Any porter who wished to help himself to anything for his own use could add it to his burden if he felt able to cope with the extra weight.   The large cook tent, which would be dismantled on the final morning, made the total up to eighteen loads.

That night we had a party. The empty crates and boxes were all piled up into a gigantic bonfire in front of the tent and, in a fit of wild abandon, all the emergency flares were fired off in a spectacular firework display.   The fire burned fiercely and the night sky was lit up by green and red flares which hung above our heads before floating gently down to earth.   The celebrations finally broke up at midnight, which was very late after the early nights we had become familiar with over the past weeks.

= = = = = = = = = = = = = = =

It was raining heavily, wet, cold and misty, as Tony and I set off at six the following morning. The porters were not expected for at least another couple of hours and the rest of the team were still asleep as we crossed the river and headed towards the cliffs above Seri. It was real monsoon weather.

We scrambled down the steep, grassy slope which would take us into the Jagatsukh Nullah.   Muddy and slippery, like a rain-soaked Lake District fell, it was difficult to believe this was the snow–covered rampart which our barefoot porters had struggled to overcome just six weeks before.

Once on the valley floor we had to cross the river, which at this lower level was swollen into a fierce torrent by all the rainwater from the higher valleys. Walking up and down the bank we found a place where the water appeared to be slightly shallower, and waded in. The swift current tugged at our legs, threatening to pull us down into the freezing water.

"The porters might need a fixed rope to get across this with their loads," shouted Tony above the sound of the rushing water, "otherwise they'll never keep their balance."

We struggled safely to the other side.

"Talking of the porters, where on earth are they?" I said as we rolled our soaked trousers back down. "If they don't appear soon, they'll never get up to Base Camp by eight o'clock."

There were so many uncertainties in the arrangements. We had sent Chamba down with a message but no word had been received in return. Maybe the message had not reached Wongdhi? Or maybe he was having difficulty in recruiting enough porters? We could not know the answer. There were no satellites or mobile phones which we could use to check that all was well. Back then we were living in an age when such things had hardly been thought of, let alone become everyday items which could be used to send and receive messages in even the most remote of places.

We trudged on towards the rocky moraine which we knew lay at the end of the valley. The river-water squelched in our sodden, fell boots. The ground was now very swampy, and around us I could make out numerous, tiny burrows.

"I think we'd better tuck our trousers into our socks," I suggested to Tony, taking my own advice as I spoke. "It looks like there are loads of leeches around here."

He simply patted his right hand pocket. The matchbox within made a rattling sound.

"The little buggers will get a shock if they try to suck my blood. I'll burn them alive."

I continued on, leaving my own trousers tucked well in to my knee-length socks. As far as I was concerned, prevention was much better than cure but, despite my precautions, I was obliged to borrow Tony's matches on a number of occasions as tell-tale patches of fresh, red blood on my clothing revealed that the leeches had breached my defences.

The heavy clouds had lifted as we were crossing the marshland, and the rain had stopped, but the air was still damp and misty. We had just reached the first of the boulders which were scattered over the moraine when half a dozen figures appeared in front of us, their approach having been hidden by the rocks between which they were now clambering.

It was the first group of porters. They all looked very young. Two of them seemed barely into their teens and I thought of all those sixty pound loads waiting for them at Base Camp.

"Some of the loads are bigger than the blooming porters," I whispered to Tony as they approached.

"Namaste. Good morning. Namaste." We waved and shouted a greeting to them.

The first group of outsiders we had seen in several weeks soon stood before us, grinning and nodding their heads in response to our welcome.

One of them spoke.

"Base Camp, Sahib? Base Camp?"

The question did not necessarily indicate that he spoke English. Everyday mountaineering terms such as Ice-axe, crampon and Base Camp had, by that time, become well-known to the Himalayan porters, just as some of their words, including verandah, bungalow and sandal, had slipped easily into our language at the time of the Raj.

We pointed up the valley towards the grey clouds which still hung over the top of the cliffs and the Base Camp valley beyond.

"Taenta Valley," said Tony. "Base Camp in Taenta Valley."

"Taenta Valley. Okay Sahib," nodded the spokesman. A couple of his companions looked a little crestfallen. It seemed that they had hoped that Base Camp might be a little lower down, perhaps below the cliffs, but their discomfiture did not last long and with a last, cheery grin the six men went on their way.

A sudden thought struck me.

"Vashisht?" I shouted after the retreating figures.

They stopped and turned round.

"Vashisht?" I repeated pointing at them. "You. From Yashisht?"

Suddenly the question was understood and a couple of them nodded.

"Vashisht Sahib. Yashisht. Yes"

That was good. They were indeed from Dharm Chand's home village which meant that he should be able to sort out any problems. I give them a thumbs-up, which was returned before they headed towards the clouds.

Over the next half hour, as we pressed on down the moraine, we passed the rest of the porters, making their way up in twos and threes. Much the same brief scenario was acted out at each successive meeting, and we remembered to give one group a note for Dharm Chand, mentioning the possible need for a fixed rope to make the river crossing safe for the heavily loaded porters.

We were soon at the site of the highest camp on the march-in. We had already descended over fifteen hundred feet and we were both feeling the benefit of the increasing oxygen levels in the air. I personally felt as if I could carry on all day, and Tony was showing no ill effects at all from his recent chest trouble. We decided not to stop but to continue as far as the shrine and rest there.

Quite soon we were below the tree line.

What a difference from when we had last been there. The warmer air, assisted by the heavier, monsoon rain, had caused the previously sparse vegetation beneath the trees to spring up at an astonishing rate. We were forced to push our way through thick, wet foliage, wading chest-deep in grasses and ferns that were more luxuriant than anything we had encountered on the march-in.

It was something of a relief when we finally reached the low, stone walls of the shrine, for this marked our exit from the mountains proper. The going should be easier the rest of the way, with well-established upland paths to follow. Before us lay the wide, high pasturelands and the long descent through the pine and deodar forest, after which we would finally be down in the Kulu Valley once again.

The garlands that our porters had woven six weeks ago still lay on the altar, the flowers now wrinkled and wet. Beside them were some fresh offerings, presumably from the men we had just met.

We sat on the wall for a few minutes.

In the distance, where the valley started to widen out, we could see animals grazing on the lush, green grass of the pastures. With them would be herdsmen from lower down, making the most of the last few days before the monsoon rains forced them to retreat to their villages.

Before long we would be down there with them, and on our way back home. The great adventure was almost over.

POSTSCRIPT

Climbing in the highest of mountains is a wonderful experience, but people still ask why anyone should want to expend so much effort just to stand upon a rocky or snowy peak?

"Because it is there."

Mallory's classic response, when he was asked why he wanted to conquer Everest, is still perhaps the best answer to that question.

Having given up the best part of a year to the enterprise, I have been asked many times whether it was worth it.

For me, personally, it was an experience which I shall never forget; both exhausting and exhilarating. It introduced me to a world I had never previously known and, as a result of the experience, doors opened for me. Three years later, in 1974, I returned to the Himalayas. I lived for several months in a Sherpa, yak-herding hut, situated in Pheriche in the Everest region. There, on behalf of the Himalayan Rescue Association, I carried out some epidemiological research into acute altitude sickness which was causing severe, and sometimes fatal, problems for members of commercial trekking parties who were trying to reach Everest Base Camp at 18,000 feet. I was also able to offer some routine medical care to local Sherpa communities.

In 1974 no more than a couple of hundred trekkers passed through Pheriche each year. Forty years on, many thousands of people attempt the same trip, and a fully-staffed, medical clinic has replaced my humble hut.

I am sure the rest of the team would agree that the success of the expedition made all the effort well worthwhile. Sadly, though, the successful ascent of the West Ridge of Indrasan was overshadowed by a great tragedy. John Brazinton was doing some climbing in the French Alps, very soon after our return, and there, on the Aiguille Verte in the Mont Blanc region, he lost his life. While collecting together his kit after a successful climb he was hit by an unexpected and sudden rock-fall. The reports indicate that he died almost instantly.

Had he lived he could have achieved much in the world of climbing and mountaineering. I hope that this book might, in some small way, act as a memorial to him.

It is the sort of risk that every climber takes and accepts but, as John had emerged unscathed from the Himalayas, it seems doubly tragic that such a simple accident should have occurred. Perhaps it would have been easier to accept and understand if the accident had happened on the expedition itself when we were always half-expecting something to go wrong.

It made me realise how very lucky I had been. As a complete novice I had ventured into the Himalayas from where, at the time of our expedition, the statistics suggested that almost one climber in eight would not return. I was with climbers of ability and experience who did their best to advise me and limit the possible consequences of my own inexperience and ignorance. Despite their support, there were many times when I was on my own and there were at least a couple of occasions when I was fortunate not to be injured. John Brazinton's accident demonstrated that the outcome could easily have been very different.

So, was it worth it? For each of us, as individuals, I am sure the answer has to be yes. But, for me, the incomparable pleasure of challenging a mountain can never be worth a person's life.

Appendix

ACUTE MOUNTAIN SICKNESS

As a result of research at Pheriche and elsewhere acute altitude sickness, also known as acute mountain sickness (A.M.S.), is better understood than was the case in the 1970s.

Mild symptoms often affect climbers and trekkers and, although such symptoms need to be monitored carefully, they will usually settle down as the individual acclimatises better. More persistent and severe symptoms can indicate that a mild episode of altitude sickness is progressing to life-threatening, high altitude cerebral oedema or high altitude pulmonary oedema. Excessive amounts of body fluid can rapidly build up in the brain and/or the lungs in just a few hours, producing a frighteningly rapid deterioration in the patient's condition.

It is no exaggeration to state that such a situation can be life-threatening. It should be regarded as a medical emergency.

Even the youngest and fittest of people can develop such symptoms, and it may be that fitter people are at a greater risk of running into serious problems because they are more capable of exceeding the recommended rates of ascent.

This is why careful acclimatisation is essential if a climb or trek which involves sleeping at above 10,000 feet is being attempted. If someone has never previously travelled to high altitude it is impossible to predict how well they will cope. If someone has previously coped well with exposure to high altitude it is likely that they will do equally well on future occasions as long as they allow time for acclimatisation.

Expert advice is that to minimise the risk of A.M.S. developing a climber or trekker should ascend slowly. A gain of no more than about 750 feet per day on average, once above 10,000 feet, will allow almost all people to acclimatise and avoid problems. Some people can safely ascend more quickly, but this cannot be guaranteed. The important thing is the height at which each night is spent. While it is acceptable to climb to higher altitudes during the day, the sleeping height each night should increase in accordance with the previously recommended acclimatisation schedule, and ideally not exceed 750 ft per day.

Such a schedule gives the body time to adapt to the lower oxygen levels and the lower barometric pressure. If symptoms develop despite a slow ascent they should not be ignored. No further ascent should be attempted until the symptoms have fully recovered, and if the symptoms persist a descent to a much lower altitude is essential.

A pressurised hyperbaric bag such as a Gamow Bag, or other similar portable device, can relieve symptoms by producing an artificial increase in oxygen and barometric pressure levels and may be useful to provide immediate, temporary relief while awaiting evacuation, but urgent descent is still essential.

Expert medical advice should be sought as soon as possible by anyone who is experiencing symptoms of altitude sickness which are persistent, or which are worsening, and descent to a lower altitude should be attempted while awaiting such advice.

SYMPTOMS OF MILD ALTITUDE SICKNESS (AMS)

- *Headache*
- *Nausea and vomiting*
- *Dizziness*
- *Excessive fatigue*
- *Loss of appetite*
- *Upset stomach and/or diarrhoea*
- *Unsteadiness*
- *Shortness of breath*

SYMPTOMS OF SEVERE ALTITUDE SICKNESS (AMS)

- *Worsening of previously mild symptoms*
- *Persistent, productive cough with blood-stained, pink or frothy white sputum*
- *Breathlessness at rest*
- *Bubbling sounds in chest when breathing*
- *Clumsiness*
- *Loss of balance and difficulty in walking*
- *Irrational behaviour or confusion*
- *Blurred or double vision*

PREVENTION OF ALTITUDE SICKNESS (AMS)

- *Adopt a conservative rate of ascent – an average ascent no more than 750 feet per day (sleeping height change) would be a safe and sensible schedule*
- *Include spare 'leeway' days in trekking or climbing schedule*
- *Know the symptoms of AMS*
- *Never continue ascending with obvious symptoms*
- *Descend if symptoms persist*
- *Ensure that group members monitor and look after each other*
- *Avoid additional unnecessary exertion*
- *Drink plenty of fluids, but no alcohol*
- *Maintain a high energy diet*

TREATMENT OF ALTITUDE SICKNESS (AMS)

- *Descent*
- *Oxygen*
- *Acetazolamide 125 mgm twice daily, Dexamethasone 8 mgm daily, Nifedipine 20 mgm six hourly*
- *A portable hyperbaric chamber (Gamow Bag or similar) can be helpful as an immediate, emergency treatment when evacuation to a lower altitude cannot immediately be achieved.*

OTHER COMMON MEDICAL PROBLEMS AT HIGH ALTITUDE

- *Irregular 'Cheyne-Stokes' breathing*
- *Upper respiratory irritation due to dry, cold air*
- *Peripheral oedema (swelling of limbs, especially ankles and feet)*
- *High altitude syncope (fainting)*
- *Migraine*
- *Emboli (blood clots) in the blood vessels of the lungs and elsewhere*
- *Oral contraceptive risk of thrombo-embolism (blood clots) may be greater because of the increased red blood cell count (polycythaemia) which occurs at high altitude*
- *Chest infection and pneumonia*
- *Gastro-intestinal infection (as may occur when travelling in many developing countries)*

MEDICAL ASSESSMENT AND PRE-EXISTING ILLNESSES

Underlying chronic illnesses such as high blood pressure, heart disease, diabetes and epilepsy are not automatically regarded as a contra-indication to routine trekking at high altitude as long as the condition is well-controlled and stable. Long-term medication must be continued and adequate time for acclimatisation must be allowed.

One thing is vitally important. Anyone who has an ongoing medical condition of any sort, or any concern about their general health and fitness, must discuss their medical condition and travel plans with a doctor who has suitable knowledge and experience. An appropriate clinical assessment can then be carried out. Obtaining such expert advice is essential before travelling to high altitude, or trekking to remote locations such as Everest Base Camp.

Printed in Great Britain
by Amazon